DR. FRÉDÉRIC
FANGET

CATHERINE
MEYER

PAULINE
AUBRY

THE ANXIETY CLUB

HOW TO SURVIVE MODERN LIFE

SELF MADE HERO

First published in English in 2024
by SelfMadeHero
139–141 Pancras Road
London NW1 1UN
www.selfmadehero.com

Written by Dr. Frédéric Fanget and Catherine Meyer
Illustrated by Pauline Aubry
© Editions Les Arènes, 2023

English Edition:
Publishing Director: Emma Hayley
Designer: Txabi Jones
Translator: Edward Gauvin
Publishing assistant: Jacob Ashbridge
Publicist: Paul Smith
With thanks to: Dan Lockwood, Nick de Somogyi
and Corinne Pearlman

A CIP record for this book is available from the British Library

ISBN 978-1-914224-21-8

10 9 8 7 6 5 4 3 2 1

Printed and bound in Slovenia

TABLE OF CONTENTS

FOREWORD

To someone who has suffered anxiety their whole life the central message of this book – that one is not alone – is very reassuring. This graphic self-help book, drawn in a loose and fluid style, gives an overview of the history and nature of this annoying condition from the perspective of a French psychiatrist. As a cartoon avatar, Dr. Fanget gives practical advice about tackling the challenges anxiety brings, and explains the different approaches to analysis and therapy. In an increasingly uncertain and media-driven world he frames our anxious states of mind in the context of our frenetic modern existence while also referencing time-tested traditions of thought – from stoicism to existentialism – and explaining the pathophysiological nature of these conditions.

Anxiety is a primal emotion, born of necessity, that is accompanied by an insurmountable feeling that one must DO SOMETHING to make the feeling go away, to avoid danger. This imperative urge is in some ways the hardest part to deal with. As Dr. Fanget points out, without any anxiety we would be a liability to ourselves, yet with a surfeit of it we become a nuisance to ourselves and others.

Everyone in *The Anxiety Club* is starring in their own disaster movie. I certainly relate to this. Our amygdala (that pesky bit of the brain that signals alarm) puts us at the centre of the narrative. Dr. Fanget is obviously a fan of film – a medium in some ways analogous to comics – and the visual content of this book makes the narrative at once more entertaining and more nuanced: the author is right there, on the page, talking to us. It is a lovely example of what I call Graphic Medicine (the word 'medicine' referring, in this context, to the healing elixir, rather than the profession of doctors).

Models of healthcare vary from nation to nation – ours in the UK is different from the French system – and the language of mental healthcare can also vary. Some of the categories used in this book sound unfamiliar to me as a British doctor, but the principles of care remain the same. Some potential readers might even baulk at the very idea of psychiatric categorization (the history of the discipline is not without controversy) but it must be remembered that the discourse of healthcare is a constantly evolving entity – a temporary framework on which to hang ideas about how to best help people.

I am a lifelong member of the Anxiety Club, and recognize aspects of myself in the characters here. I also recognize the faintly ridiculous quandaries they find themselves in, and the objectification of these mental trials forms part of the basis of cognitive behavioural therapy. I don't expect to ever be able to relinquish my membership – there is, as the good doctor notes, no magical solution, but mutual support is important and it is good to know that there are professionals like Dr. Fanget out there who understand us members so well, helping us to help ourselves.

Dr. Ian Williams
Cartoonist and Doctor
Founder of graphicmedicine.org

ANY RESEMBLANCE TO ACTUAL PEOPLE OR SITUATIONS IS ENTIRELY INTENTIONAL — IT'S THE WHOLE POINT OF THIS COMIC! STILL, WE'VE PRESERVED THEIR ANONYMITY... THAT IS, FOR EVERYONE EXCEPT DR. FANGET, OUR SUPERHERO PSYCHIATRIST!

CHAPTER 1
THE FACES OF ANXIETY

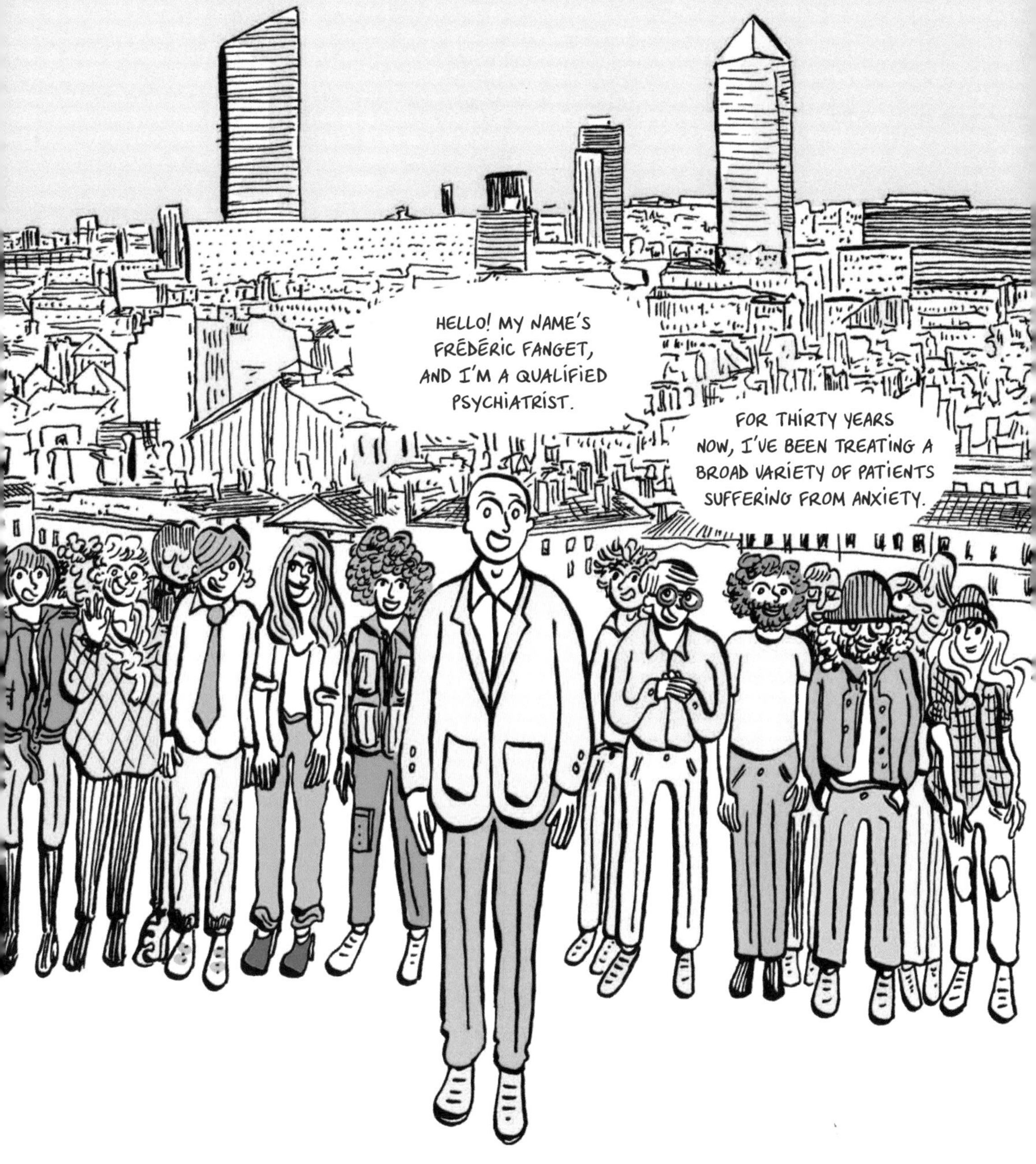
HELLO! MY NAME'S FRÉDÉRIC FANGET, AND I'M A QUALIFIED PSYCHIATRIST.
FOR THIRTY YEARS NOW, I'VE BEEN TREATING A BROAD VARIETY OF PATIENTS SUFFERING FROM ANXIETY.

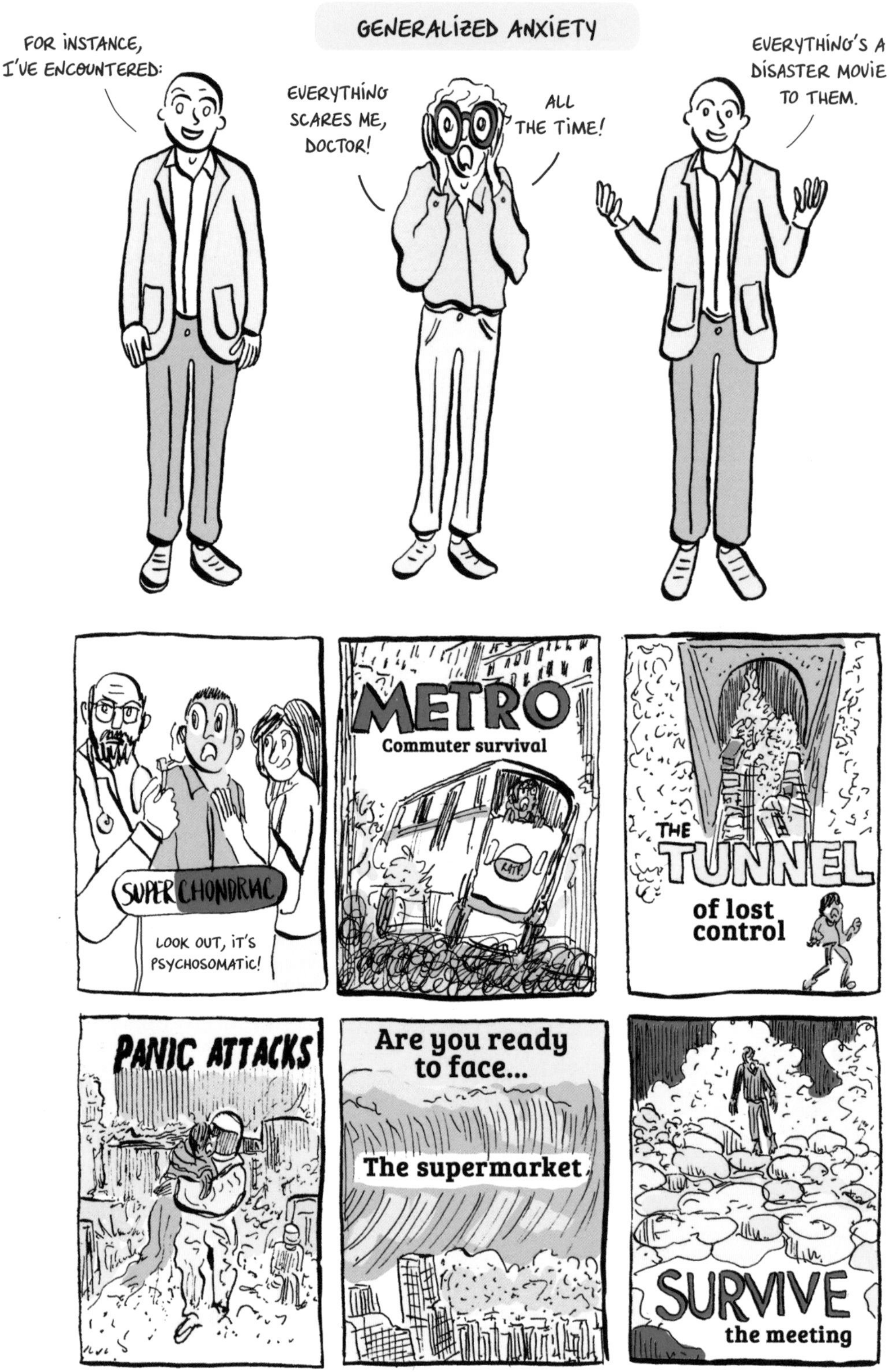
GENERALIZED ANXIETY
FOR INSTANCE, I'VE ENCOUNTERED:
EVERYTHING SCARES ME, DOCTOR!
ALL THE TIME!
EVERYTHING'S A DISASTER MOVIE TO THEM.
SUPERCHONDRIAC
LOOK OUT, IT'S PSYCHOSOMATIC!
METRO
Commuter survival
RATP
THE TUNNEL
of lost control
PANIC ATTACKS
Are you ready to face...
The supermarket
SURVIVE
the meeting

PANIC DISORDER

WHEN WE'RE ANXIOUS WE FEEL LIKE SOMETHING BAD IS GOING TO HAPPEN TO US.

WE THINK WE WON'T BE SAVED.

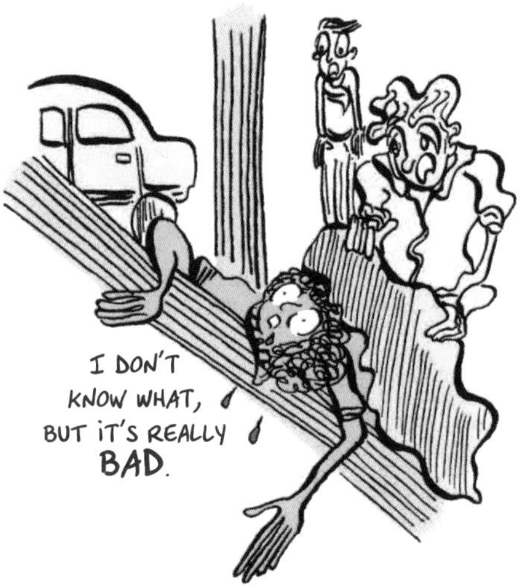
I DON'T KNOW WHAT, BUT IT'S REALLY BAD.

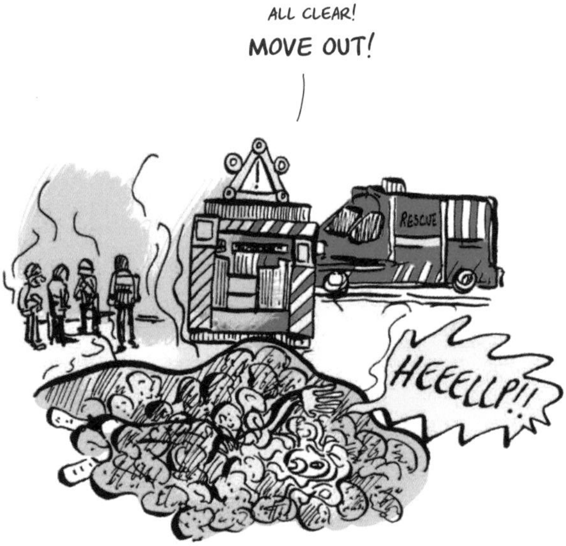
ALL CLEAR!
MOVE OUT!
RESCUE
HEEELLP!!

SOME OF US HAVE PANIC ATTACKS FOR NO REASON.

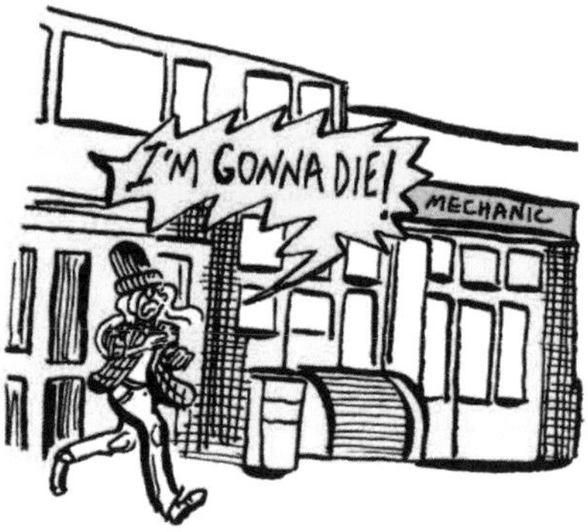
I'M GONNA DIE!
MECHANIC

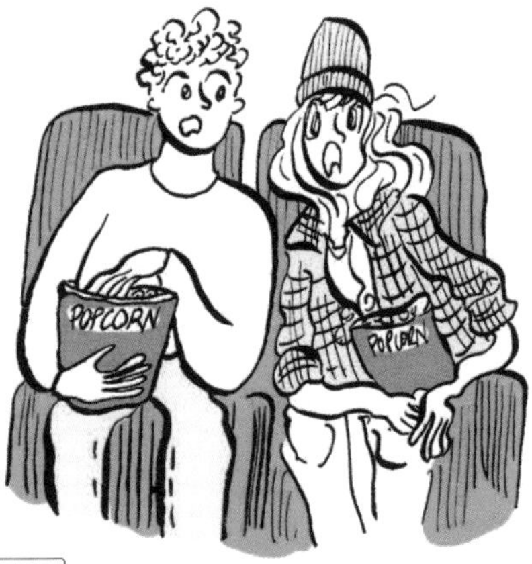
POPCORN

ANYWHERE, ANYTIME.

AGORAPHOBIA

"WHEN THE SUPERMARKET'S REALLY CROWDED, I FEEL LIKE MY END IS NIGH."

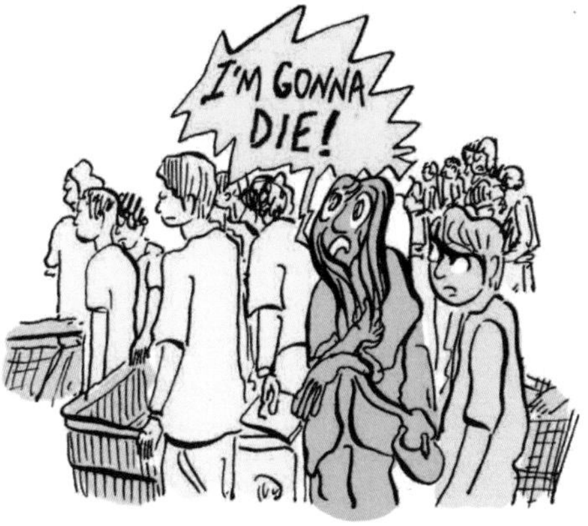
I'M GONNA DIE!

AUTOPHOBIA

"IF I CAN'T FIND A LIFE PARTNER, I'M GOING TO DIE ALONE, EATEN BY DOGS, LIKE BRIDGET JONES."

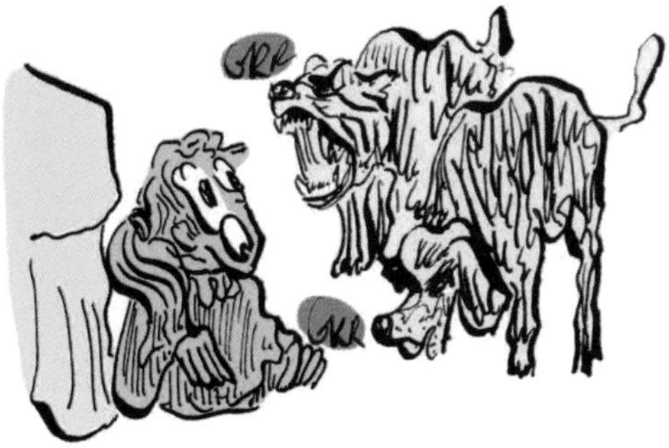

PHOBIAS

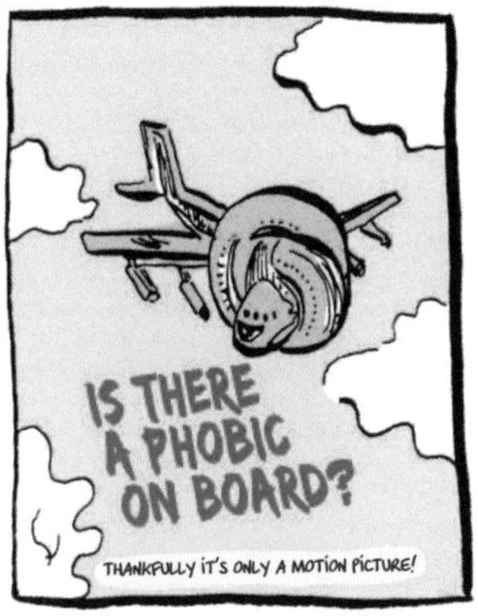
IS THERE A PHOBIC ON BOARD?
THANKFULLY IT'S ONLY A MOTION PICTURE!

OBSESSIVE-COMPULSIVE

"I HAVE TO BE IN TOTAL CONTROL, ON TOP OF EVERYTHING, TO PREVENT DISASTER."

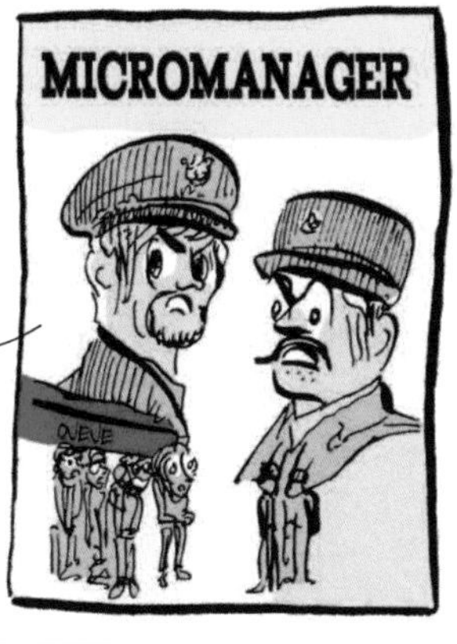
MICROMANAGER
QUEUE

SELF-ESTEEM ISSUES

"I'M ALWAYS AFRAID OF MESSING UP AT WORK."

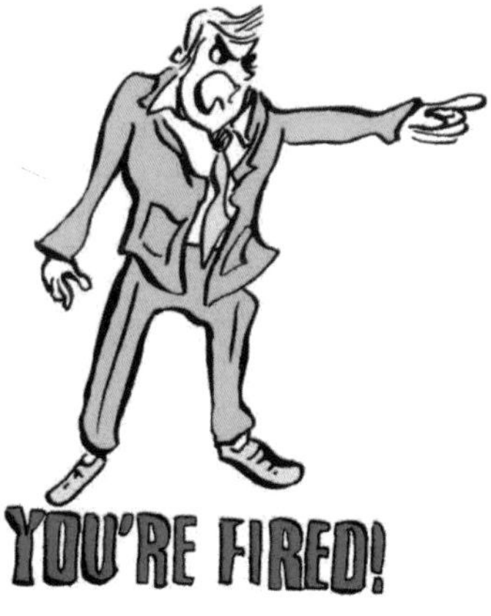
YOU'RE FIRED!

"I'M SCARED MY PARTNER WILL FIND OUT THE TRUTH."

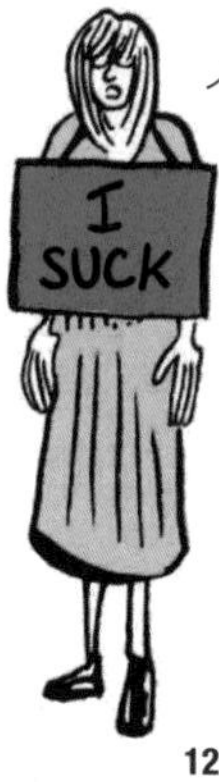
I SUCK

FEELING UNSAFE

"I'M SCARED OF HOME INVASION. I'VE GOT DOUBLE BOLTS."

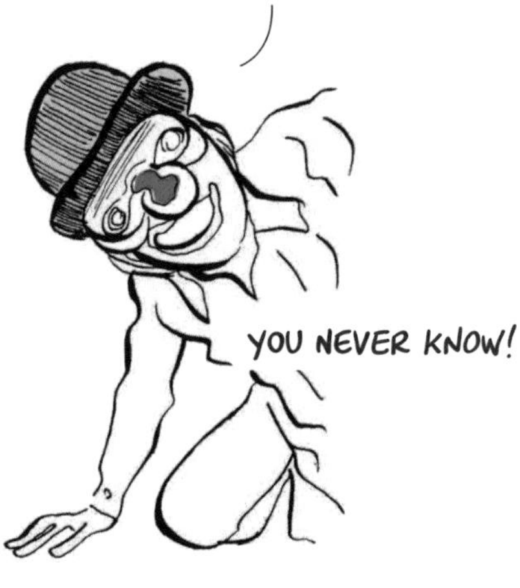
YOU NEVER KNOW!

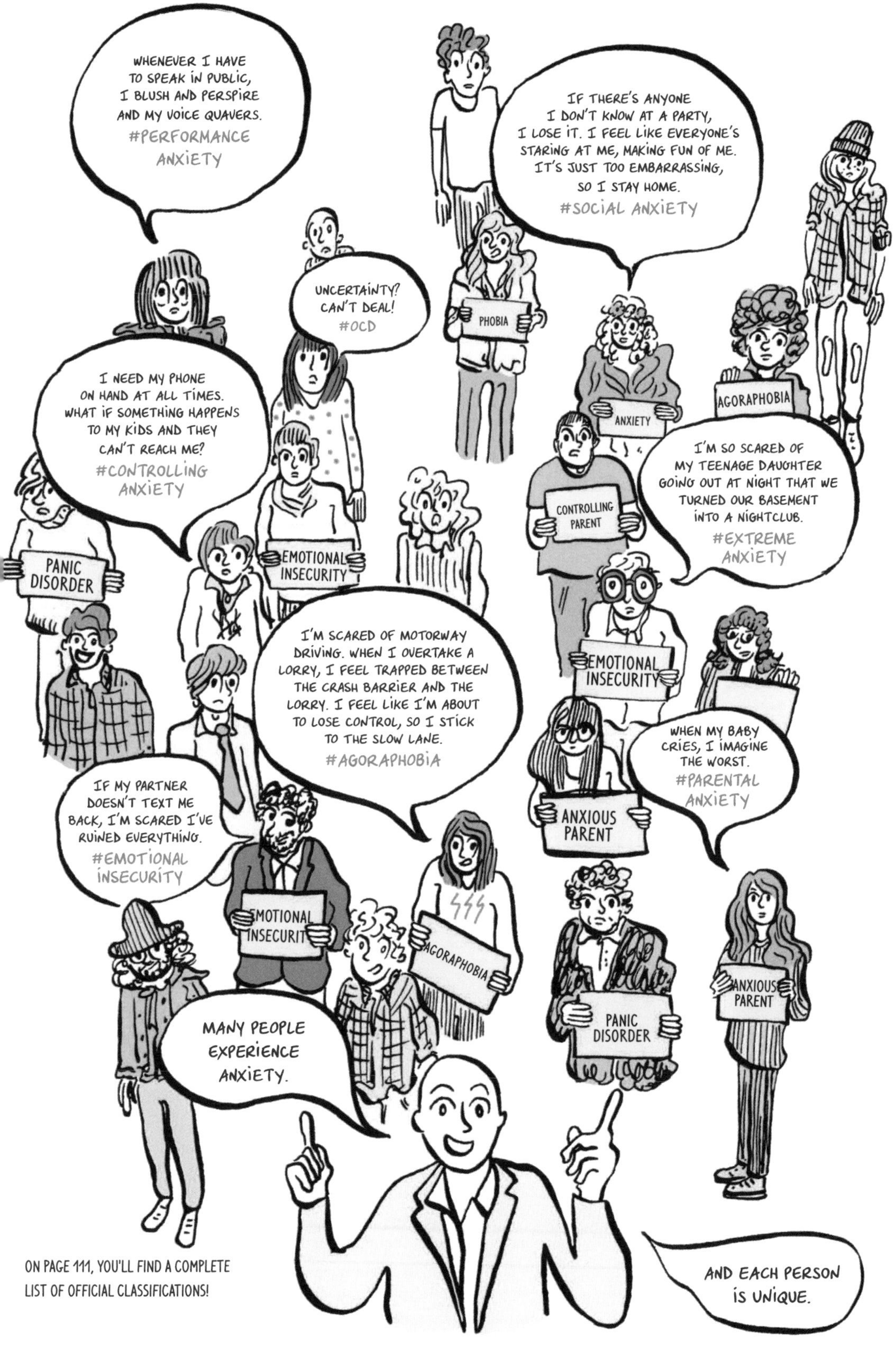
WHENEVER I HAVE TO SPEAK IN PUBLIC, I BLUSH AND PERSPIRE AND MY VOICE QUAVERS. #PERFORMANCE ANXIETY
UNCERTAINTY? CAN'T DEAL! #OCD
IF THERE'S ANYONE I DON'T KNOW AT A PARTY, I LOSE IT. I FEEL LIKE EVERYONE'S STARING AT ME, MAKING FUN OF ME. IT'S JUST TOO EMBARRASSING, SO I STAY HOME. #SOCIAL ANXIETY
PHOBIA
ANXIETY
AGORAPHOBIA
I NEED MY PHONE ON HAND AT ALL TIMES. WHAT IF SOMETHING HAPPENS TO MY KIDS AND THEY CAN'T REACH ME? #CONTROLLING ANXIETY
CONTROLLING PARENT
I'M SO SCARED OF MY TEENAGE DAUGHTER GOING OUT AT NIGHT THAT WE TURNED OUR BASEMENT INTO A NIGHTCLUB. #EXTREME ANXIETY
PANIC DISORDER
EMOTIONAL INSECURITY
I'M SCARED OF MOTORWAY DRIVING. WHEN I OVERTAKE A LORRY, I FEEL TRAPPED BETWEEN THE CRASH BARRIER AND THE LORRY. I FEEL LIKE I'M ABOUT TO LOSE CONTROL, SO I STICK TO THE SLOW LANE. #AGORAPHOBIA
EMOTIONAL INSECURITY
WHEN MY BABY CRIES, I IMAGINE THE WORST. #PARENTAL ANXIETY
ANXIOUS PARENT
IF MY PARTNER DOESN'T TEXT ME BACK, I'M SCARED I'VE RUINED EVERYTHING. #EMOTIONAL INSECURITY
EMOTIONAL INSECURIT
AGORAPHOBIA
PANIC DISORDER
ANXIOUS PARENT
MANY PEOPLE EXPERIENCE ANXIETY.
AND EACH PERSON IS UNIQUE.

ON PAGE 111, YOU'LL FIND A COMPLETE LIST OF OFFICIAL CLASSIFICATIONS!

CHAPTER 2

SOME KEYS TO UNDERSTANDING

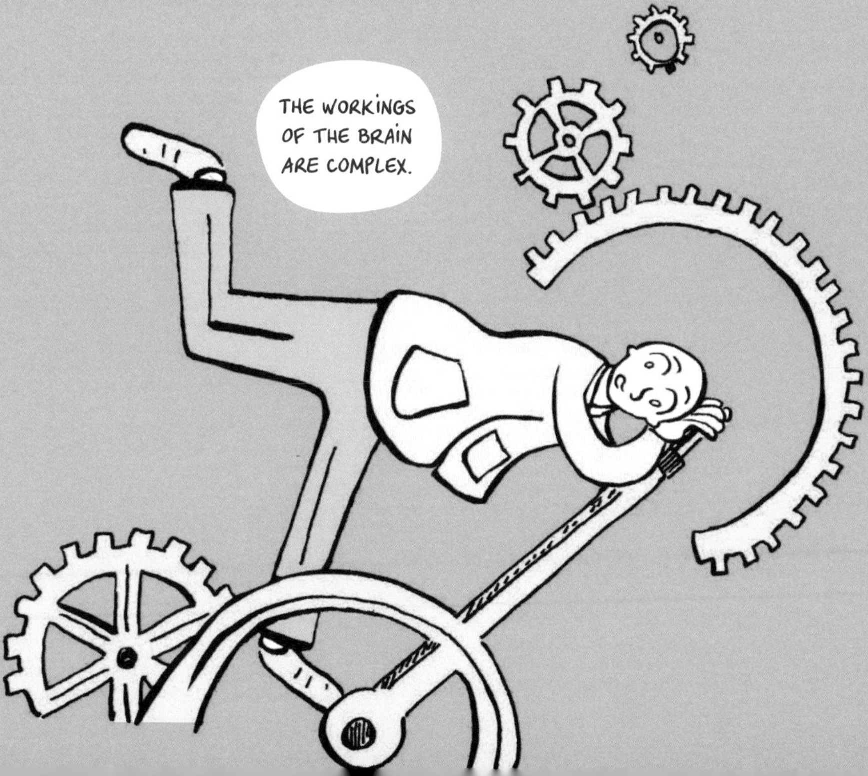
THE WORKINGS OF THE BRAIN ARE COMPLEX.

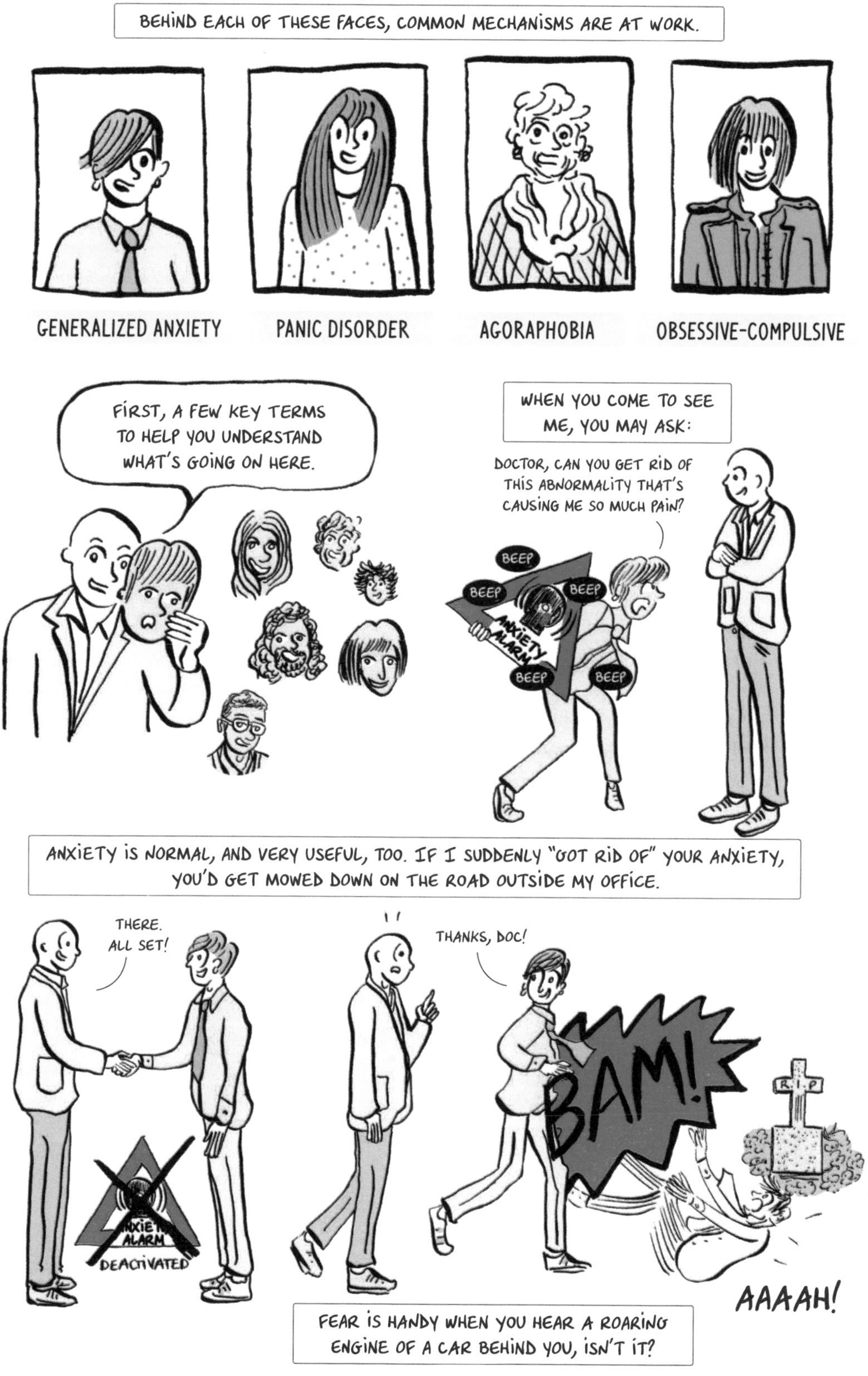
BEHIND EACH OF THESE FACES, COMMON MECHANISMS ARE AT WORK.
GENERALIZED ANXIETY
PANIC DISORDER
AGORAPHOBIA
OBSESSIVE-COMPULSIVE
FIRST, A FEW KEY TERMS TO HELP YOU UNDERSTAND WHAT'S GOING ON HERE.
WHEN YOU COME TO SEE ME, YOU MAY ASK:
DOCTOR, CAN YOU GET RID OF THIS ABNORMALITY THAT'S CAUSING ME SO MUCH PAIN?
BEEP
BEEP
BEEP
ANXIETY ALARM
BEEP
BEEP
ANXIETY IS NORMAL, AND VERY USEFUL, TOO. IF I SUDDENLY "GOT RID OF" YOUR ANXIETY, YOU'D GET MOWED DOWN ON THE ROAD OUTSIDE MY OFFICE.
THERE. ALL SET!
DEACTIVATED
THANKS, DOC!
BAM!
R.I.P.
AAAAH!
FEAR IS HANDY WHEN YOU HEAR A ROARING ENGINE OF A CAR BEHIND YOU, ISN'T IT?

1. IT'S ALL A MATTER OF SETTINGS...

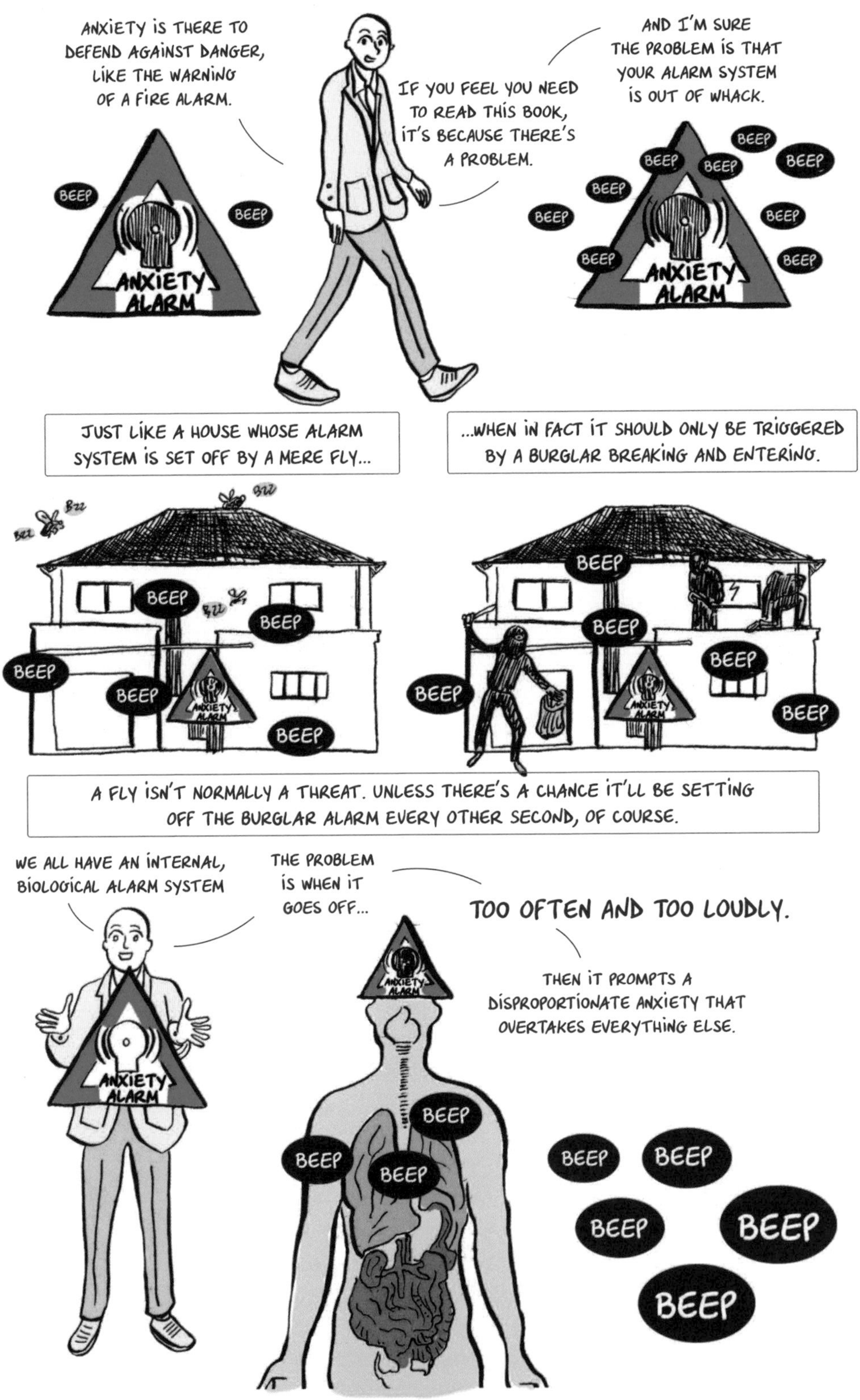
ANXIETY IS THERE TO DEFEND AGAINST DANGER, LIKE THE WARNING OF A FIRE ALARM.
BEEP
BEEP
ANXIETY ALARM
IF YOU FEEL YOU NEED TO READ THIS BOOK, IT'S BECAUSE THERE'S A PROBLEM.
AND I'M SURE THE PROBLEM IS THAT YOUR ALARM SYSTEM IS OUT OF WHACK.
BEEP
ANXIETY ALARM
JUST LIKE A HOUSE WHOSE ALARM SYSTEM IS SET OFF BY A MERE FLY...
...WHEN IN FACT IT SHOULD ONLY BE TRIGGERED BY A BURGLAR BREAKING AND ENTERING.
BZZ
BEEP
BEEP
A FLY ISN'T NORMALLY A THREAT. UNLESS THERE'S A CHANCE IT'LL BE SETTING OFF THE BURGLAR ALARM EVERY OTHER SECOND, OF COURSE.
WE ALL HAVE AN INTERNAL, BIOLOGICAL ALARM SYSTEM
THE PROBLEM IS WHEN IT GOES OFF...
TOO OFTEN AND TOO LOUDLY.
THEN IT PROMPTS A DISPROPORTIONATE ANXIETY THAT OVERTAKES EVERYTHING ELSE.
ANXIETY ALARM
BEEP
BEEP
BEEP

2. OVERTHINKING THINGS: ANTICIPATING AND BROODING

APART FROM OUR «BIOLOGICAL ALARM SYSTEM», THERE ARE OTHER INDIVIDUAL PSYCHOLOGICAL FACTORS...

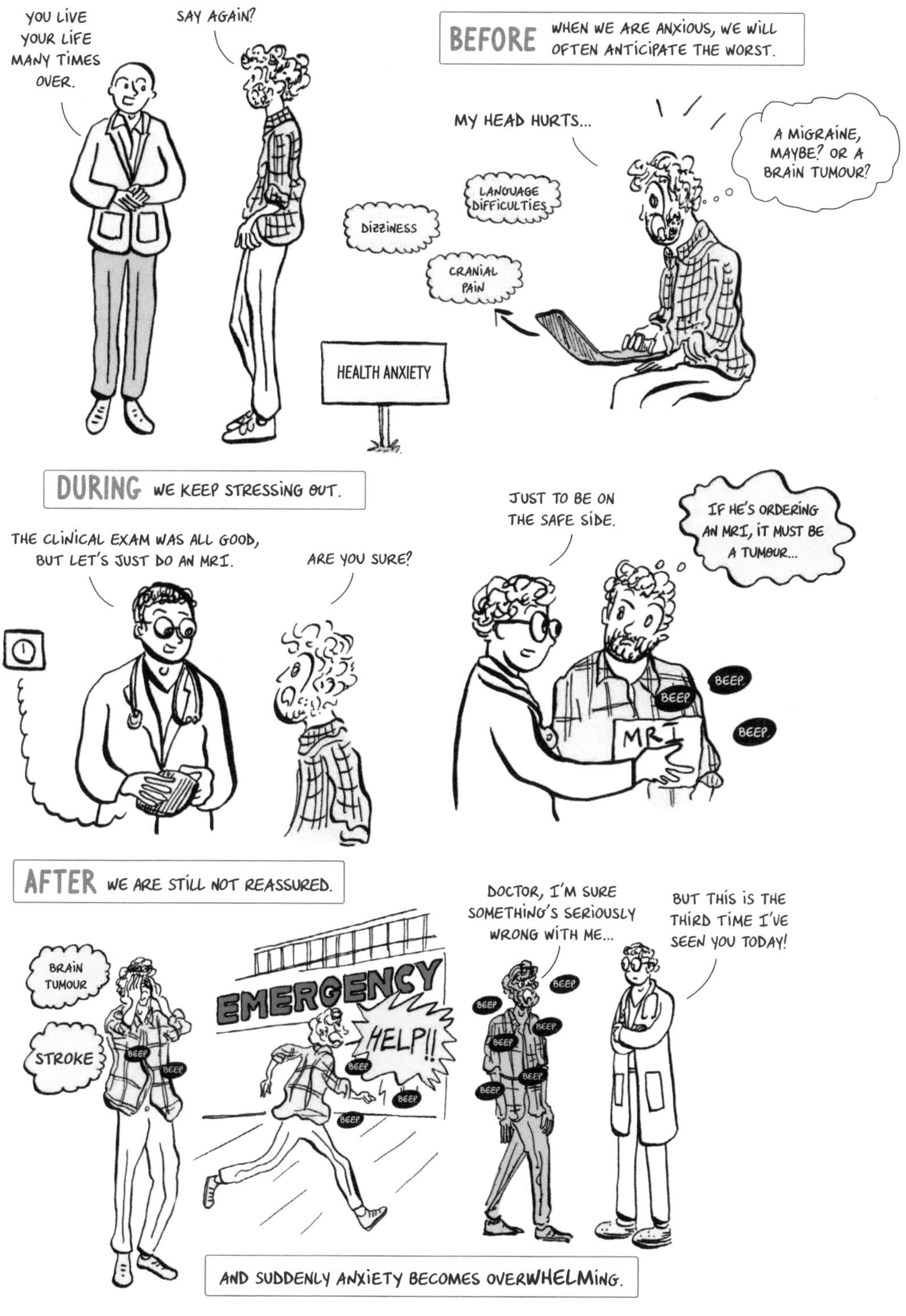
YOU LIVE YOUR LIFE MANY TIMES OVER.
SAY AGAIN?
HEALTH ANXIETY
BEFORE WHEN WE ARE ANXIOUS, WE WILL OFTEN ANTICIPATE THE WORST.
MY HEAD HURTS...
A MIGRAINE, MAYBE? OR A BRAIN TUMOUR?
LANGUAGE DIFFICULTIES
DIZZINESS
CRANIAL PAIN
DURING WE KEEP STRESSING OUT.
THE CLINICAL EXAM WAS ALL GOOD, BUT LET'S JUST DO AN MRI.
ARE YOU SURE?
JUST TO BE ON THE SAFE SIDE.
IF HE'S ORDERING AN MRI, IT MUST BE A TUMOUR...
BEEP
BEEP
BEEP
MRI
AFTER WE ARE STILL NOT REASSURED.
BRAIN TUMOUR
STROKE
BEEP
BEEP
EMERGENCY
HELP!!
BEEP
BEEP
BEEP
DOCTOR, I'M SURE SOMETHING'S SERIOUSLY WRONG WITH ME...
BUT THIS IS THE THIRD TIME I'VE SEEN YOU TODAY!
BEEP
BEEP
BEEP
BEEP
BEEP
BEEP
AND SUDDENLY ANXIETY BECOMES OVERWHELMING.

3. THE MAGNIFIER EFFECT

I EXPLAIN TO MY PATIENTS THAT OUR ANXIETIES ARE DOWN TO A PROBLEM OF SCALE.

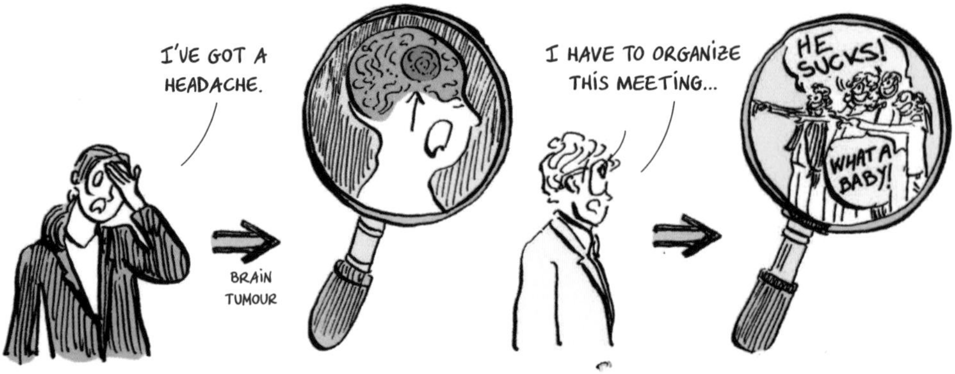

I'VE GOT A HEADACHE.
BRAIN TUMOUR
I HAVE TO ORGANIZE THIS MEETING...
HE SUCKS!
WHAT A BABY!

ON ONE HAND, WE OVERESTIMATE THE DANGER.

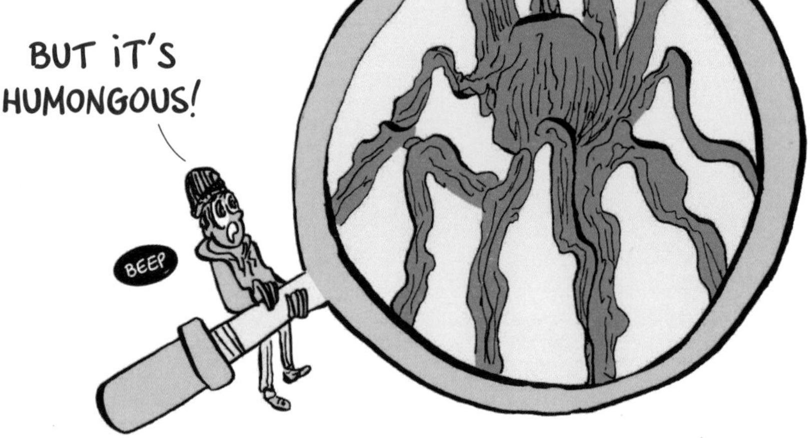

BUT IT'S HUMONGOUS!
BEEP

ON THE OTHER, WE UNDERESTIMATE OUR OWN CAPACITY TO FACE IT.

WE NEVER REMEMBER ALL THE TIMES WE WERE ABLE TO SUCCEED.

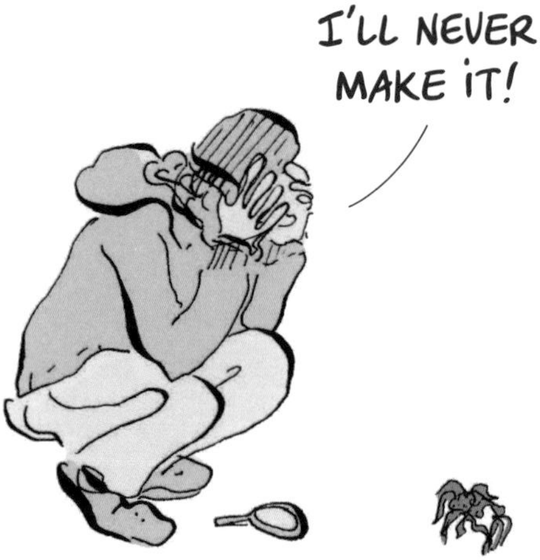

I'LL NEVER MAKE IT!

4. IS THIS NORMAL OR ABNORMAL?

HARD TO SAY. WHEN IT COMES TO ANXIETY, WE ALL HAVE DIFFERENT SETTINGS, AND WE ALL SPEND DIFFERENT AMOUNTS OF TIME WORRYING.

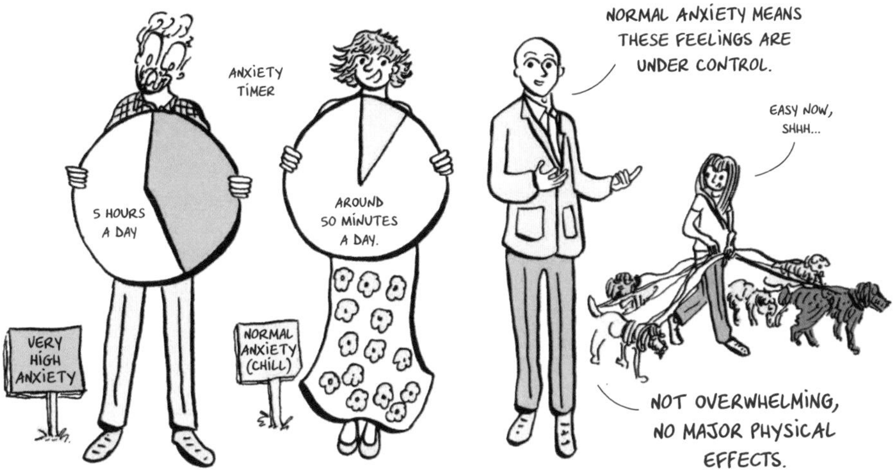

ANXIETY TIMER
5 HOURS A DAY
VERY HIGH ANXIETY
AROUND 50 MINUTES A DAY.
NORMAL ANXIETY (CHILL)
NORMAL ANXIETY MEANS THESE FEELINGS ARE UNDER CONTROL.
EASY NOW, SHHH...
NOT OVERWHELMING, NO MAJOR PHYSICAL EFFECTS.

PATHOLOGICAL ANXIETY IS WHEN OUR WARNING SYSTEM IS SEVERAL LEVELS OFF.

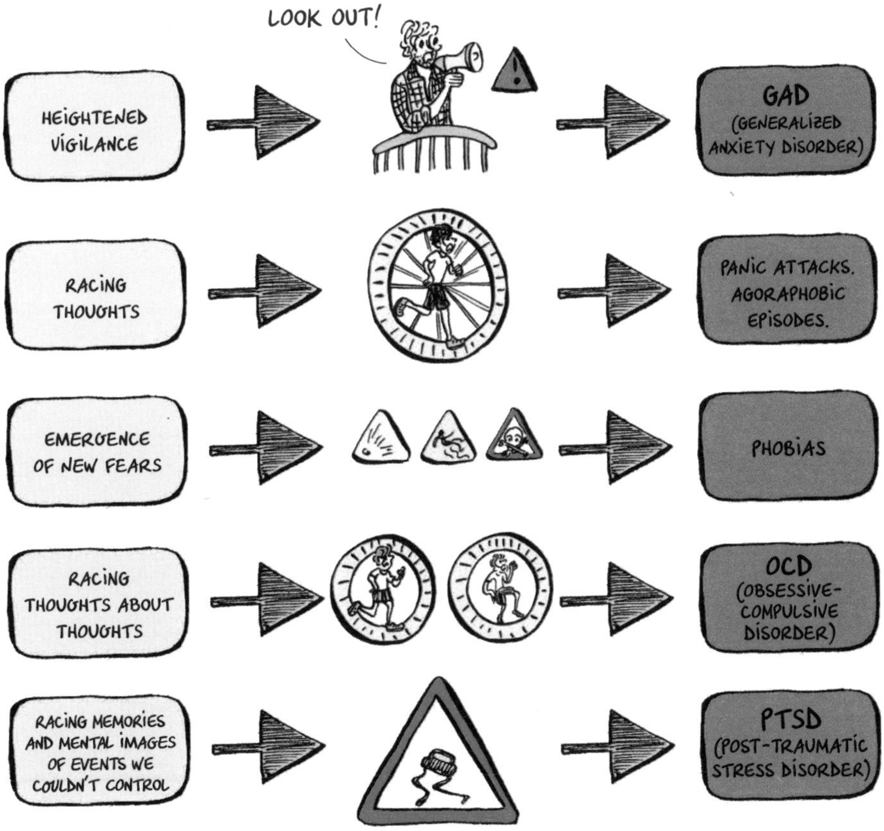

LOOK OUT!
HEIGHTENED VIGILANCE
GAD (GENERALIZED ANXIETY DISORDER)
RACING THOUGHTS
PANIC ATTACKS. AGORAPHOBIC EPISODES.
EMERGENCE OF NEW FEARS
PHOBIAS
RACING THOUGHTS ABOUT THOUGHTS
OCD (OBSESSIVE-COMPULSIVE DISORDER)
RACING MEMORIES AND MENTAL IMAGES OF EVENTS WE COULDN'T CONTROL
PTSD (POST-TRAUMATIC STRESS DISORDER)

CHAPTER 3
ANXIETY'S DISASTER CINEMA

ANXIETY SUFFERERS ALWAYS TURN EVERYTHING INTO A MOVIE — A DISASTER MOVIE, THAT IS.

EXAGGERATING THREATS, ANTICIPATING DANGERS, AND NEVER BEING REASSURED EVEN WHEN EVERYTHING'S BEEN CHECKED.

DOESN'T SOUND LIKE A COMEDY, DOES IT?

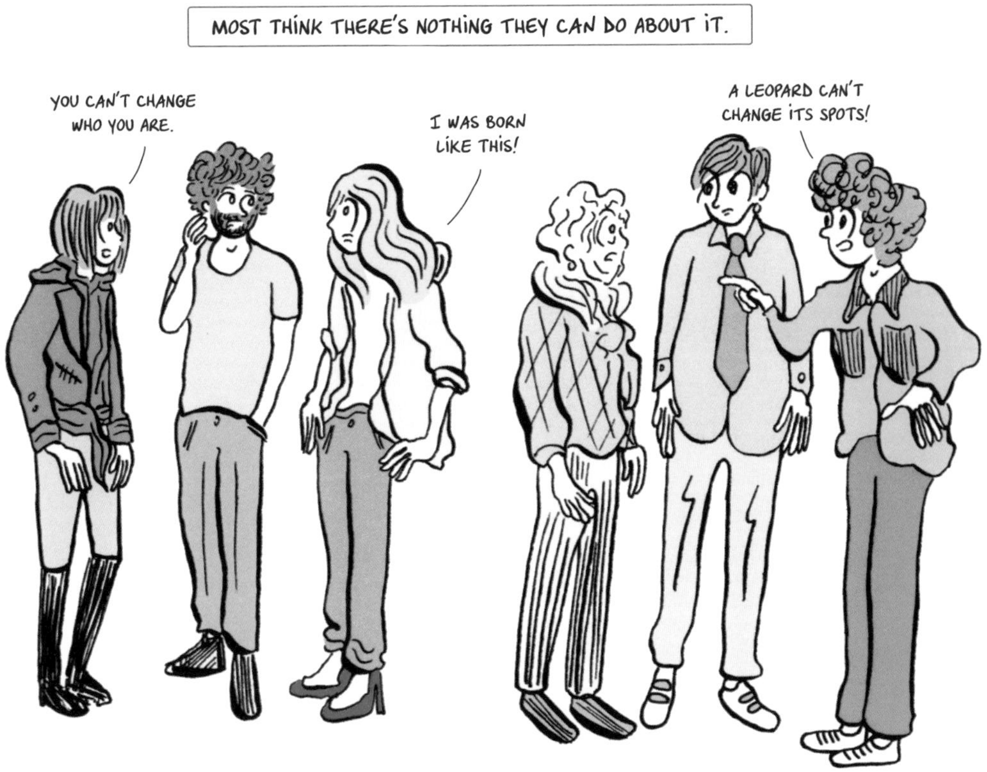
MOST THINK THERE'S NOTHING THEY CAN DO ABOUT IT.
YOU CAN'T CHANGE WHO YOU ARE.
I WAS BORN LIKE THIS!
A LEOPARD CAN'T CHANGE ITS SPOTS!

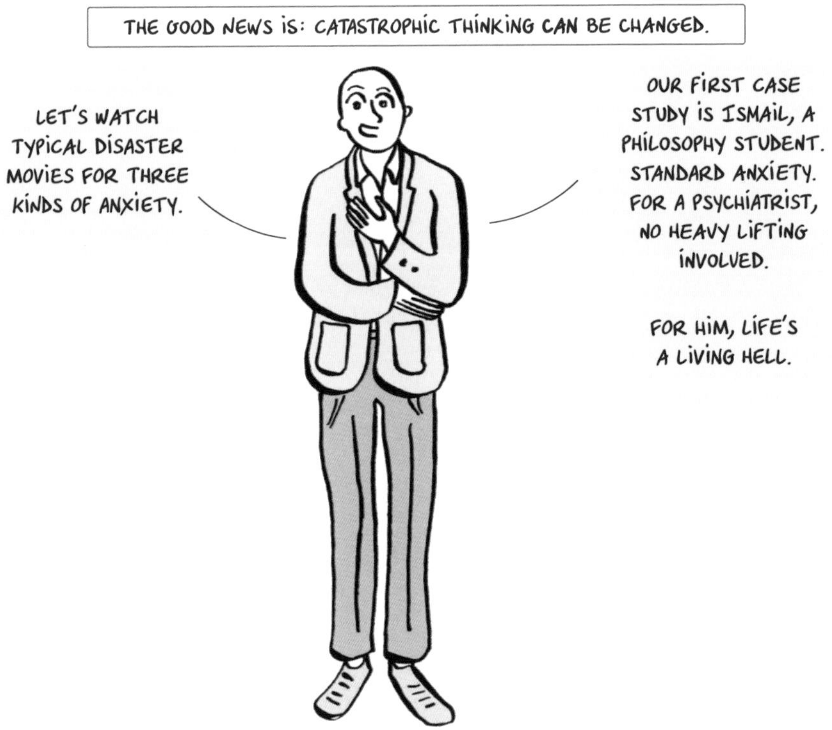
THE GOOD NEWS IS: CATASTROPHIC THINKING CAN BE CHANGED.
LET'S WATCH TYPICAL DISASTER MOVIES FOR THREE KINDS OF ANXIETY.
OUR FIRST CASE STUDY IS ISMAIL, A PHILOSOPHY STUDENT. STANDARD ANXIETY. FOR A PSYCHIATRIST, NO HEAVY LIFTING INVOLVED.
FOR HIM, LIFE'S A LIVING HELL.

ANXIETY CLUB PRODUCTIONS PRESENTS

ISMAIL'S

FEAR OF SLEEPLESS NIGHTS

BASED ON HENRY FUSELI'S "THE NIGHTMARE"

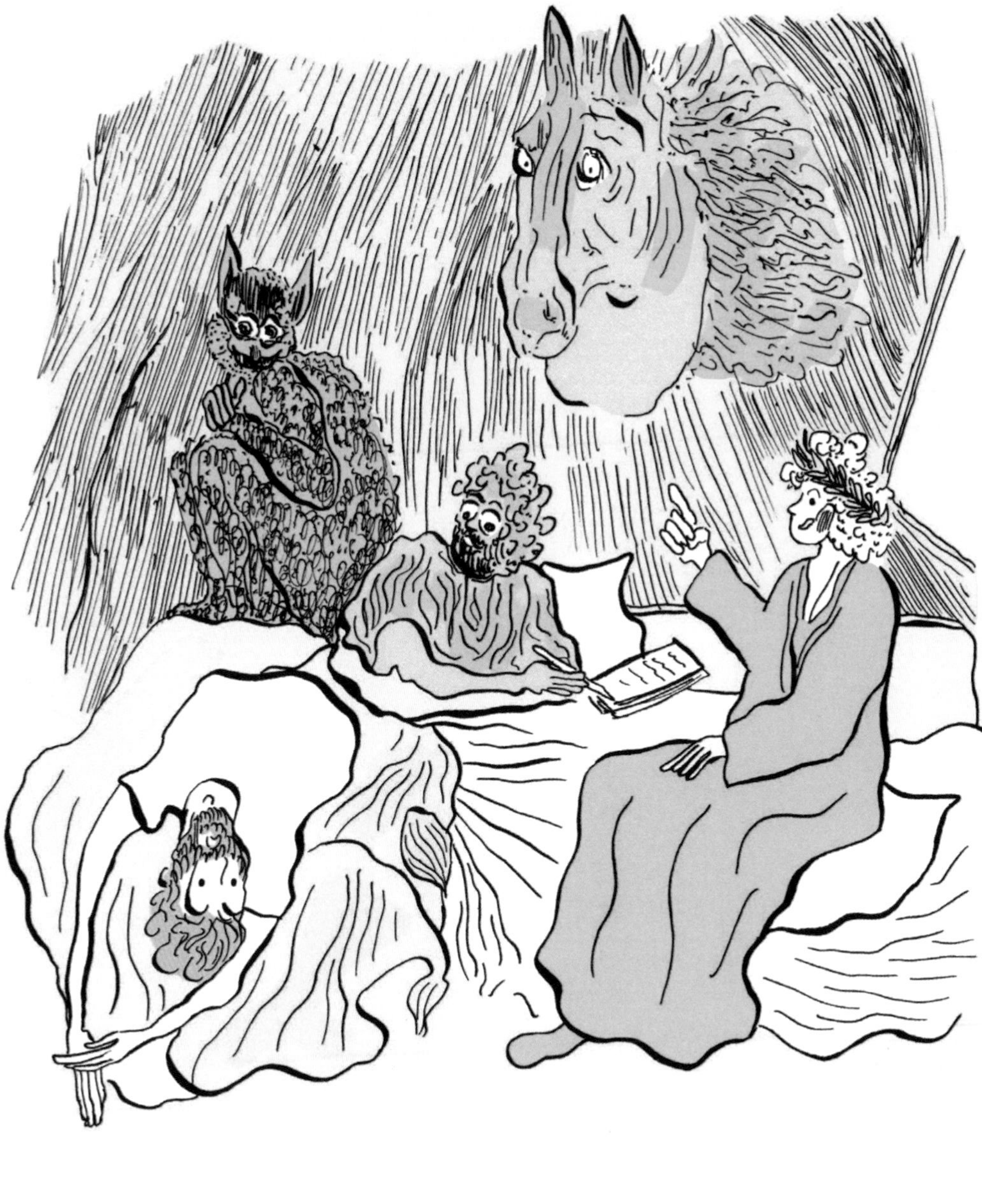

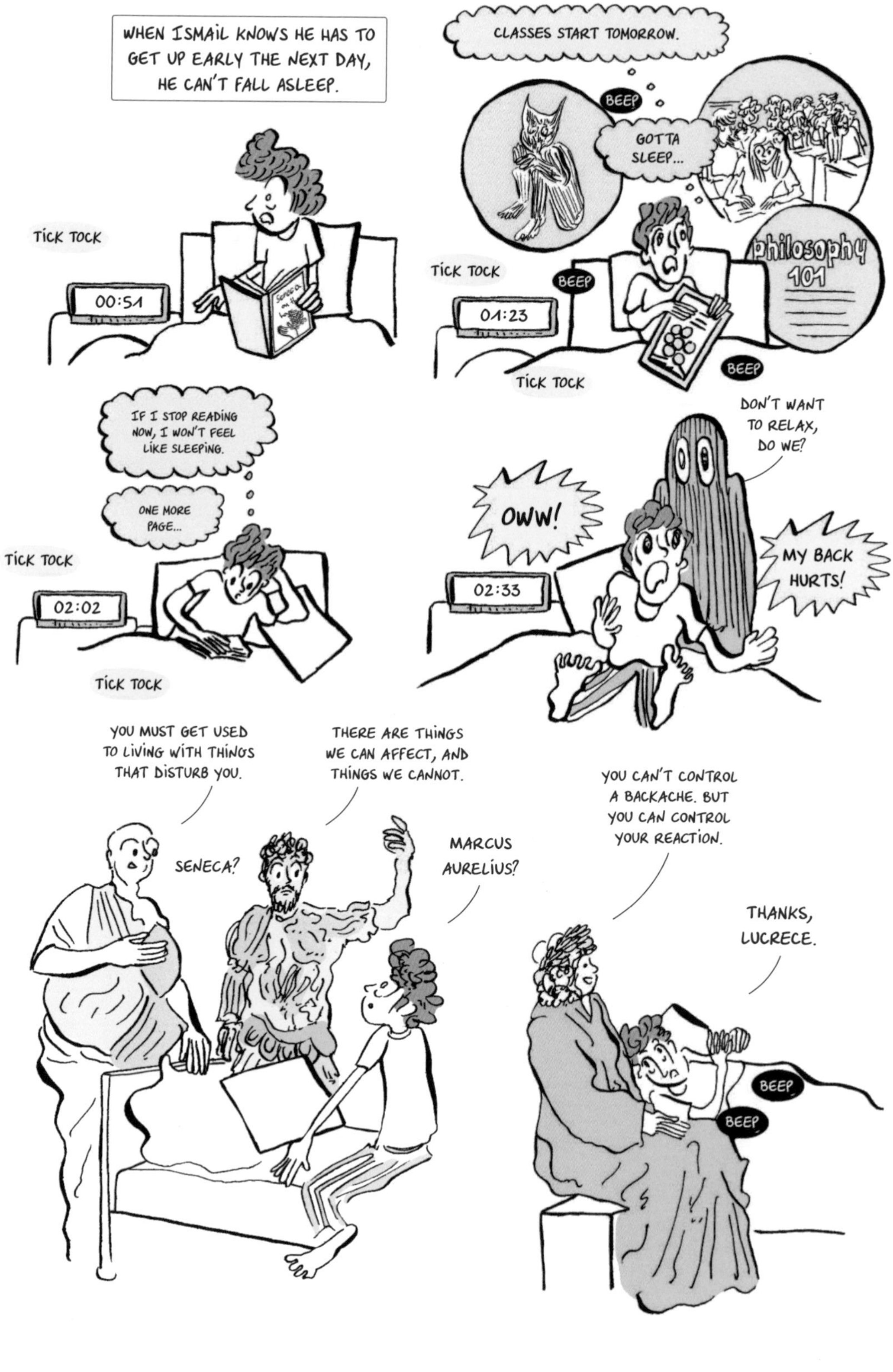
WHEN ISMAIL KNOWS HE HAS TO GET UP EARLY THE NEXT DAY, HE CAN'T FALL ASLEEP.
TICK TOCK
00:51
CLASSES START TOMORROW.
BEEP
GOTTA SLEEP...
TICK TOCK
BEEP
01:23
philosophy 101
TICK TOCK
BEEP
IF I STOP READING NOW, I WON'T FEEL LIKE SLEEPING.
ONE MORE PAGE...
TICK TOCK
02:02
TICK TOCK
DON'T WANT TO RELAX, DO WE?
OWW!
02:33
MY BACK HURTS!
YOU MUST GET USED TO LIVING WITH THINGS THAT DISTURB YOU.
SENECA?
THERE ARE THINGS WE CAN AFFECT, AND THINGS WE CANNOT.
MARCUS AURELIUS?
YOU CAN'T CONTROL A BACKACHE. BUT YOU CAN CONTROL YOUR REACTION.
THANKS, LUCRECE.
BEEP
BEEP

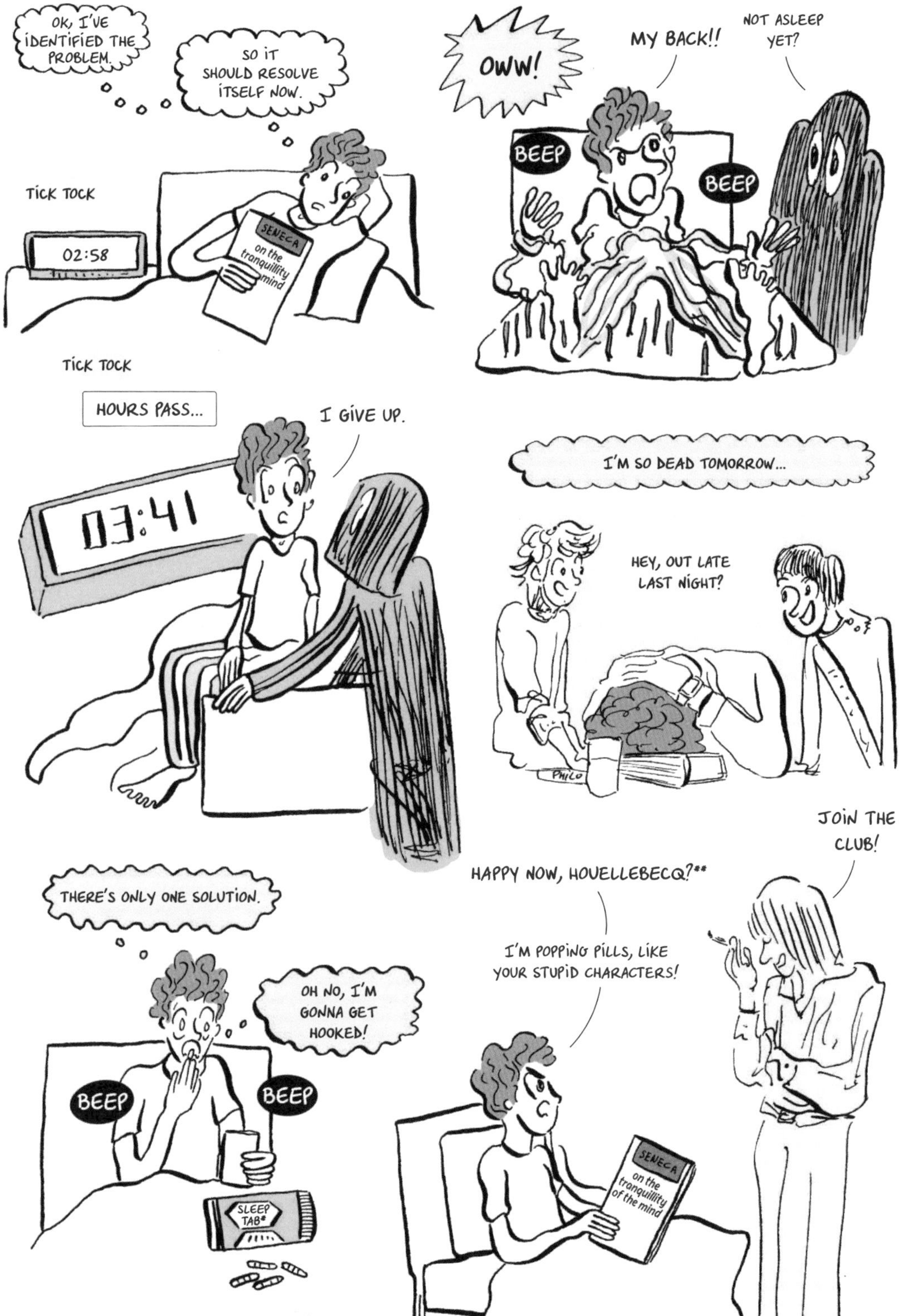
OK, I'VE IDENTIFIED THE PROBLEM.
SO IT SHOULD RESOLVE ITSELF NOW.
TICK TOCK
02:58
SENECA on the tranquillity of the mind
TICK TOCK
OWW!
MY BACK!!
NOT ASLEEP YET?
BEEP
BEEP
HOURS PASS...
I GIVE UP.
03:41
I'M SO DEAD TOMORROW...
HEY, OUT LATE LAST NIGHT?
PHILO
THERE'S ONLY ONE SOLUTION.
OH NO, I'M GONNA GET HOOKED!
BEEP
BEEP
SLEEP TAB*
HAPPY NOW, HOUELLEBECQ?**
JOIN THE CLUB!
I'M POPPING PILLS, LIKE YOUR STUPID CHARACTERS!
SENECA on the tranquillity of the mind

*ALWAYS CONSULT YOUR DOCTOR/MEDICAL PRACTITIONER BEFORE TAKING ANY DRUGS.

**MICHEL HOUELLEBECQ IS A FRENCH ESSAYIST AND NOVELIST.

SPEC SHEET: ANXIETY'S VICIOUS CYCLE

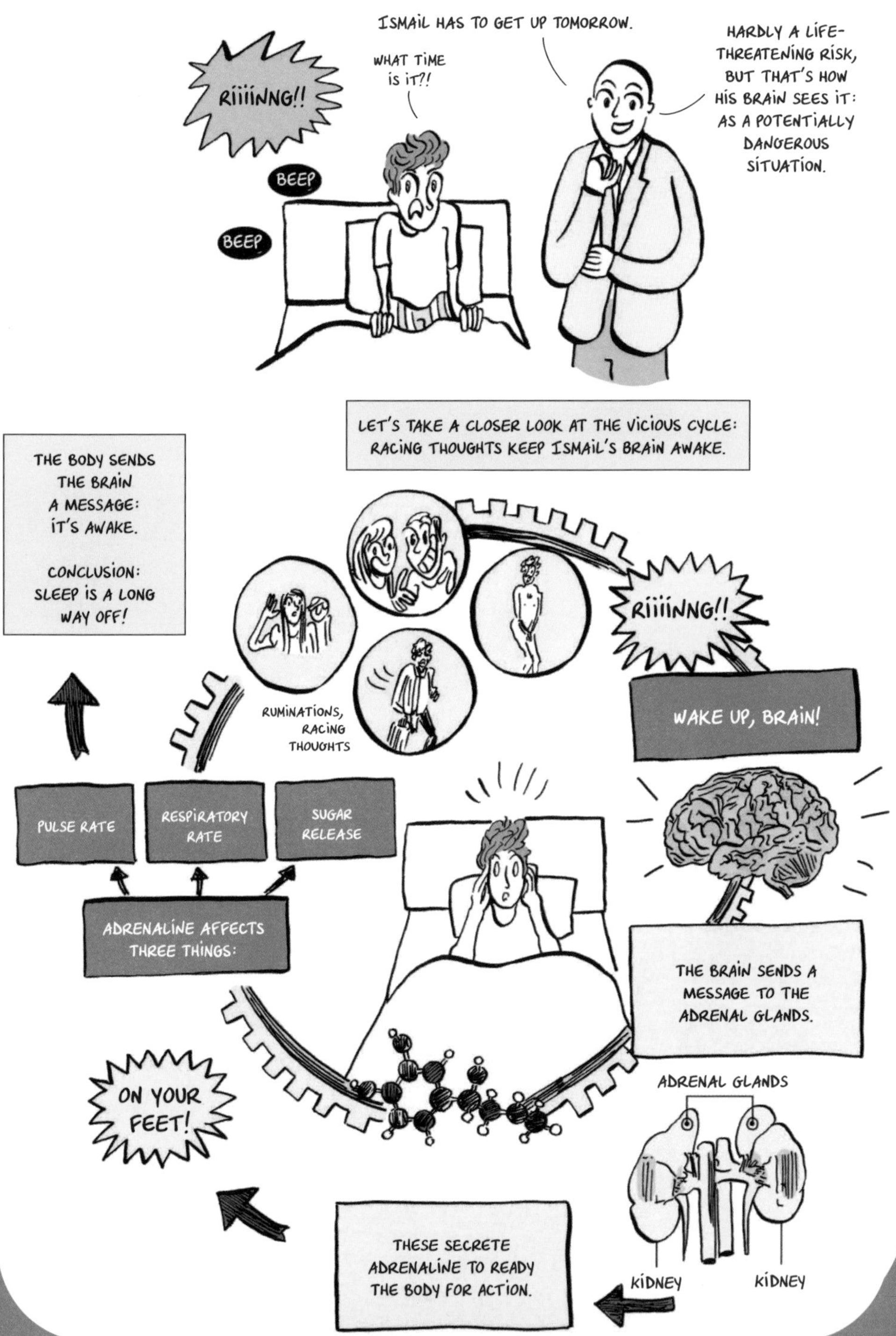
RIiiiNNG!!
BEEP
BEEP
WHAT TIME IS IT?!
ISMAIL HAS TO GET UP TOMORROW.
HARDLY A LIFE-THREATENING RISK, BUT THAT'S HOW HIS BRAIN SEES IT: AS A POTENTIALLY DANGEROUS SITUATION.
LET'S TAKE A CLOSER LOOK AT THE VICIOUS CYCLE: RACING THOUGHTS KEEP ISMAIL'S BRAIN AWAKE.
RIiiiNNG!!
WAKE UP, BRAIN!
THE BRAIN SENDS A MESSAGE TO THE ADRENAL GLANDS.
ADRENAL GLANDS
KIDNEY
KIDNEY
THESE SECRETE ADRENALINE TO READY THE BODY FOR ACTION.
ON YOUR FEET!
ADRENALINE AFFECTS THREE THINGS:
PULSE RATE
RESPIRATORY RATE
SUGAR RELEASE
THE BODY SENDS THE BRAIN A MESSAGE: IT'S AWAKE.
CONCLUSION: SLEEP IS A LONG WAY OFF!
RUMINATIONS, RACING THOUGHTS

AS ISMAIL'S THERAPIST, I CAN ACT ON TWO FRONTS: BODY AND THOUGHTS.

1. BODY

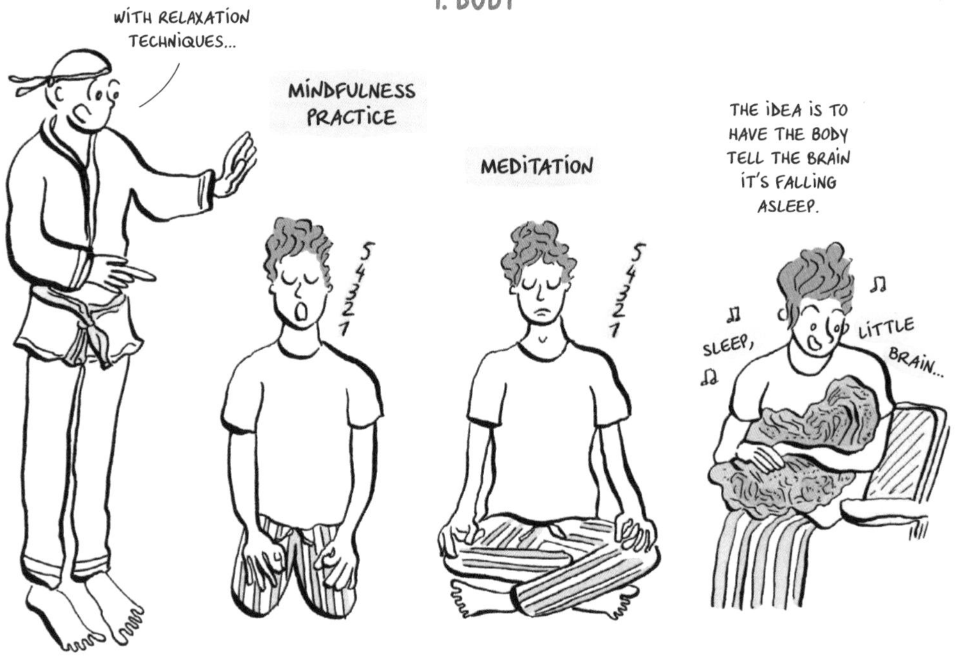

WITH RELAXATION TECHNIQUES...
MINDFULNESS PRACTICE
5 4 3 2 1
MEDITATION
5 4 3 2 1
THE IDEA IS TO HAVE THE BODY TELL THE BRAIN IT'S FALLING ASLEEP.
SLEEP, LITTLE BRAIN...

2. CATASTROPHIC THOUGHTS

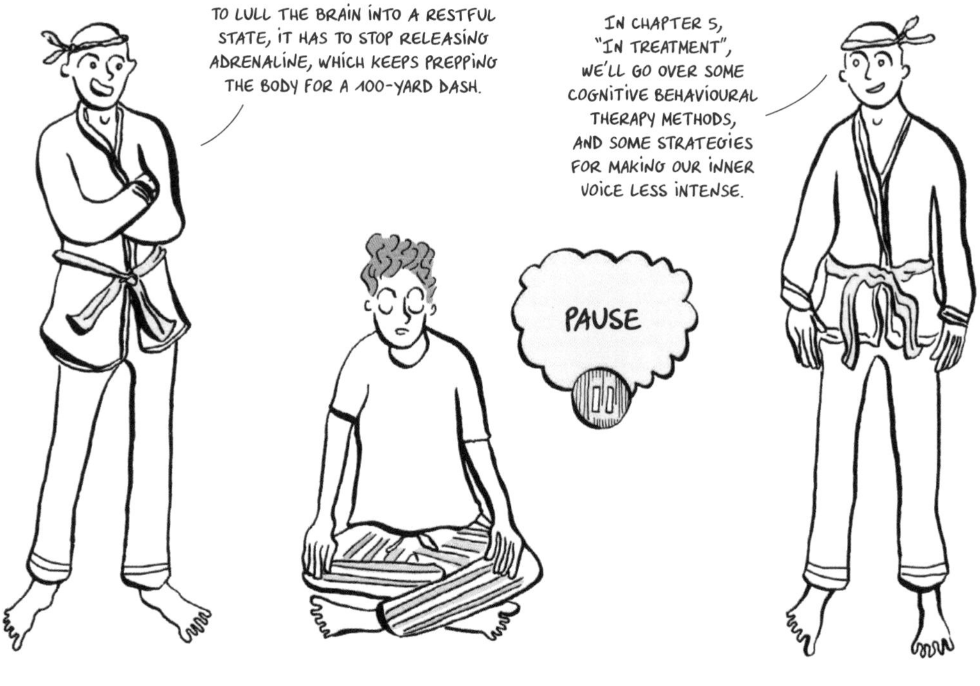

TO LULL THE BRAIN INTO A RESTFUL STATE, IT HAS TO STOP RELEASING ADRENALINE, WHICH KEEPS PREPPING THE BODY FOR A 100-YARD DASH.
IN CHAPTER 5, "IN TREATMENT", WE'LL GO OVER SOME COGNITIVE BEHAVIOURAL THERAPY METHODS, AND SOME STRATEGIES FOR MAKING OUR INNER VOICE LESS INTENSE.
PAUSE

AND NOW FOR OUR
SECOND CASE, MONA.

SHE'S A BOOKSELLER.
HER ANXIETY BEGAN
TO OVERWHELM HER IN
ENCLOSED SPACES, LIKE
THE SUBWAY.

ANXIETY CLUB PRODUCTIONS PRESENTS

A FILM BY MONA

ENCLOSED
SUBWAY OF DOOM

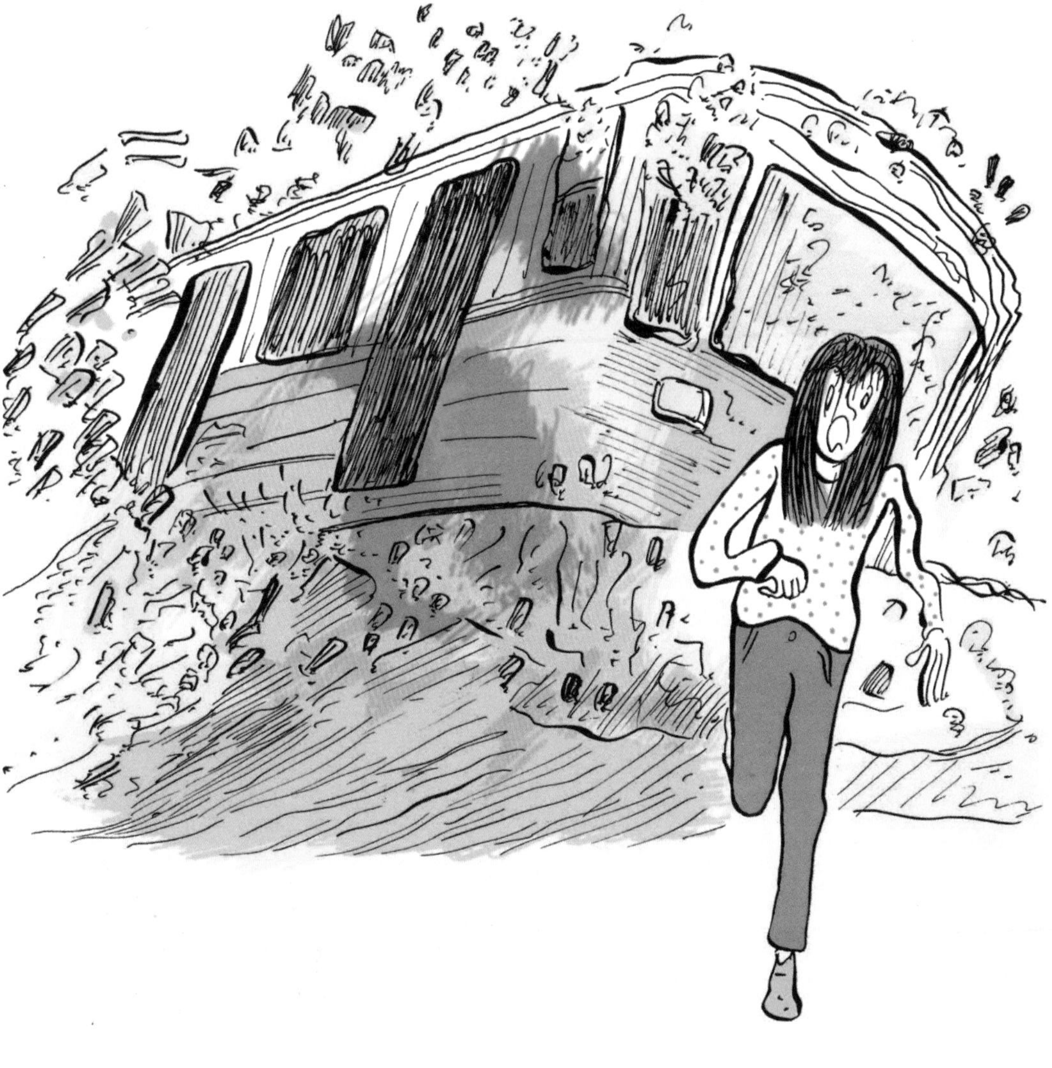

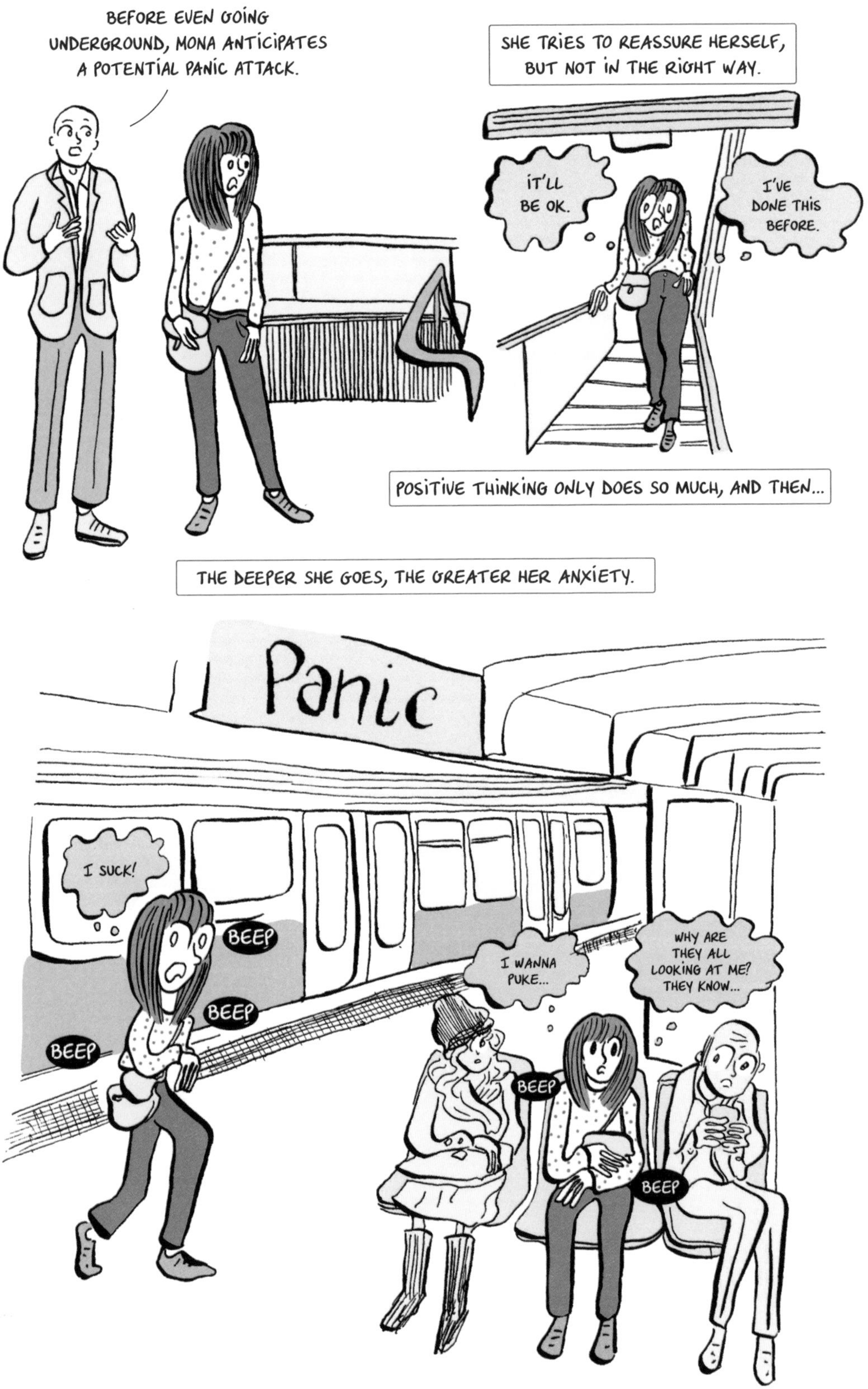
BEFORE EVEN GOING UNDERGROUND, MONA ANTICIPATES A POTENTIAL PANIC ATTACK.
SHE TRIES TO REASSURE HERSELF, BUT NOT IN THE RIGHT WAY.
IT'LL BE OK.
I'VE DONE THIS BEFORE.
POSITIVE THINKING ONLY DOES SO MUCH, AND THEN...
THE DEEPER SHE GOES, THE GREATER HER ANXIETY.
Panic
I SUCK!
BEEP
BEEP
BEEP
I WANNA PUKE...
WHY ARE THEY ALL LOOKING AT ME? THEY KNOW...
BEEP
BEEP

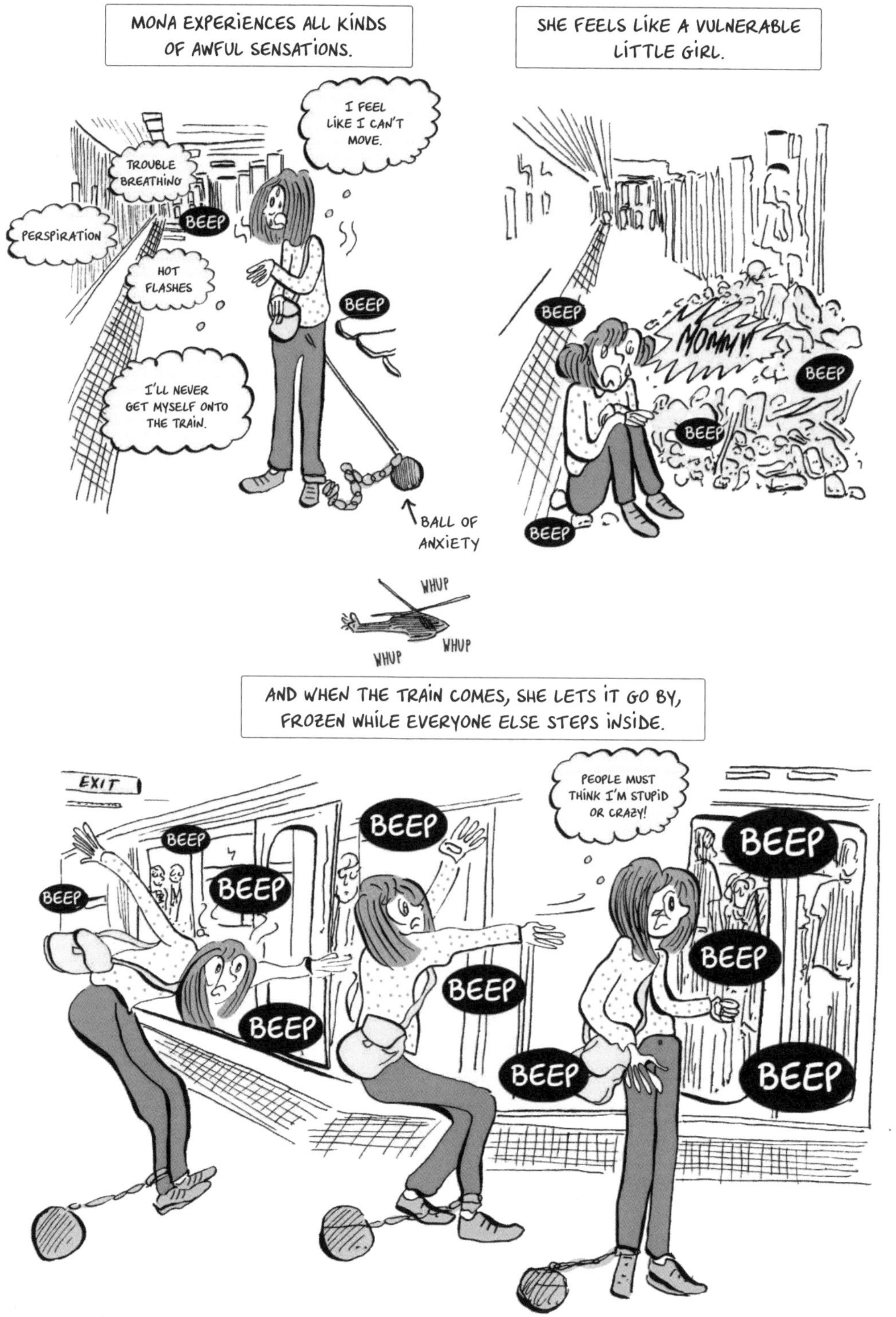
MONA EXPERIENCES ALL KINDS OF AWFUL SENSATIONS.
I FEEL LIKE I CAN'T MOVE.
TROUBLE BREATHING
PERSPIRATION
BEEP
HOT FLASHES
BEEP
I'LL NEVER GET MYSELF ONTO THE TRAIN.
BALL OF ANXIETY
SHE FEELS LIKE A VULNERABLE LITTLE GIRL.
BEEP
MOMMY!
BEEP
BEEP
BEEP
WHUP
WHUP
WHUP
AND WHEN THE TRAIN COMES, SHE LETS IT GO BY, FROZEN WHILE EVERYONE ELSE STEPS INSIDE.
EXIT
BEEP
BEEP
BEEP
BEEP
BEEP
PEOPLE MUST THINK I'M STUPID OR CRAZY!
BEEP
BEEP
BEEP
BEEP
BEEP

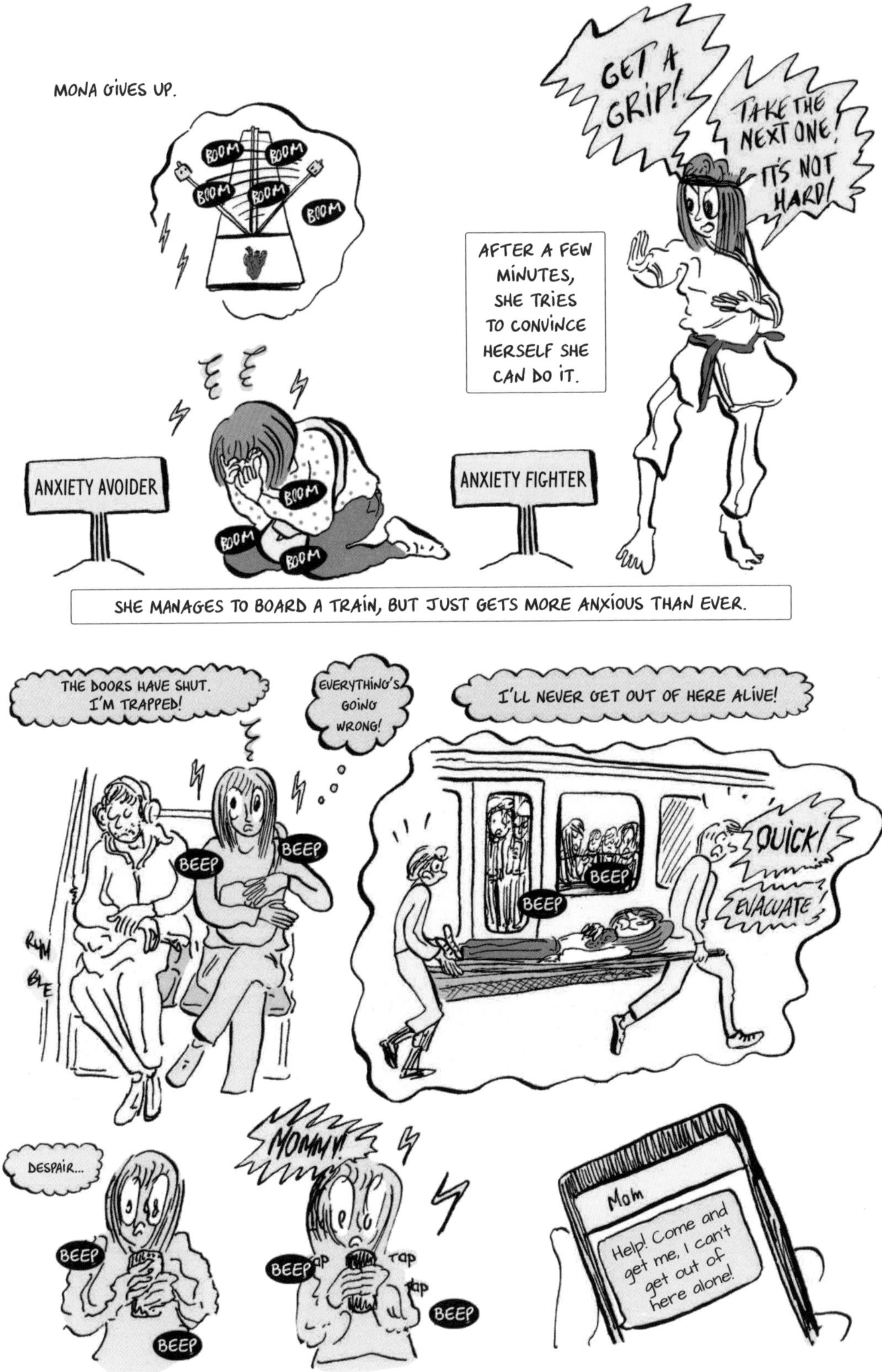
MONA GIVES UP.
BOOM
BOOM
BOOM
BOOM
BOOM
ANXIETY AVOIDER
BOOM
BOOM
BOOM
ANXIETY FIGHTER
AFTER A FEW MINUTES, SHE TRIES TO CONVINCE HERSELF SHE CAN DO IT.
GET A GRIP!
TAKE THE NEXT ONE! IT'S NOT HARD!
SHE MANAGES TO BOARD A TRAIN, BUT JUST GETS MORE ANXIOUS THAN EVER.
THE DOORS HAVE SHUT. I'M TRAPPED!
EVERYTHING'S GOING WRONG!
I'LL NEVER GET OUT OF HERE ALIVE!
RUM BLE
BEEP
BEEP
BEEP
BEEP
QUICK!
EVACUATE!
DESPAIR...
BEEP
BEEP
MOMMY!
BEEP
tap
tap
tap
BEEP
Mom
Help! Come and get me, I can't get out of here alone!

AT THE NEXT STATION, MONA RUNS OUT.

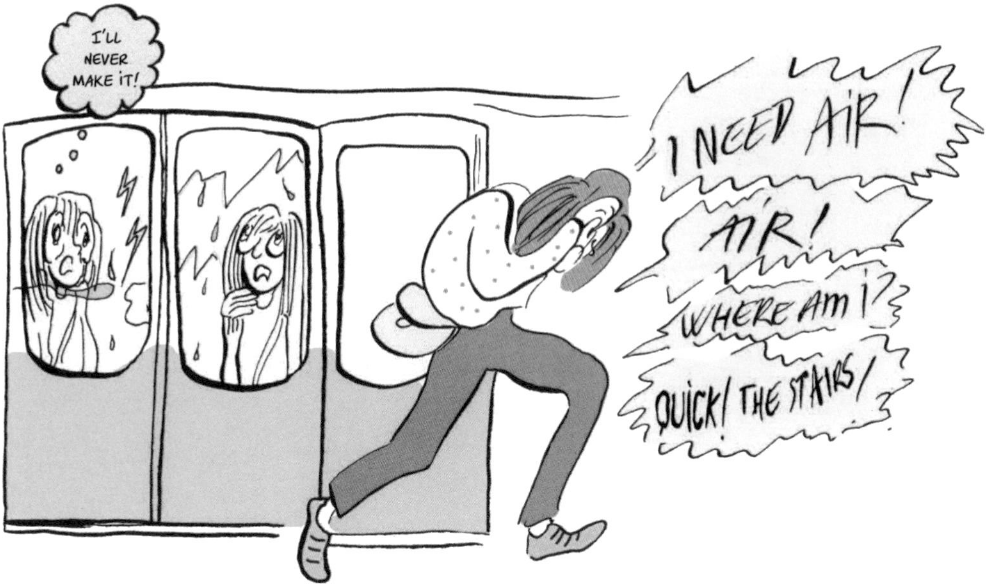
I'LL NEVER MAKE IT!
I NEED AIR!
AIR!
WHERE AM I?
QUICK! THE STAIRS!

SHE'S EXHAUSTED, AS IF SHE'D RUN A MARATHON!

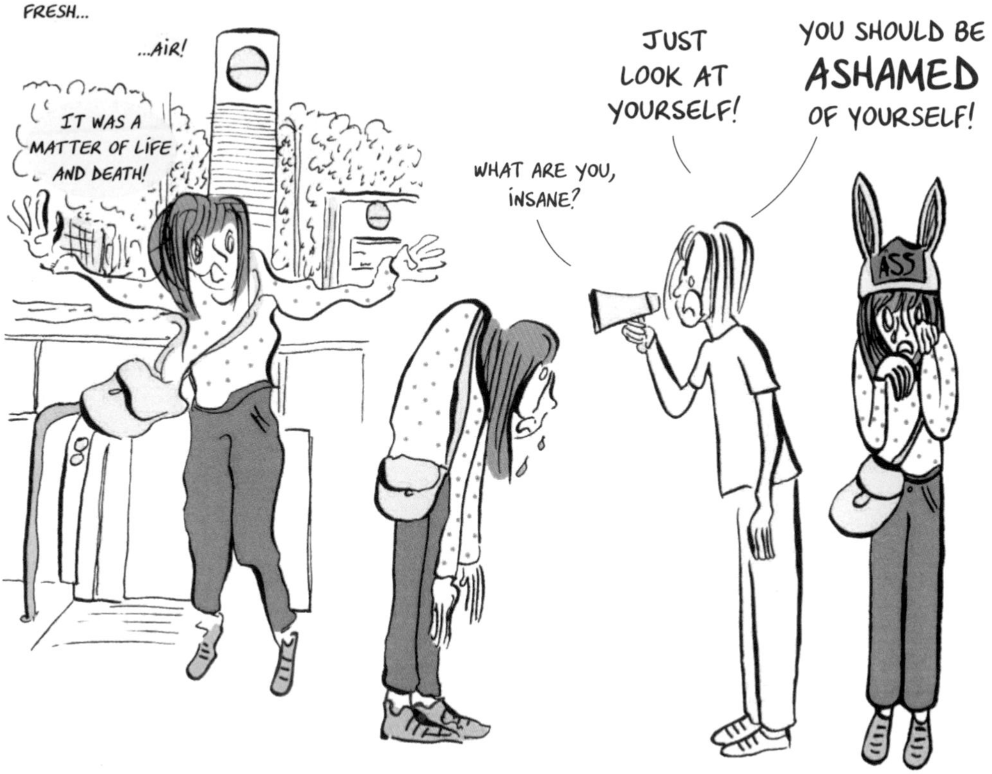
FRESH...
...AIR!
IT WAS A MATTER OF LIFE AND DEATH!
WHAT ARE YOU, INSANE?
JUST LOOK AT YOURSELF!
YOU SHOULD BE **ASHAMED** OF YOURSELF!
ASS

SPEC SHEET: SYMPTOMS OF A PANIC ATTACK

PANIC ATTACKS PRESENT IN BOTH COGNITIVE (CATASTROPHIZING) AND PHYSICAL WAYS. THEY'RE NOT JUST IN YOUR HEAD.

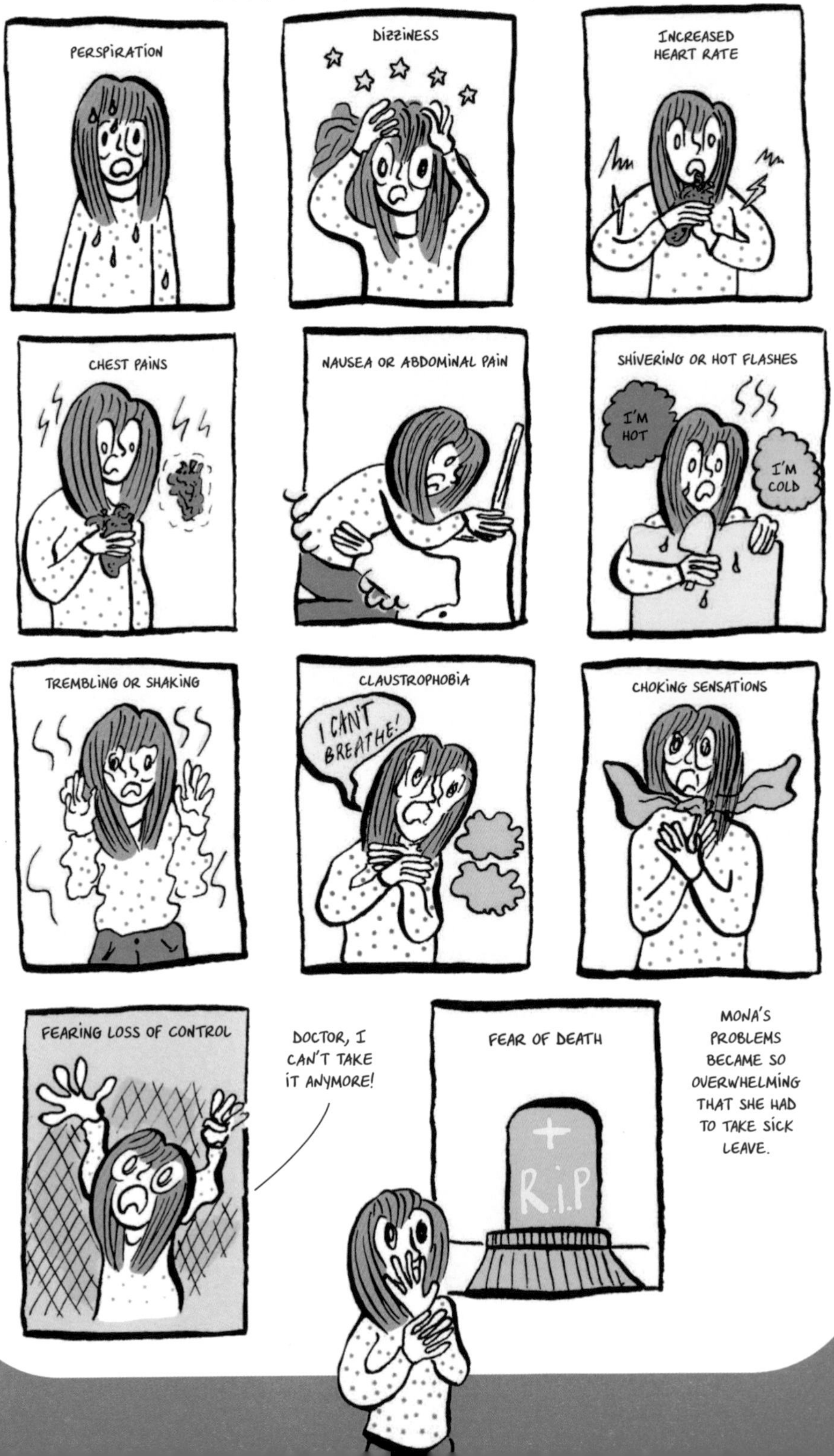
PERSPIRATION
DIZZINESS
INCREASED HEART RATE
CHEST PAINS
NAUSEA OR ABDOMINAL PAIN
SHIVERING OR HOT FLASHES
I'M HOT
I'M COLD
TREMBLING OR SHAKING
CLAUSTROPHOBIA
I CAN'T BREATHE!
CHOKING SENSATIONS
FEARING LOSS OF CONTROL
DOCTOR, I CAN'T TAKE IT ANYMORE!
FEAR OF DEATH
R.I.P
MONA'S PROBLEMS BECAME SO OVERWHELMING THAT SHE HAD TO TAKE SICK LEAVE.

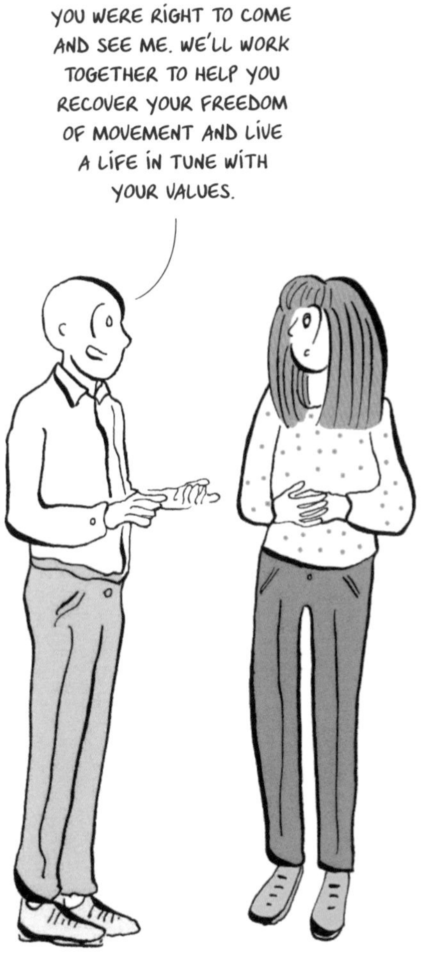
YOU WERE RIGHT TO COME AND SEE ME. WE'LL WORK TOGETHER TO HELP YOU RECOVER YOUR FREEDOM OF MOVEMENT AND LIVE A LIFE IN TUNE WITH YOUR VALUES.

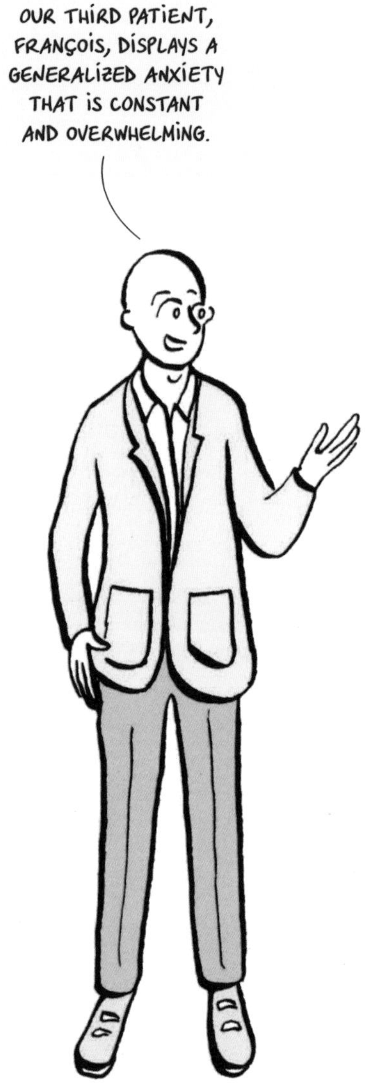
OUR THIRD PATIENT, FRANÇOIS, DISPLAYS A GENERALIZED ANXIETY THAT IS CONSTANT AND OVERWHELMING.

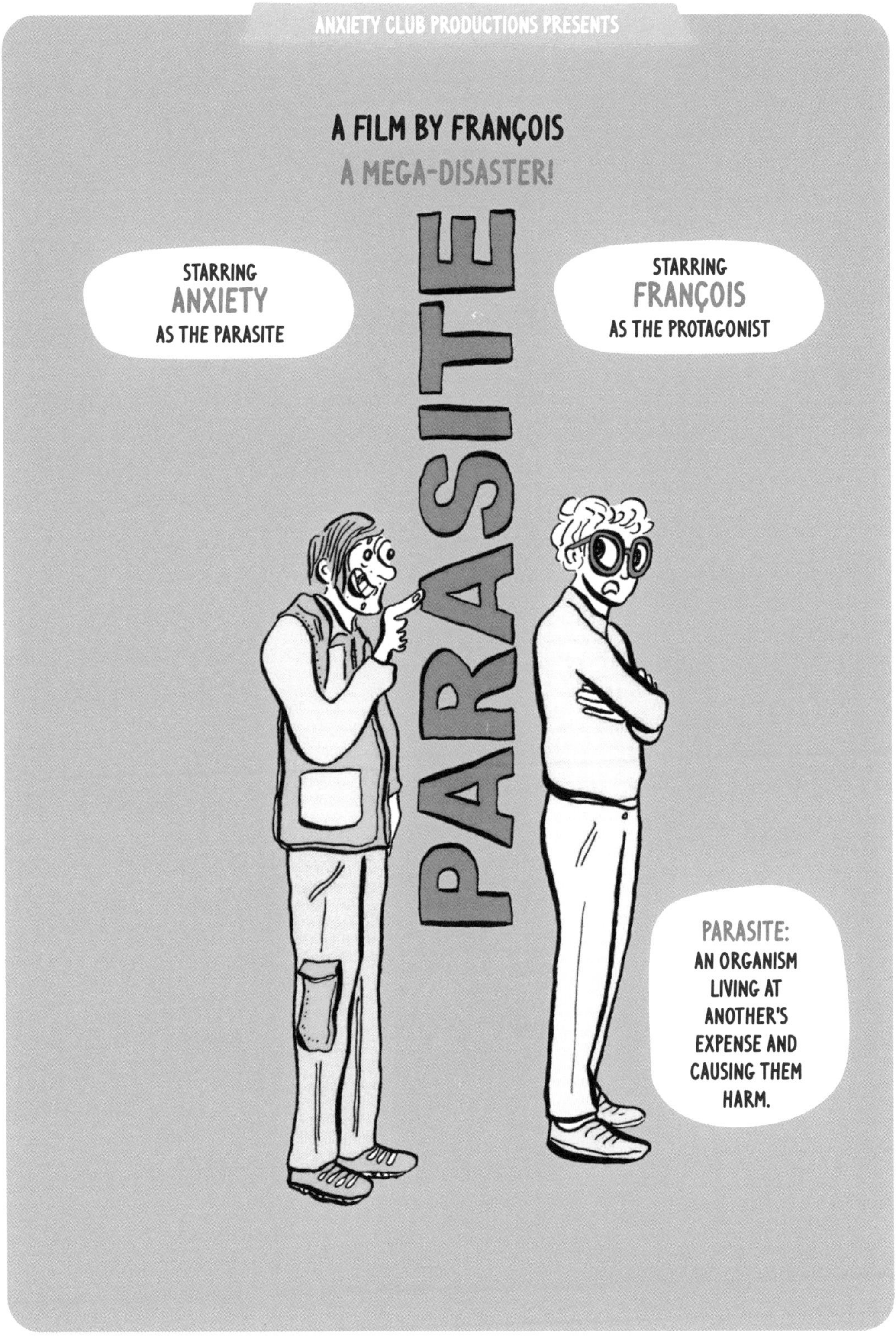
ANXIETY CLUB PRODUCTIONS PRESENTS
A FILM BY FRANÇOIS
A MEGA-DISASTER!
PARASITE
STARRING ANXIETY AS THE PARASITE
STARRING FRANÇOIS AS THE PROTAGONIST
PARASITE: AN ORGANISM LIVING AT ANOTHER'S EXPENSE AND CAUSING THEM HARM.

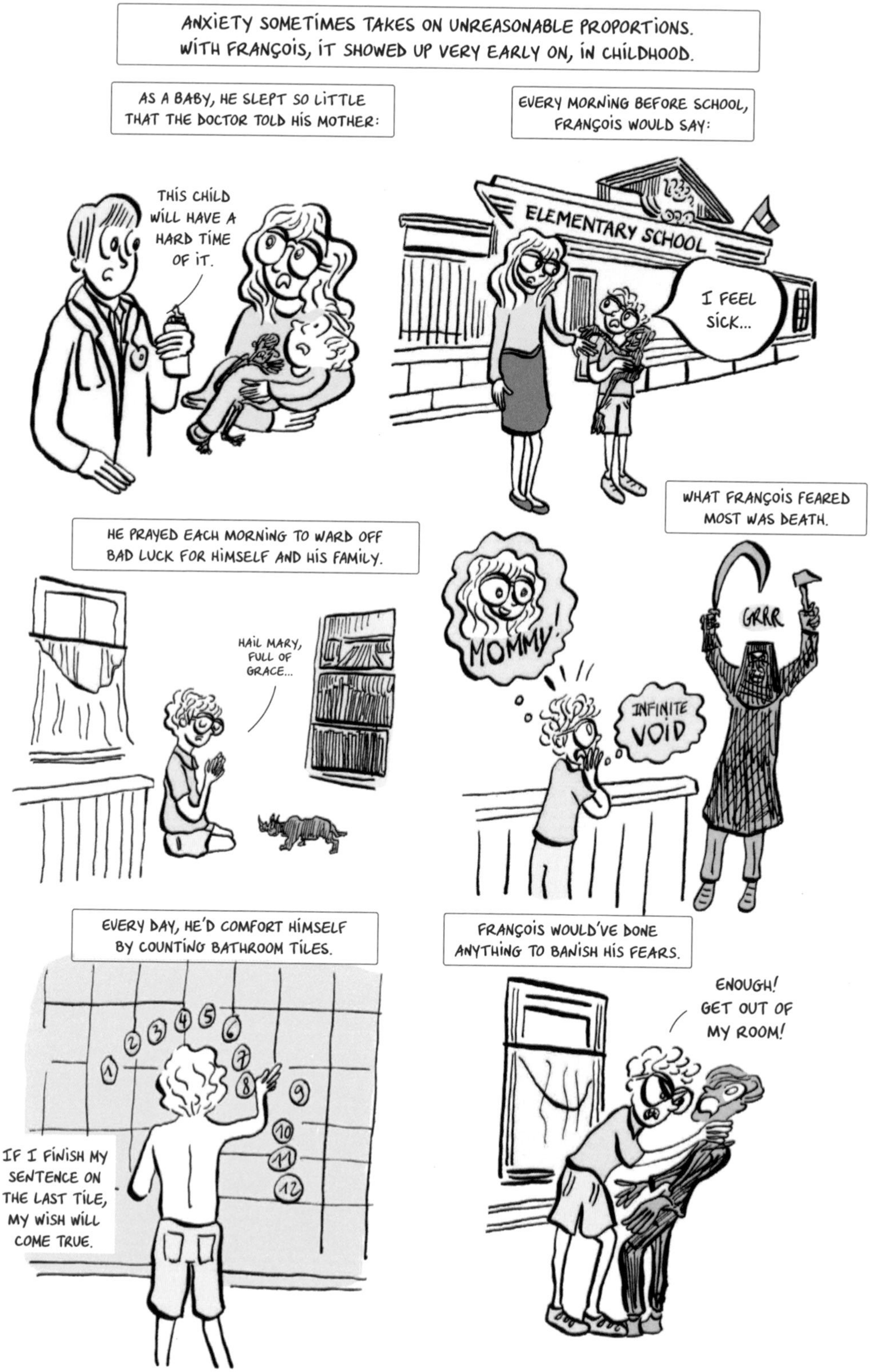
ANXIETY SOMETIMES TAKES ON UNREASONABLE PROPORTIONS. WITH FRANÇOIS, IT SHOWED UP VERY EARLY ON, IN CHILDHOOD.
AS A BABY, HE SLEPT SO LITTLE THAT THE DOCTOR TOLD HIS MOTHER:
THIS CHILD WILL HAVE A HARD TIME OF IT.
EVERY MORNING BEFORE SCHOOL, FRANÇOIS WOULD SAY:
ELEMENTARY SCHOOL
I FEEL SICK...
HE PRAYED EACH MORNING TO WARD OFF BAD LUCK FOR HIMSELF AND HIS FAMILY.
HAIL MARY, FULL OF GRACE...
WHAT FRANÇOIS FEARED MOST WAS DEATH.
MOMMY!
INFINITE VOID
GRRR
EVERY DAY, HE'D COMFORT HIMSELF BY COUNTING BATHROOM TILES.
1 2 3 4 5 6 7 8 9 10 11 12
IF I FINISH MY SENTENCE ON THE LAST TILE, MY WISH WILL COME TRUE.
FRANÇOIS WOULD'VE DONE ANYTHING TO BANISH HIS FEARS.
ENOUGH! GET OUT OF MY ROOM!

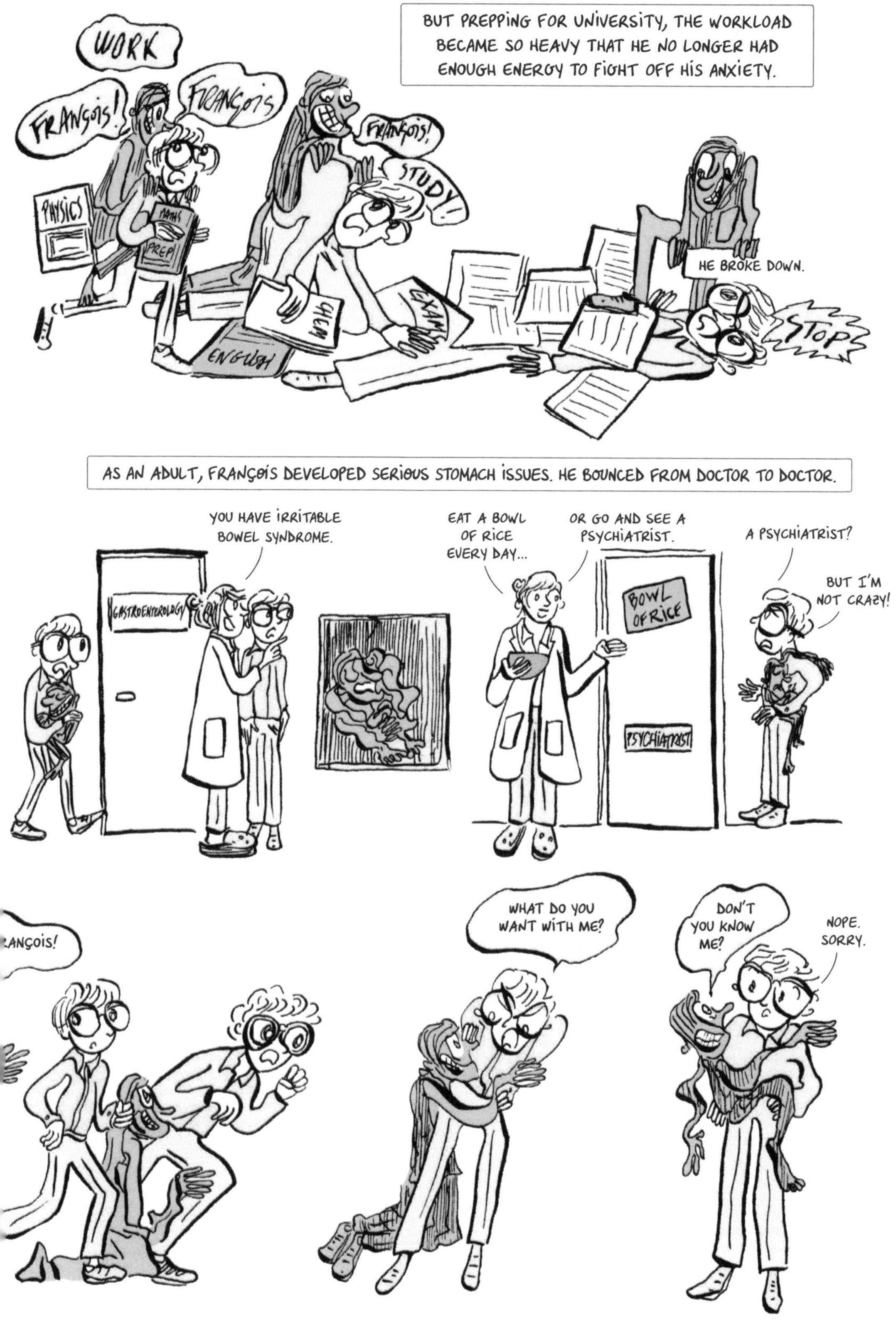
BUT PREPPING FOR UNIVERSITY, THE WORKLOAD BECAME SO HEAVY THAT HE NO LONGER HAD ENOUGH ENERGY TO FIGHT OFF HIS ANXIETY.
WORK
FRANÇOIS!
FRANÇOIS
FRANÇOIS!
STUDY!
PHYSICS
MATHS
PREP
CHEM
ENGLISH
EXAM
HE BROKE DOWN.
STOP
AS AN ADULT, FRANÇOIS DEVELOPED SERIOUS STOMACH ISSUES. HE BOUNCED FROM DOCTOR TO DOCTOR.
YOU HAVE IRRITABLE BOWEL SYNDROME.
GASTROENTEROLOGY
EAT A BOWL OF RICE EVERY DAY...
OR GO AND SEE A PSYCHIATRIST.
BOWL OF RICE
PSYCHIATRIST
A PSYCHIATRIST?
BUT I'M NOT CRAZY!
ANÇOIS!
WHAT DO YOU WANT WITH ME?
DON'T YOU KNOW ME?
NOPE. SORRY.

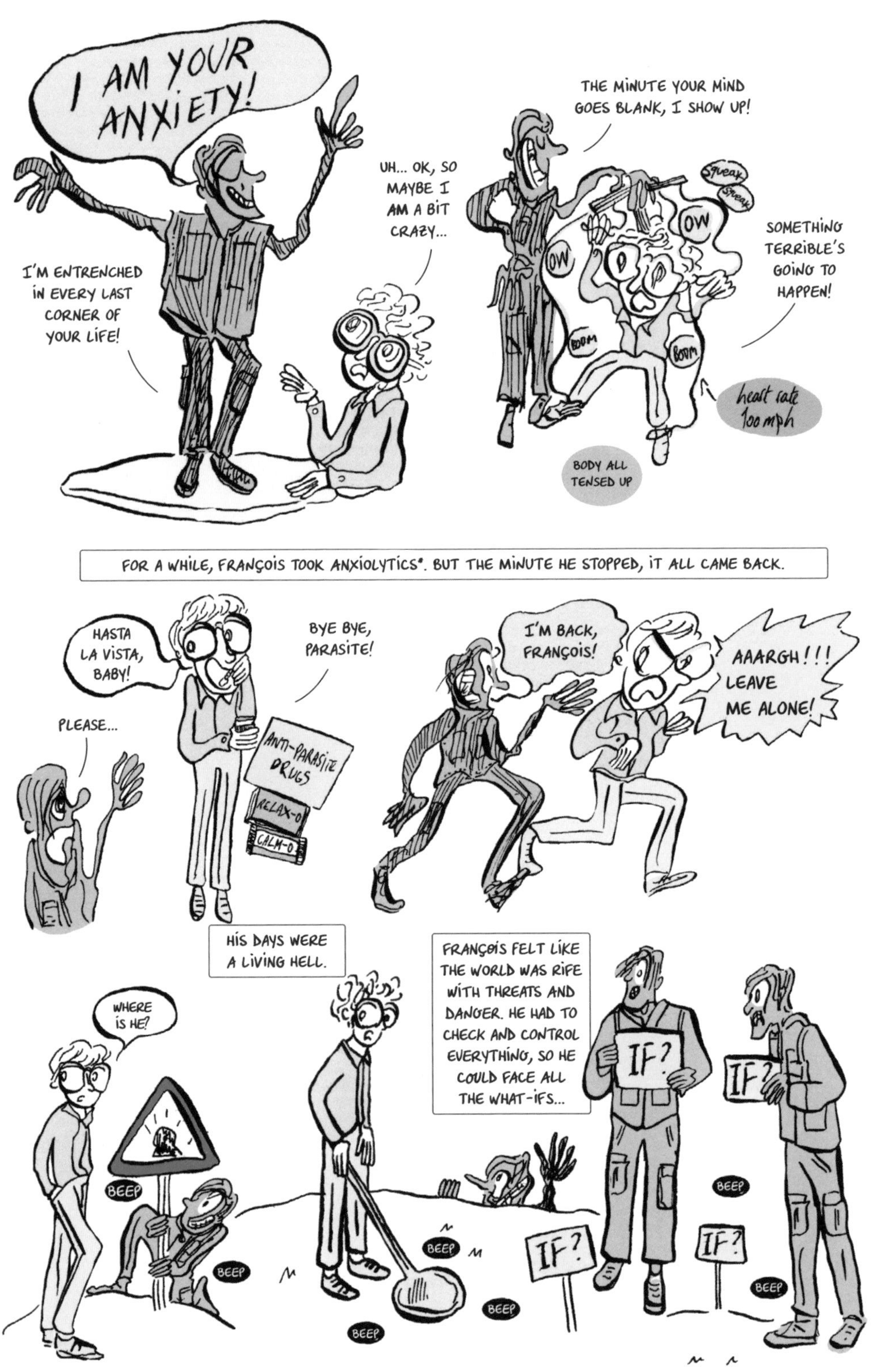
I AM YOUR ANXIETY!
I'M ENTRENCHED IN EVERY LAST CORNER OF YOUR LIFE!
UH... OK, SO MAYBE I AM A BIT CRAZY...
THE MINUTE YOUR MIND GOES BLANK, I SHOW UP!
squeak
squeak
OW
OW
SOMETHING TERRIBLE'S GOING TO HAPPEN!
BOOM
BOOM
heart rate 100 mph
BODY ALL TENSED UP
FOR A WHILE, FRANÇOIS TOOK ANXIOLYTICS*. BUT THE MINUTE HE STOPPED, IT ALL CAME BACK.
HASTA LA VISTA, BABY!
PLEASE...
BYE BYE, PARASITE!
ANTI-PARASITE DRUGS
RELAX-O
CALM-O
I'M BACK, FRANÇOIS!
AAARGH!!! LEAVE ME ALONE!
HIS DAYS WERE A LIVING HELL.
FRANÇOIS FELT LIKE THE WORLD WAS RIFE WITH THREATS AND DANGER. HE HAD TO CHECK AND CONTROL EVERYTHING, SO HE COULD FACE ALL THE WHAT-IFS...
WHERE IS HE?
IF?
IF?
BEEP
BEEP
BEEP
BEEP
BEEP
IF?
IF?
BEEP
BEEP

*ANTI-ANXIETY MEDICATION. ALWAYS CONSULT YOUR DOCTOR/MEDICAL PRACTITIONER BEFORE TAKING ANY DRUGS.

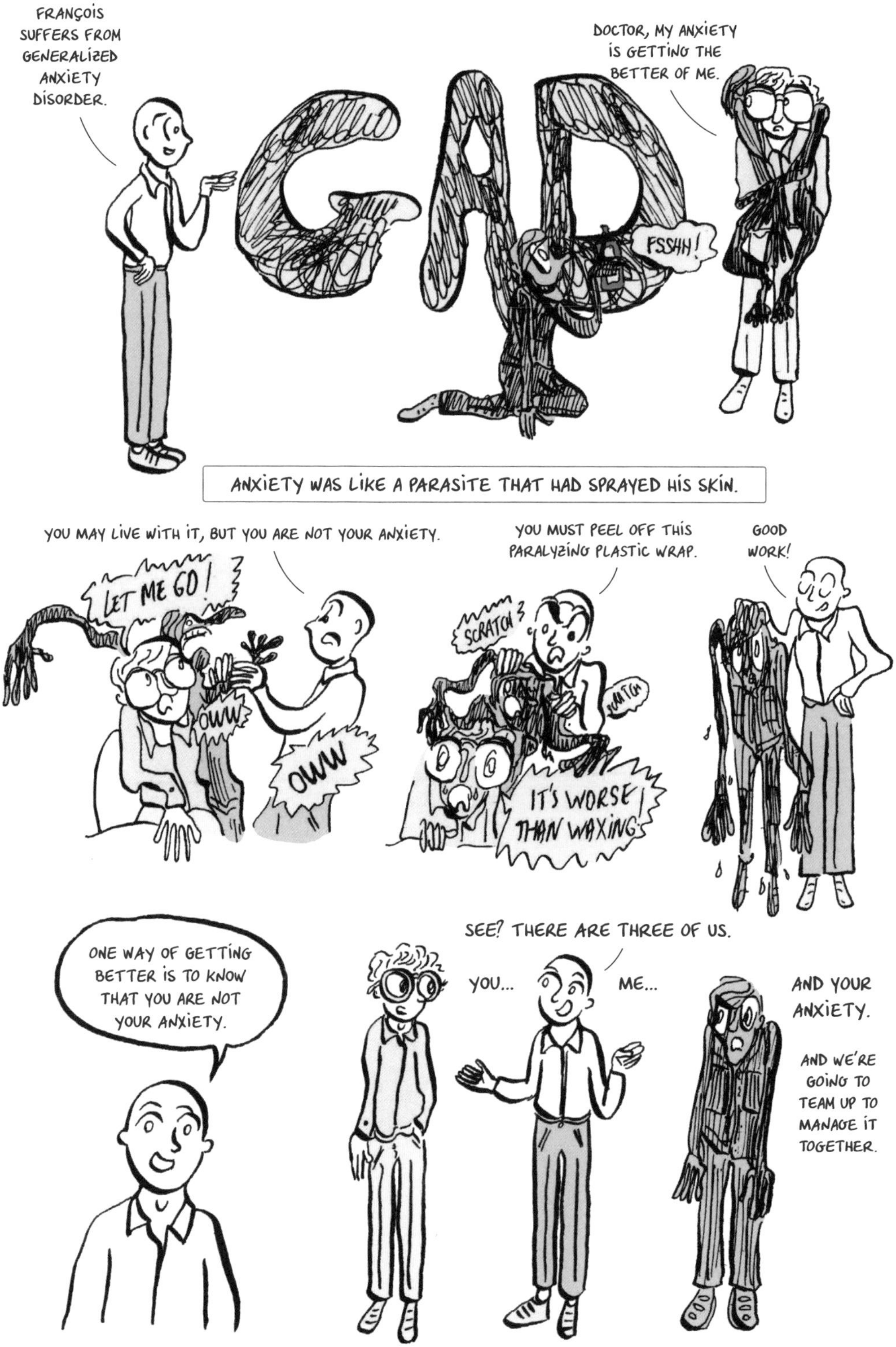
FRANÇOIS SUFFERS FROM GENERALIZED ANXIETY DISORDER.
GAD
DOCTOR, MY ANXIETY IS GETTING THE BETTER OF ME.
FSSHH!
ANXIETY WAS LIKE A PARASITE THAT HAD SPRAYED HIS SKIN.
YOU MAY LIVE WITH IT, BUT YOU ARE NOT YOUR ANXIETY.
LET ME GO!
OWW
OWW
YOU MUST PEEL OFF THIS PARALYZING PLASTIC WRAP.
SCRATCH
IT'S WORSE THAN WAXING!
GOOD WORK!
ONE WAY OF GETTING BETTER IS TO KNOW THAT YOU ARE NOT YOUR ANXIETY.
SEE? THERE ARE THREE OF US.
YOU...
ME...
AND YOUR ANXIETY.
AND WE'RE GOING TO TEAM UP TO MANAGE IT TOGETHER.

CHAPTER 4
THE CAUSES OF ANXIETY

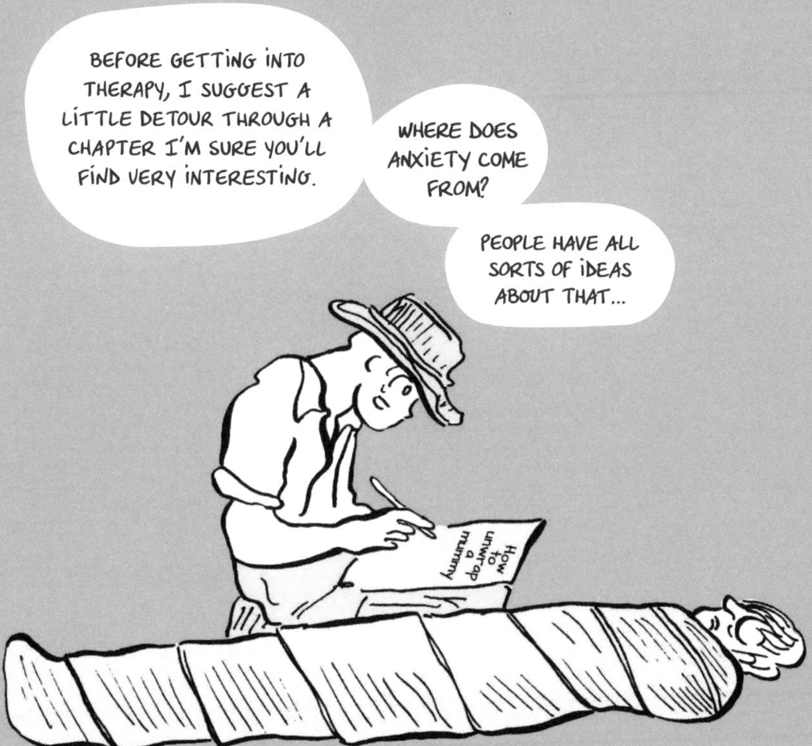
BEFORE GETTING INTO THERAPY, I SUGGEST A LITTLE DETOUR THROUGH A CHAPTER I'M SURE YOU'LL FIND VERY INTERESTING.
WHERE DOES ANXIETY COME FROM?
PEOPLE HAVE ALL SORTS OF IDEAS ABOUT THAT...
How to unwrap a mummy

NATURE VS. NURTURE: THE OLD DEBATE

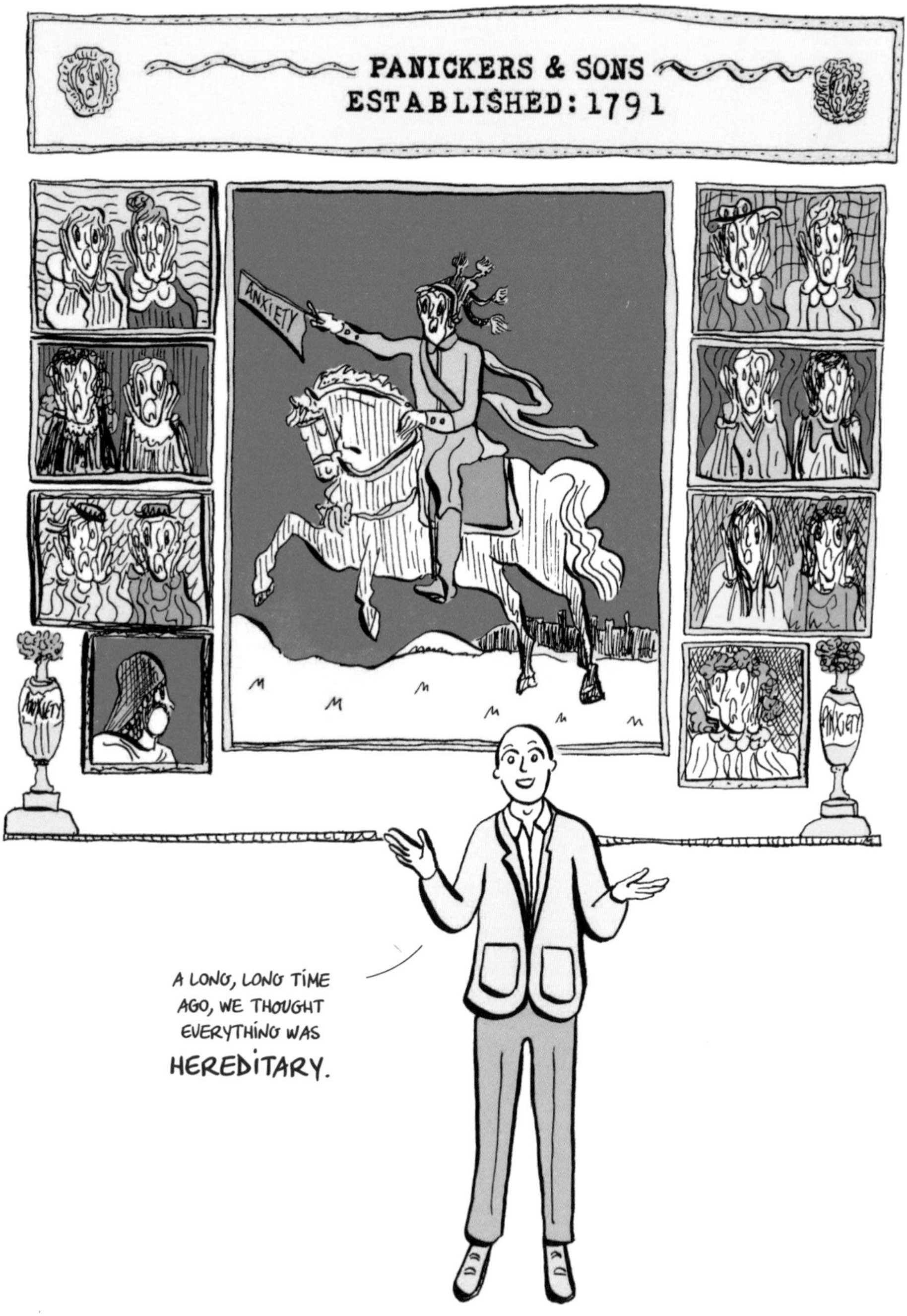
PANICKERS & SONS
ESTABLISHED: 1791
ANXIETY
ANXIETY
ANXIETY
A LONG, LONG TIME AGO, WE THOUGHT EVERYTHING WAS HEREDITARY.

THEN, WITH THE ADVENT OF PSYCHOANALYSIS, WE THOUGHT EVERYTHING WAS A MATTER OF **UPBRINGING** BY OUR PARENTS, ESPECIALLY OUR MOTHER.

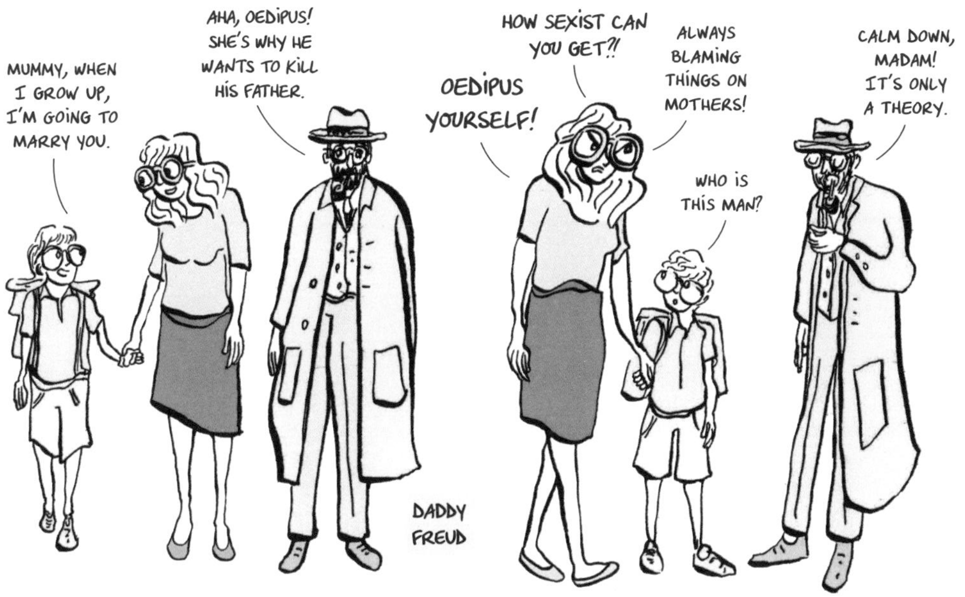
MUMMY, WHEN I GROW UP, I'M GOING TO MARRY YOU.
AHA, OEDIPUS! SHE'S WHY HE WANTS TO KILL HIS FATHER.
DADDY FREUD
OEDIPUS YOURSELF!
HOW SEXIST CAN YOU GET?!
ALWAYS BLAMING THINGS ON MOTHERS!
WHO IS THIS MAN?
CALM DOWN, MADAM! IT'S ONLY A THEORY.

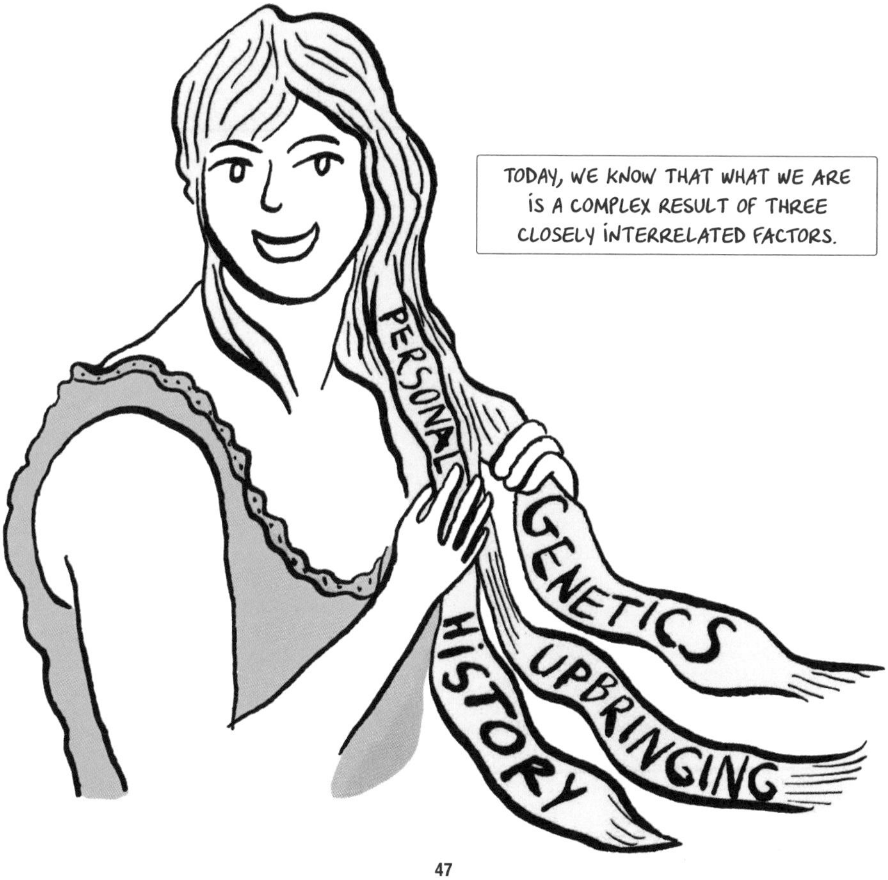
TODAY, WE KNOW THAT WHAT WE ARE IS A COMPLEX RESULT OF THREE CLOSELY INTERRELATED FACTORS.
PERSONAL HISTORY
GENETICS
UPBRINGING

FACTOR ONE: BIOLOGY

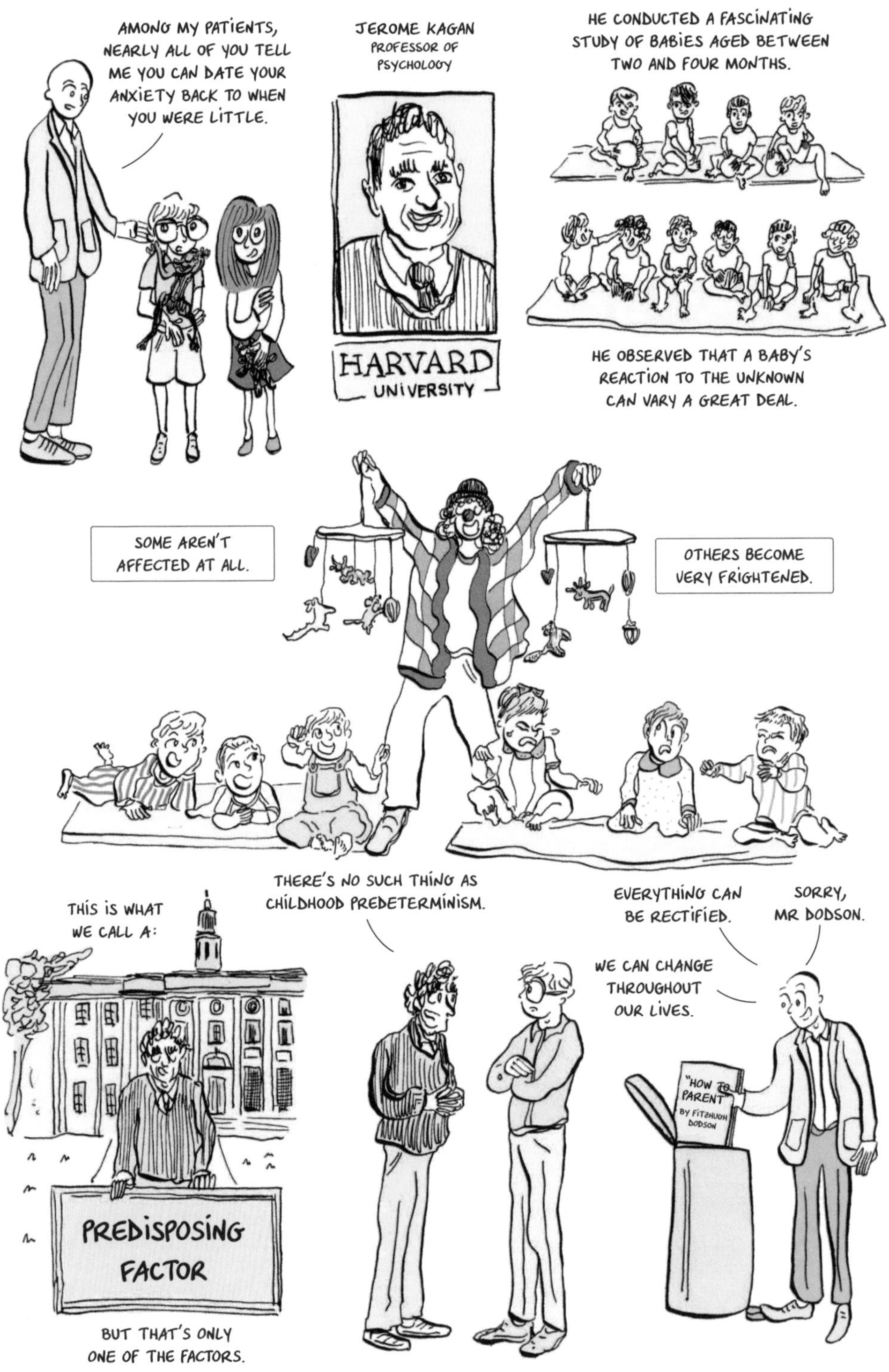
AMONG MY PATIENTS, NEARLY ALL OF YOU TELL ME YOU CAN DATE YOUR ANXIETY BACK TO WHEN YOU WERE LITTLE.
JEROME KAGAN
PROFESSOR OF PSYCHOLOGY
HARVARD UNIVERSITY
HE CONDUCTED A FASCINATING STUDY OF BABIES AGED BETWEEN TWO AND FOUR MONTHS.
HE OBSERVED THAT A BABY'S REACTION TO THE UNKNOWN CAN VARY A GREAT DEAL.
SOME AREN'T AFFECTED AT ALL.
OTHERS BECOME VERY FRIGHTENED.
THIS IS WHAT WE CALL A:
PREDISPOSING FACTOR
BUT THAT'S ONLY ONE OF THE FACTORS.
THERE'S NO SUCH THING AS CHILDHOOD PREDETERMINISM.
EVERYTHING CAN BE RECTIFIED.
WE CAN CHANGE THROUGHOUT OUR LIVES.
SORRY, MR DODSON.
"HOW TO PARENT" BY FITZHUGH DODSON

FACTOR TWO: UPBRINGING

THE FAMILIAL COCOON IS CLEARLY A KEY FACTOR. AMONG MY PATIENTS, MANY HAVE BEEN SUBJECTED TO ENORMOUS PRESSURES, PERHAPS AN EXCESS OF PARENTAL AUTHORITY, SINCE CHILDHOOD.

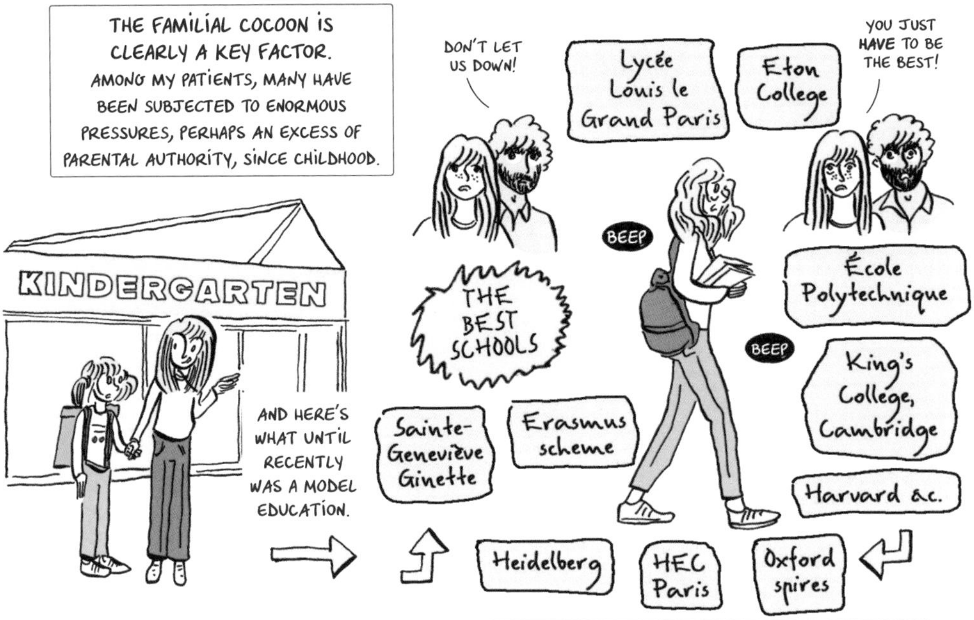
DON'T LET US DOWN!
Lycée Louis le Grand Paris
Eton College
YOU JUST HAVE TO BE THE BEST!
KINDERGARTEN
BEEP
THE BEST SCHOOLS
École Polytechnique
BEEP
King's College, Cambridge
AND HERE'S WHAT UNTIL RECENTLY WAS A MODEL EDUCATION.
Sainte-Geneviève Ginette
Erasmus scheme
Harvard &c.
Heidelberg
HEC Paris
Oxford spires

RESULT: THE CHILD LIVES IN AN ATMOSPHERE OF CONSTANT ANXIETY AT NOT LIVING UP TO THEIR PARENTS' EXPECTATIONS AND SO PROVOKING THEIR ANGER.

OTHERS OF YOU HAVE BEEN BROUGHT UP IN OVERPROTECTIVE FAMILY ENVIRONMENTS.

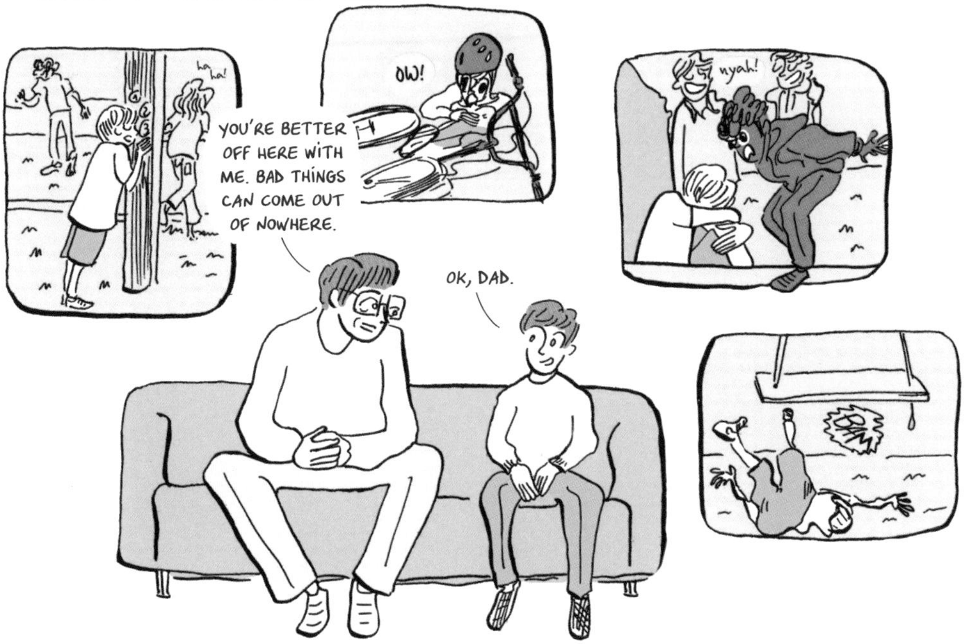
ha ha!
OW!
nyah!
YOU'RE BETTER OFF HERE WITH ME. BAD THINGS CAN COME OUT OF NOWHERE.
OK, DAD.

RESULT: THE CHILD WILL DEVELOP A TENDENCY TO VIEW THE EXTERNAL WORLD AS A SOURCE OF CONSTANT DANGER.

FACTOR THREE: TRAUMA

THIS PLAYS A CRUCIAL ROLE IN MOST CASES OF ANXIETY.
MEMORIES OF BAD SOCIAL EXPERIENCES OFTEN HAUNT US.

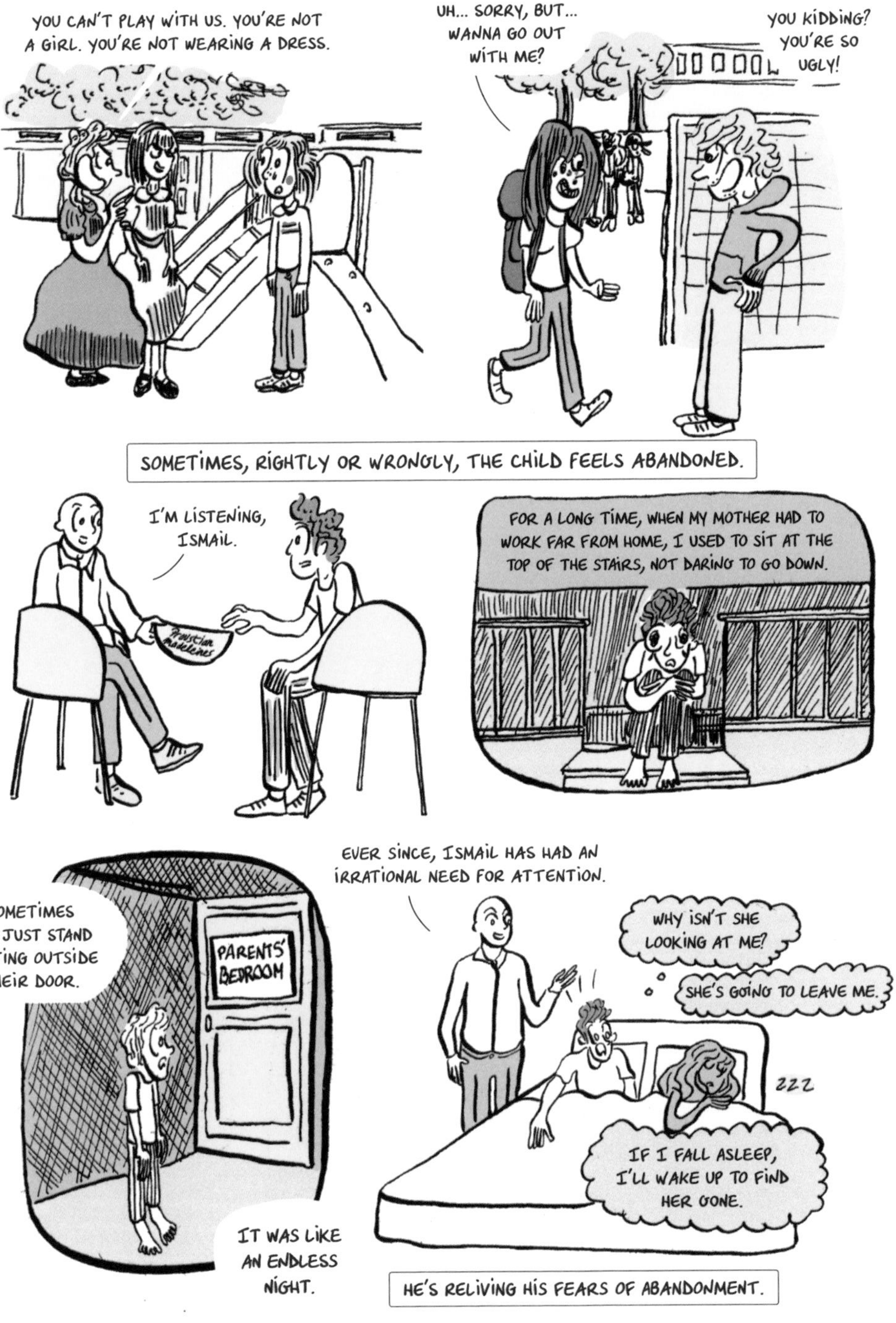

YOU CAN'T PLAY WITH US. YOU'RE NOT A GIRL. YOU'RE NOT WEARING A DRESS.
UH... SORRY, BUT... WANNA GO OUT WITH ME?
YOU KIDDING? YOU'RE SO UGLY!
SOMETIMES, RIGHTLY OR WRONGLY, THE CHILD FEELS ABANDONED.
I'M LISTENING, ISMAIL.
Proustian madeleines
FOR A LONG TIME, WHEN MY MOTHER HAD TO WORK FAR FROM HOME, I USED TO SIT AT THE TOP OF THE STAIRS, NOT DARING TO GO DOWN.
SOMETIMES I'D JUST STAND WAITING OUTSIDE THEIR DOOR.
PARENTS' BEDROOM
IT WAS LIKE AN ENDLESS NIGHT.
EVER SINCE, ISMAIL HAS HAD AN IRRATIONAL NEED FOR ATTENTION.
WHY ISN'T SHE LOOKING AT ME?
SHE'S GOING TO LEAVE ME.
ZZZ
IF I FALL ASLEEP, I'LL WAKE UP TO FIND HER GONE.
HE'S RELIVING HIS FEARS OF ABANDONMENT.

ANOTHER DEEP CAUSE: THE HUMAN CONDITION

IT'S WORTH ADDING THAT, FOR ALL OF US, BEHIND ALL OUR ANXIETIES LIES THE CENTRAL HUMAN FEAR OF DEATH.

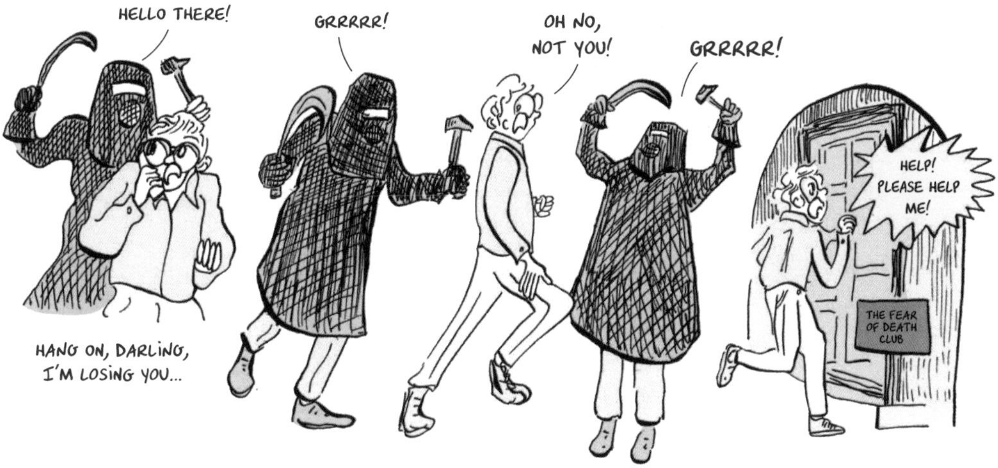
HELLO THERE!
HANG ON, DARLING, I'M LOSING YOU...
GRRRRR!
OH NO, NOT YOU!
GRRRRR!
HELP! PLEASE HELP ME!
THE FEAR OF DEATH CLUB

ALL THE GREAT AND ENDURING PHILOSOPHERS HAVE SOUGHT TO DEAL WITH THIS FEAR.

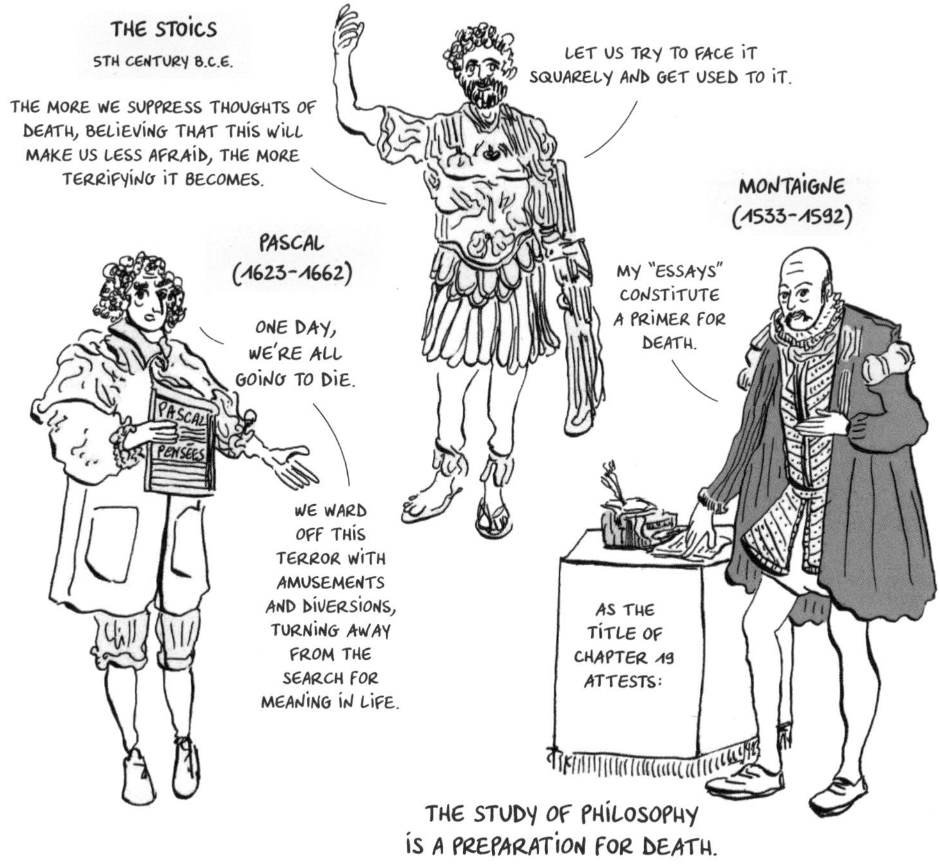
THE STOICS
5TH CENTURY B.C.E.
THE MORE WE SUPPRESS THOUGHTS OF DEATH, BELIEVING THAT THIS WILL MAKE US LESS AFRAID, THE MORE TERRIFYING IT BECOMES.
LET US TRY TO FACE IT SQUARELY AND GET USED TO IT.
PASCAL
(1623-1662)
ONE DAY, WE'RE ALL GOING TO DIE.
PASCAL PENSÉES
WE WARD OFF THIS TERROR WITH AMUSEMENTS AND DIVERSIONS, TURNING AWAY FROM THE SEARCH FOR MEANING IN LIFE.
MONTAIGNE
(1533-1592)
MY "ESSAYS" CONSTITUTE A PRIMER FOR DEATH.
AS THE TITLE OF CHAPTER 19 ATTESTS:
THE STUDY OF PHILOSOPHY IS A PREPARATION FOR DEATH.

PHILOSOPHERS HAVE ALSO EVOKED THE BEWILDERING ANXIETY THAT FREE WILL CAN PROMPT IN US.

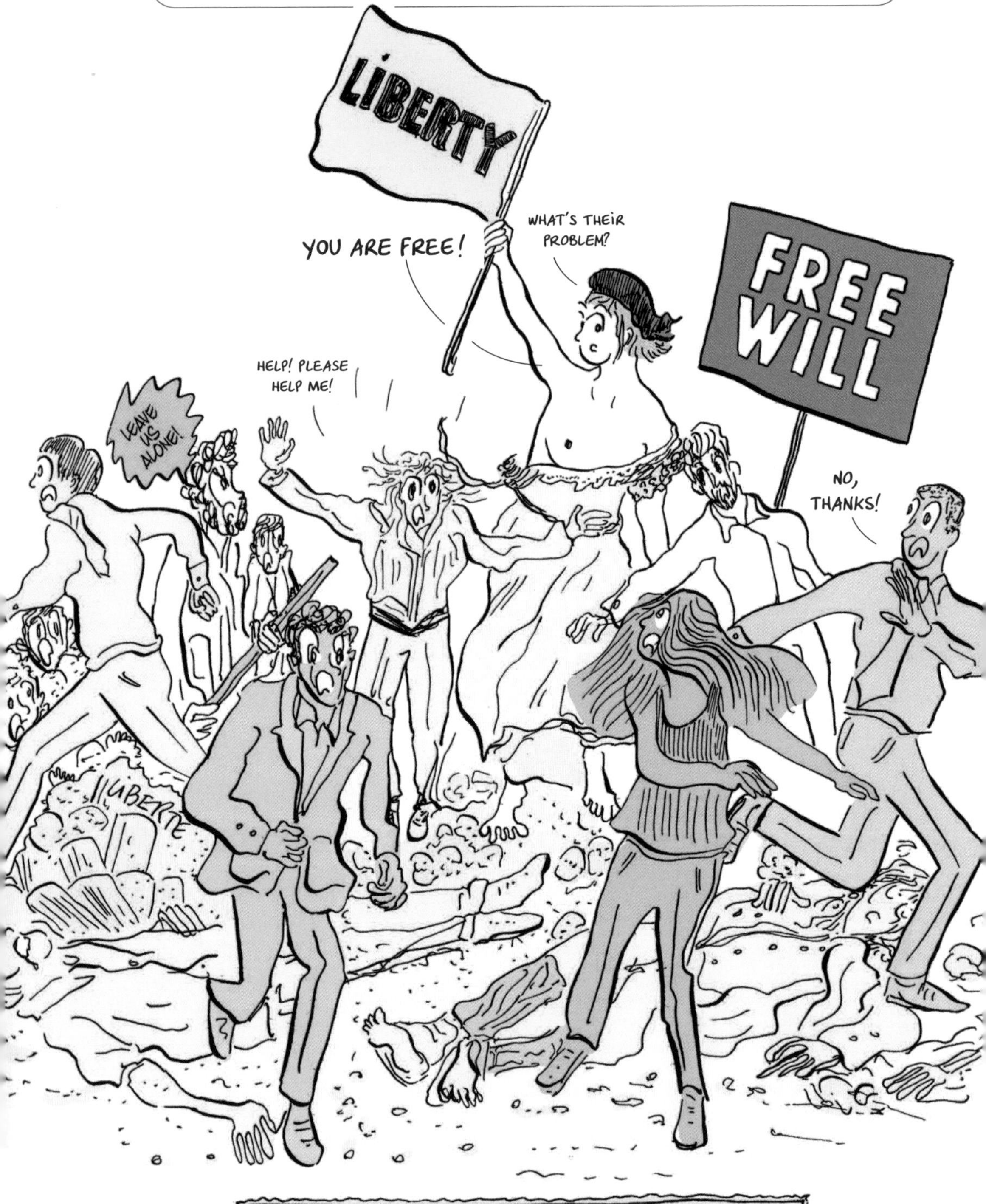
LIBERTY
YOU ARE FREE!
WHAT'S THEIR PROBLEM?
FREE WILL
HELP! PLEASE HELP ME!
LEAVE US ALONE!
NO, THANKS!
LIBERTÉ

LIBERTY TERRIFYING THE PEOPLE.
(AFTER DELACROIX)

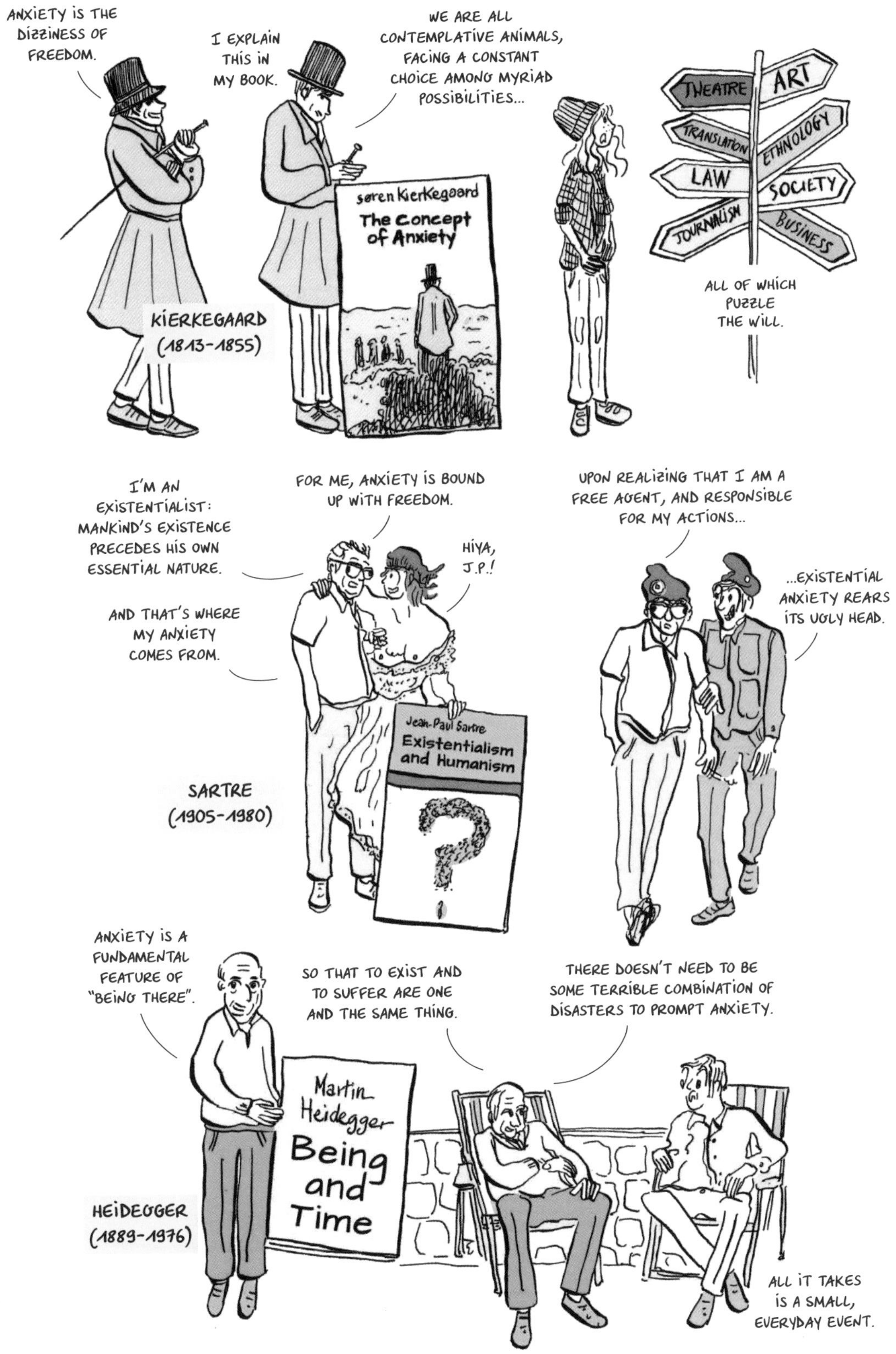
ANXIETY IS THE DIZZINESS OF FREEDOM.
I EXPLAIN THIS IN MY BOOK.
WE ARE ALL CONTEMPLATIVE ANIMALS, FACING A CONSTANT CHOICE AMONG MYRIAD POSSIBILITIES...
KIERKEGAARD (1813-1855)
SØREN KIERKEGAARD The Concept of Anxiety
THEATRE
ART
TRANSLATION
ETHNOLOGY
LAW
SOCIETY
JOURNALISM
BUSINESS
ALL OF WHICH PUZZLE THE WILL.
I'M AN EXISTENTIALIST: MANKIND'S EXISTENCE PRECEDES HIS OWN ESSENTIAL NATURE.
AND THAT'S WHERE MY ANXIETY COMES FROM.
FOR ME, ANXIETY IS BOUND UP WITH FREEDOM.
HIYA, J.P.!
SARTRE (1905-1980)
Jean-Paul Sartre Existentialism and Humanism
UPON REALIZING THAT I AM A FREE AGENT, AND RESPONSIBLE FOR MY ACTIONS...
...EXISTENTIAL ANXIETY REARS ITS UGLY HEAD.
ANXIETY IS A FUNDAMENTAL FEATURE OF "BEING THERE".
HEIDEGGER (1889-1976)
Martin Heidegger Being and Time
SO THAT TO EXIST AND TO SUFFER ARE ONE AND THE SAME THING.
THERE DOESN'T NEED TO BE SOME TERRIBLE COMBINATION OF DISASTERS TO PROMPT ANXIETY.
ALL IT TAKES IS A SMALL, EVERYDAY EVENT.

CHAPTER 5
IN TREATMENT
A THREE-SEASON LIMITED SERIES

IT'S NOT THE END OF THE WORLD. WE CAN LEARN TO DECATASTROPHIZE OUR THOUGHTS! I'VE HAD TO ABBREVIATE THE PROCESS GREATLY HERE, BUT WE WILL STILL SEE THE THREE MAJOR FRONTS.

1. COGNITIVE
CHANGE OUR MENTAL PROGRAMMING

2. BEHAVIOURAL
LEARN TO TAME OUR FEARS

3. EMOTIONAL
FULL AWARENESS, VALUES, MEANING IN LIFE

LET'S START OUR "IN TREATMENT" SECTION WITH ISMAIL, THE STUDENT INSOMNIAC..

HIS CASE IS TYPICAL OF WHAT WE MIGHT CONSIDER AS MILD ANXIETY.

WITH TIME, THERE'S THE POSSIBILITY THAT IT WILL BECOME UNMANAGEABLE, A BURDEN TOO HEAVY TO BEAR.

SEASON 1 — MINOR ANXIETY

In Treatment

WITH ISMAIL

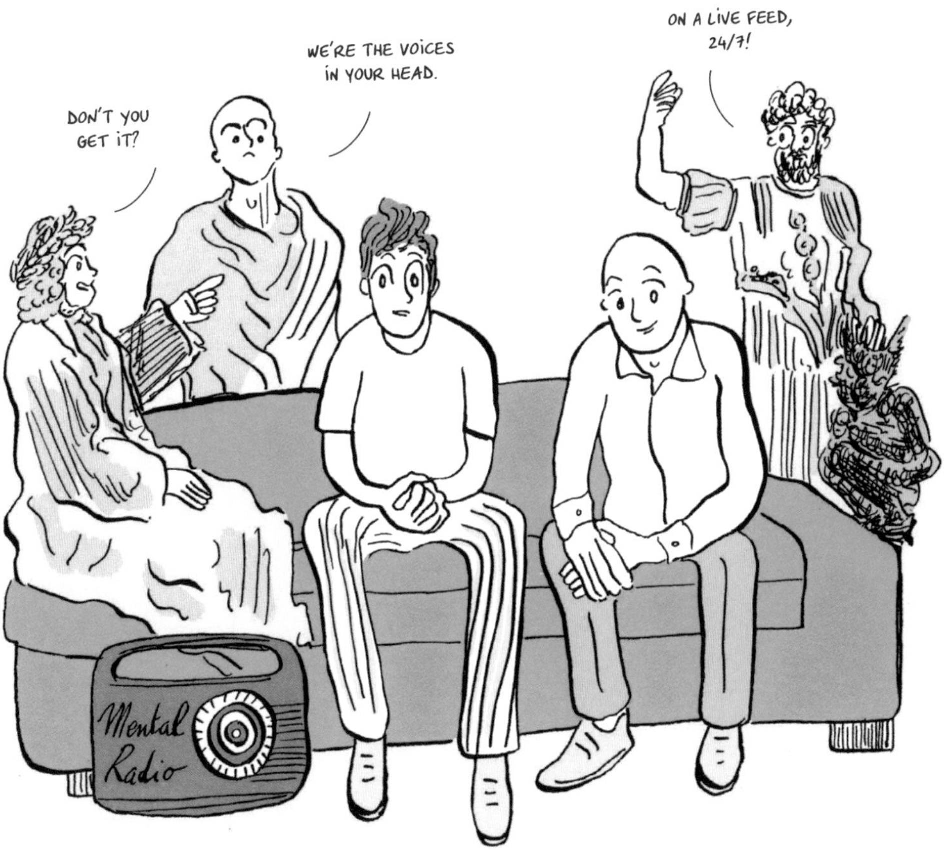
DON'T YOU GET IT?
WE'RE THE VOICES IN YOUR HEAD.
ON A LIVE FEED, 24/7!
Mental Radio

HOW DO YOU LOWER THE VOLUME ON YOUR MENTAL RADIO'S ANXIETY BROADCASTS?

OUR MENTAL RADIO

THE SITUATIONS WE EXPERIENCE TRIGGER OUR ANXIETIES, BUT IT'S OUR INTERPRETATION THAT EXACERBATES THEM. WE ALL HAVE A LITTLE VOICE INSIDE US CONSTANTLY INTERPRETING SITUATIONS AND COMMENTING ON OUR ACTIONS, LIKE A MENTAL RADIO THAT HAS INSINUATED ITSELF INTO EVERY ASPECT OF OUR LIVES.

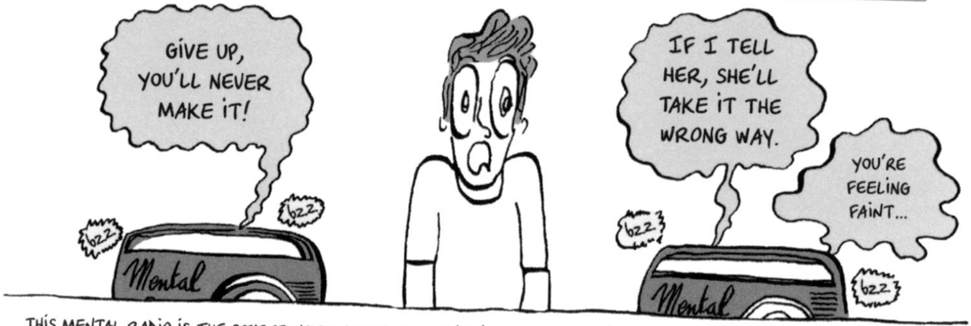
GIVE UP, YOU'LL NEVER MAKE IT!
bzz
bzz
Mental
IF I TELL HER, SHE'LL TAKE IT THE WRONG WAY.
YOU'RE FEELING FAINT...
bzz
bzz
Mental

THIS MENTAL RADIO IS THE SOURCE NOT ONLY OF OUR ANXIETIES, BUT OF OUR INDECISIVENESS AND INHIBITIONS AS WELL.

IT OFTEN STEMS FROM OUR CHILDHOOD AND ITS DEEPLY ROOTED PATTERNS WITHIN US, LIKE THE VOICE OF A PARENT WHO HAS DOUBTED US, OR ANOTHER WHO OVERPROTECTED US.

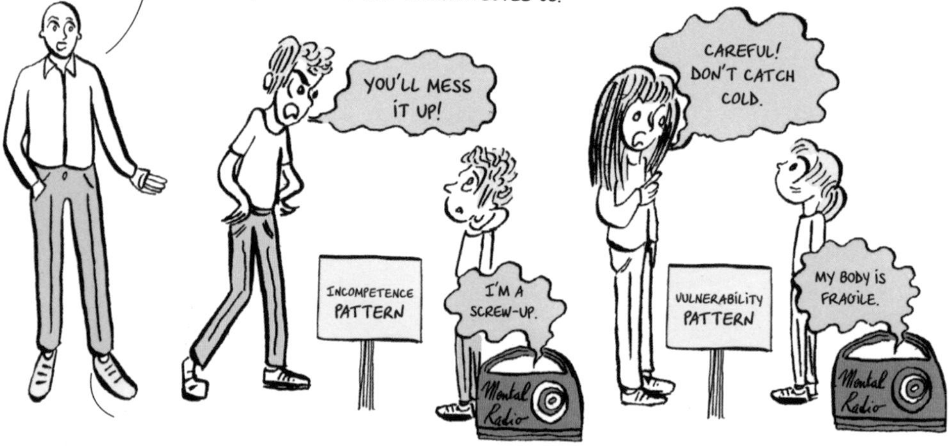
YOU'LL MESS IT UP!
INCOMPETENCE PATTERN
I'M A SCREW-UP.
Mental Radio
CAREFUL! DON'T CATCH COLD.
VULNERABILITY PATTERN
MY BODY IS FRAGILE.
Mental Radio

OR THAT OF A PARENT WHO TOLD US THE WORLD WAS FULL OF DANGERS.

OUR MENTAL RADIO CAN ALSO ARISE FROM CONDITIONING THAT MARKED US EMOTIONALLY.

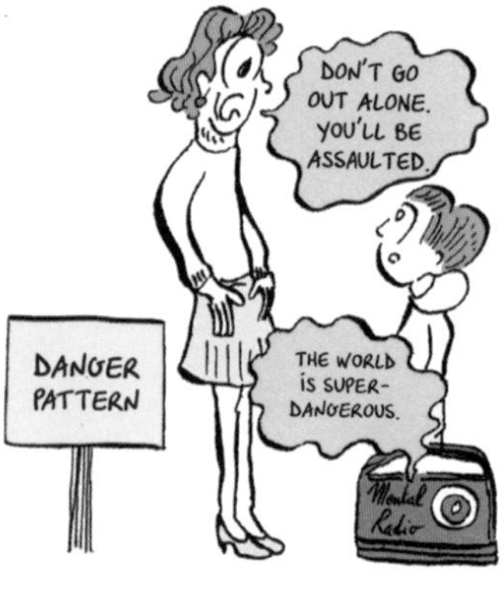
DON'T GO OUT ALONE. YOU'LL BE ASSAULTED.
DANGER PATTERN
THE WORLD IS SUPER-DANGEROUS.
Mental Radio

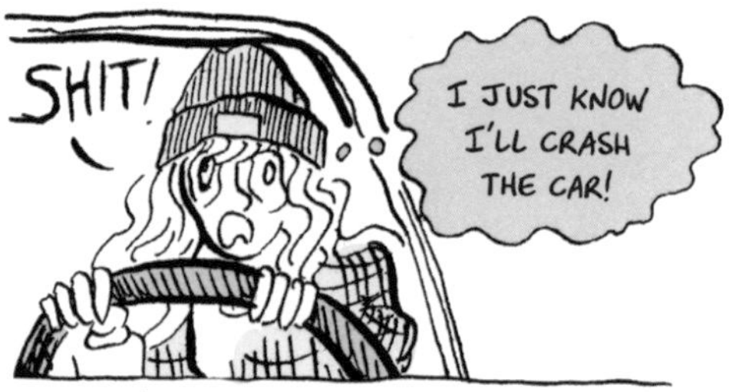
SHIT!
I JUST KNOW I'LL CRASH THE CAR!

FOR INSTANCE, A PANIC ATTACK IN ONE LOCATION CAN PRODUCE AN INSTINCTIVE FEAR IN ALL SIMILAR LOCATIONS.

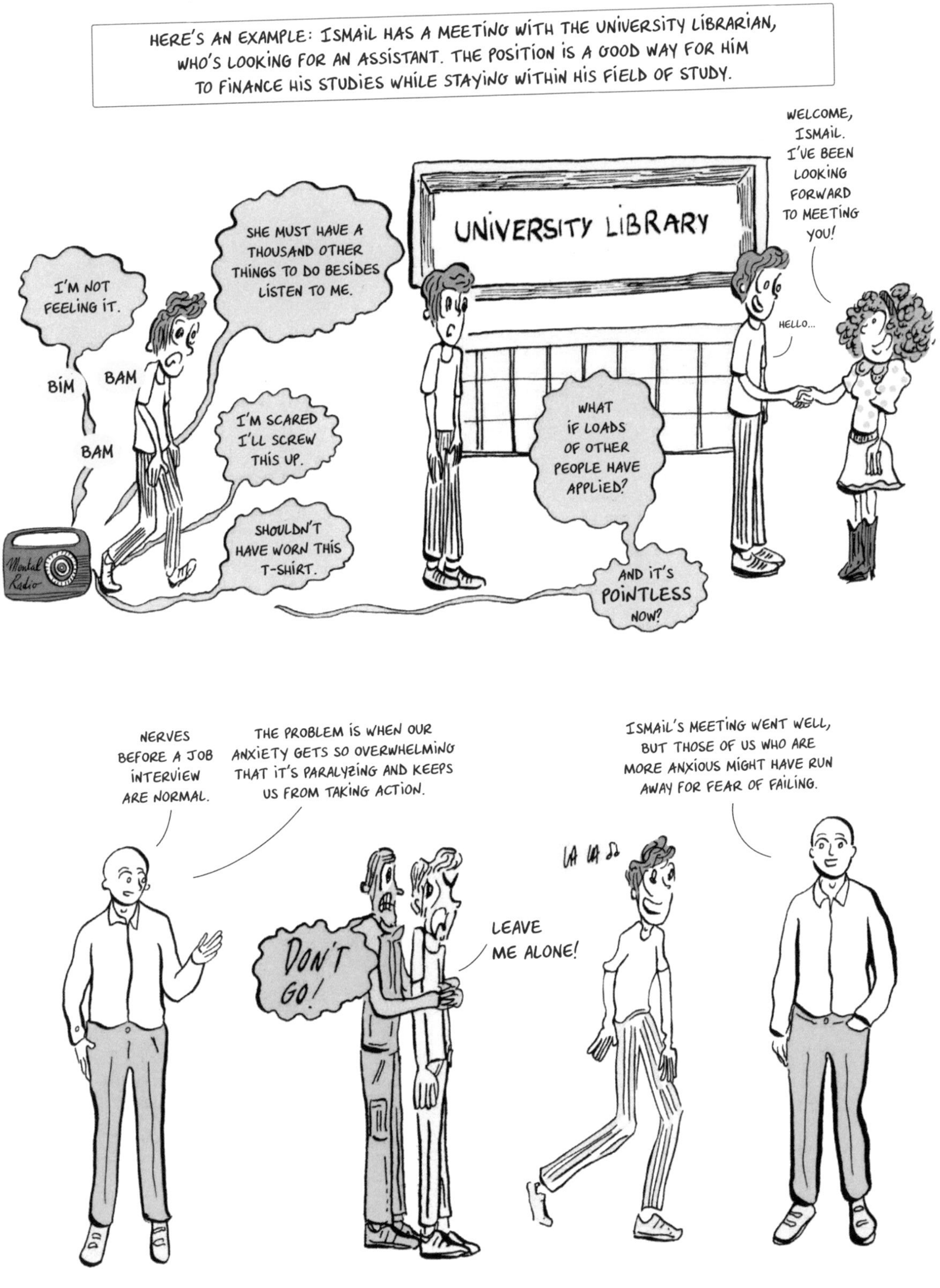
HERE'S AN EXAMPLE: ISMAIL HAS A MEETING WITH THE UNIVERSITY LIBRARIAN, WHO'S LOOKING FOR AN ASSISTANT. THE POSITION IS A GOOD WAY FOR HIM TO FINANCE HIS STUDIES WHILE STAYING WITHIN HIS FIELD OF STUDY.
I'M NOT FEELING IT.
BIM
BAM
BAM
Mental Radio
SHE MUST HAVE A THOUSAND OTHER THINGS TO DO BESIDES LISTEN TO ME.
I'M SCARED I'LL SCREW THIS UP.
SHOULDN'T HAVE WORN THIS T-SHIRT.
UNIVERSITY LIBRARY
WHAT IF LOADS OF OTHER PEOPLE HAVE APPLIED?
AND IT'S POINTLESS NOW?
WELCOME, ISMAIL. I'VE BEEN LOOKING FORWARD TO MEETING YOU!
HELLO...
NERVES BEFORE A JOB INTERVIEW ARE NORMAL.
THE PROBLEM IS WHEN OUR ANXIETY GETS SO OVERWHELMING THAT IT'S PARALYZING AND KEEPS US FROM TAKING ACTION.
DON'T GO!
LEAVE ME ALONE!
LA LA
ISMAIL'S MEETING WENT WELL, BUT THOSE OF US WHO ARE MORE ANXIOUS MIGHT HAVE RUN AWAY FOR FEAR OF FAILING.

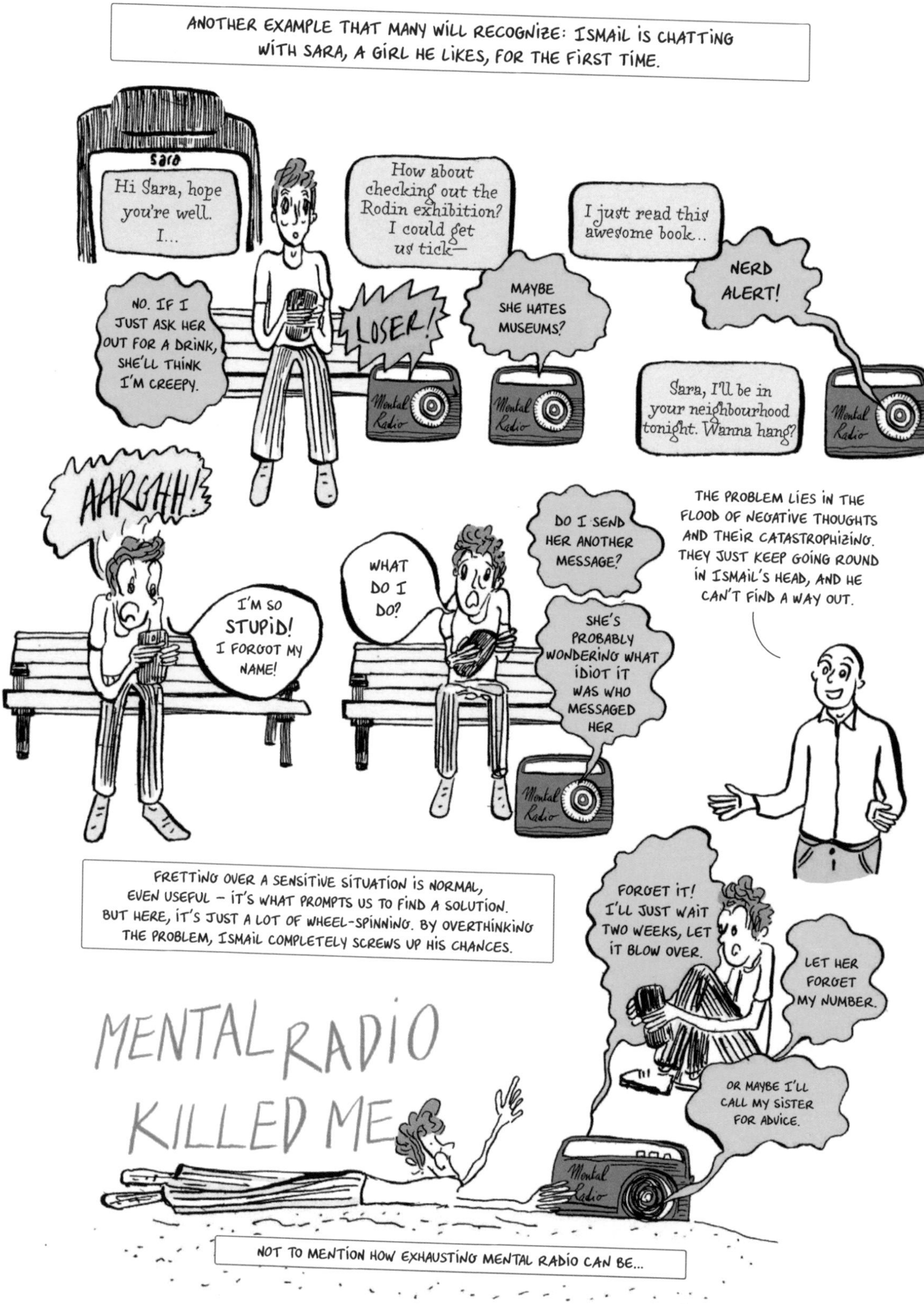
ANOTHER EXAMPLE THAT MANY WILL RECOGNIZE: ISMAIL IS CHATTING WITH SARA, A GIRL HE LIKES, FOR THE FIRST TIME.
Sara
Hi Sara, hope you're well. I...
NO. IF I JUST ASK HER OUT FOR A DRINK, SHE'LL THINK I'M CREEPY.
How about checking out the Rodin exhibition? I could get us tick—
LOSER!
MAYBE SHE HATES MUSEUMS?
I just read this awesome book...
NERD ALERT!
Sara, I'll be in your neighbourhood tonight. Wanna hang?
AARGHH!
I'M SO STUPID! I FORGOT MY NAME!
WHAT DO I DO?
DO I SEND HER ANOTHER MESSAGE?
SHE'S PROBABLY WONDERING WHAT IDIOT IT WAS WHO MESSAGED HER
THE PROBLEM LIES IN THE FLOOD OF NEGATIVE THOUGHTS AND THEIR CATASTROPHIZING. THEY JUST KEEP GOING ROUND IN ISMAIL'S HEAD, AND HE CAN'T FIND A WAY OUT.
FRETTING OVER A SENSITIVE SITUATION IS NORMAL, EVEN USEFUL – IT'S WHAT PROMPTS US TO FIND A SOLUTION. BUT HERE, IT'S JUST A LOT OF WHEEL-SPINNING. BY OVERTHINKING THE PROBLEM, ISMAIL COMPLETELY SCREWS UP HIS CHANCES.
FORGET IT! I'LL JUST WAIT TWO WEEKS, LET IT BLOW OVER.
LET HER FORGET MY NUMBER.
OR MAYBE I'LL CALL MY SISTER FOR ADVICE.
MENTAL RADIO KILLED ME
NOT TO MENTION HOW EXHAUSTING MENTAL RADIO CAN BE...

HOW TO LOWER THE VOLUME ON OUR MENTAL RADIO

ONCE AGAIN, IT'S ALL A MATTER OF PRACTICE. HERE ARE SEVEN STEPS FOR LEARNING HOW TO STOP THAT VOICE BOTHERING US.

1. AWARENESS OF THE VOICES

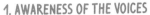

FIRST OF ALL, WE HAVE TO TELL TWO VOICES APART.

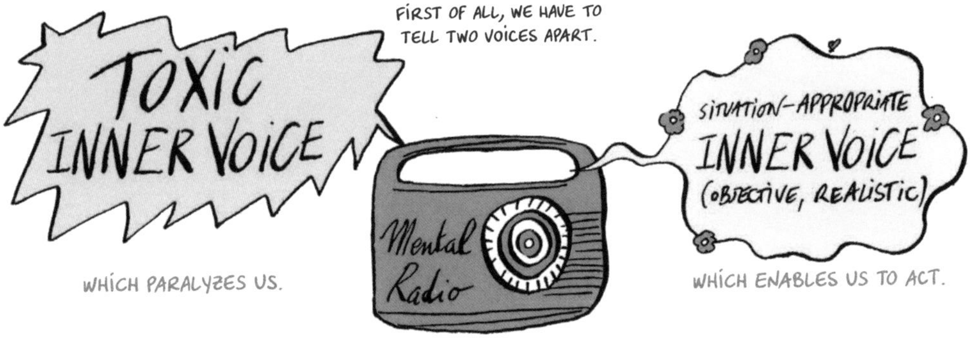

TOXIC INNER VOICE
WHICH PARALYZES US.
Mental Radio
SITUATION-APPROPRIATE INNER VOICE (OBJECTIVE, REALISTIC)
WHICH ENABLES US TO ACT.

IT'S ONLY NATURAL THAT ISMAIL SHOULD FRET OVER HIS TEXT MESSAGE: ALL SITUATIONS INVOLVING SEDUCTION ARE STRESSFUL. A WELL-ADJUSTED MENTAL RADIO WOULD LEAD HIM TO THINK BEFOREHAND.

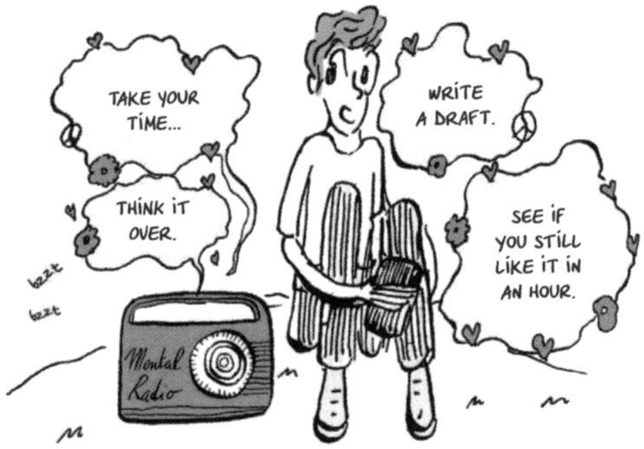

TAKE YOUR TIME...
THINK IT OVER.
WRITE A DRAFT.
SEE IF YOU STILL LIKE IT IN AN HOUR.
bzzt
bzzt
Mental Radio

BUT ISMAIL HAS TWO OTHER MENTAL RADIOS:

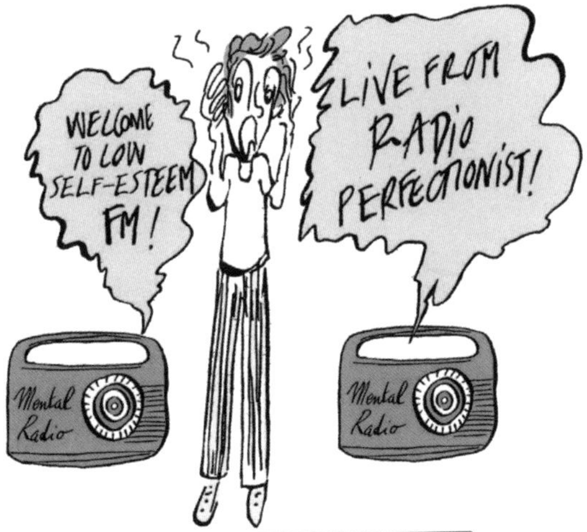

WELCOME TO LOW SELF-ESTEEM FM!
LIVE FROM RADIO PERFECTIONIST!
Mental Radio
Mental Radio

THESE DRAG HIM DOWN INTO INDECISIVENESS AND NEGATIVE EMOTIONS THAT PUSH HIM FURTHER INTO DOUBT WHEN COMPOSING HIS MESSAGE. IT'S A VICIOUS CIRCLE. THESE TWO FREQUENCIES ARE NOT CONNECTED TO HIS SITUATION, BUT RATHER TO HIS ACCUSTOMED PATTERNS.

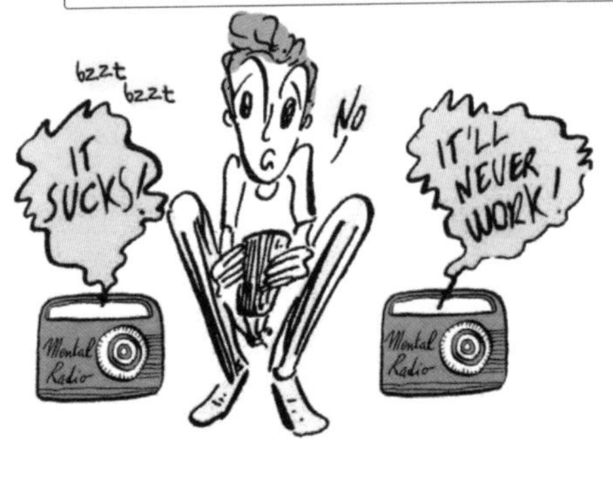

bzzt
bzzt
IT SUCKS!
NO
IT'LL NEVER WORK!
Mental Radio
Mental Radio

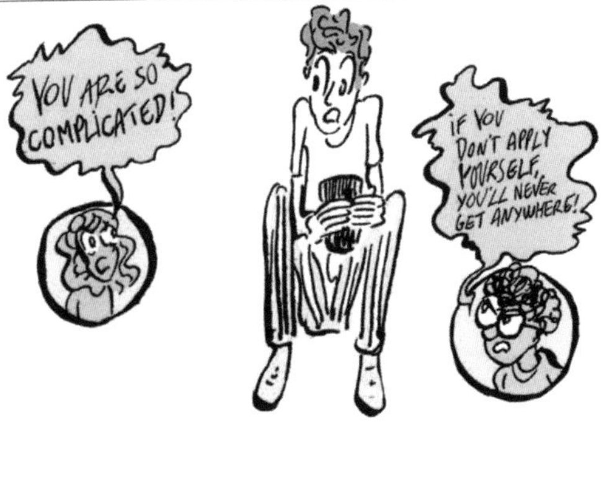

YOU ARE SO COMPLICATED!
IF YOU DON'T APPLY YOURSELF, YOU'LL NEVER GET ANYWHERE!

2. AWARENESS OF MENTAL RADIO'S HARMFUL EFFECTS

MAKE A LIST OF THE WAYS THESE VOICES ARE RUINING OUR LIVES.

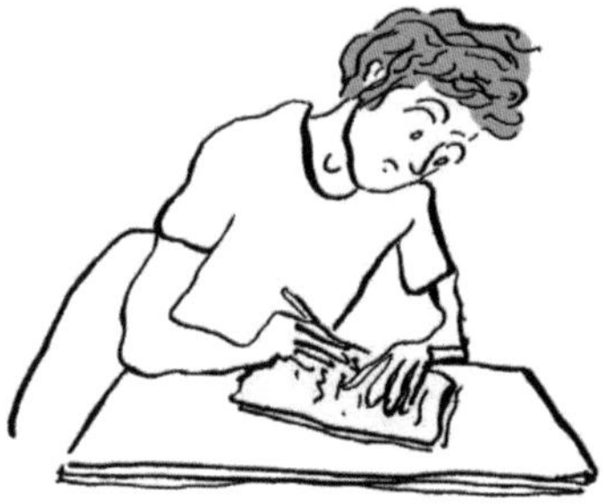

- *lots of negative emotions and excessive doubts*
- *negative cognitive bias*
- *indecisiveness*
- *avoidance of situations that create fear*
- *negative self-image*
- *it wears out my friends*
- *it makes me drink or smoke*

3. TELL OUR MENTAL RADIO TO STOP

STANDING UP TO OUR INNER VOICE HELPS US NOT TO LET IT PARALYZE US.

IF THE VOICE IS VERY NEGATIVE, THAT LIKELY MEANS WE'RE RELIVING A SITUATION WE DIDN'T FEEL UP TO, OR SOME TRAUMA.

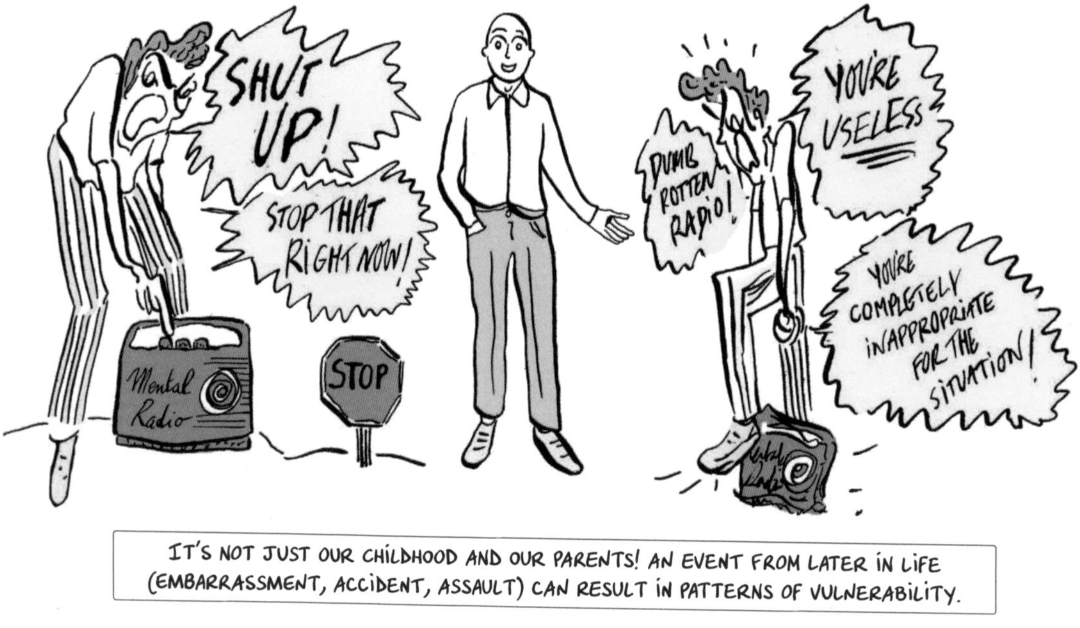

SHUT UP!
STOP THAT RIGHT NOW!
Mental Radio
STOP
DUMB ROTTEN RADIO!
YOU'RE USELESS
YOU'RE COMPLETELY INAPPROPRIATE FOR THE SITUATION!

IT'S NOT JUST OUR CHILDHOOD AND OUR PARENTS! AN EVENT FROM LATER IN LIFE (EMBARRASSMENT, ACCIDENT, ASSAULT) CAN RESULT IN PATTERNS OF VULNERABILITY.

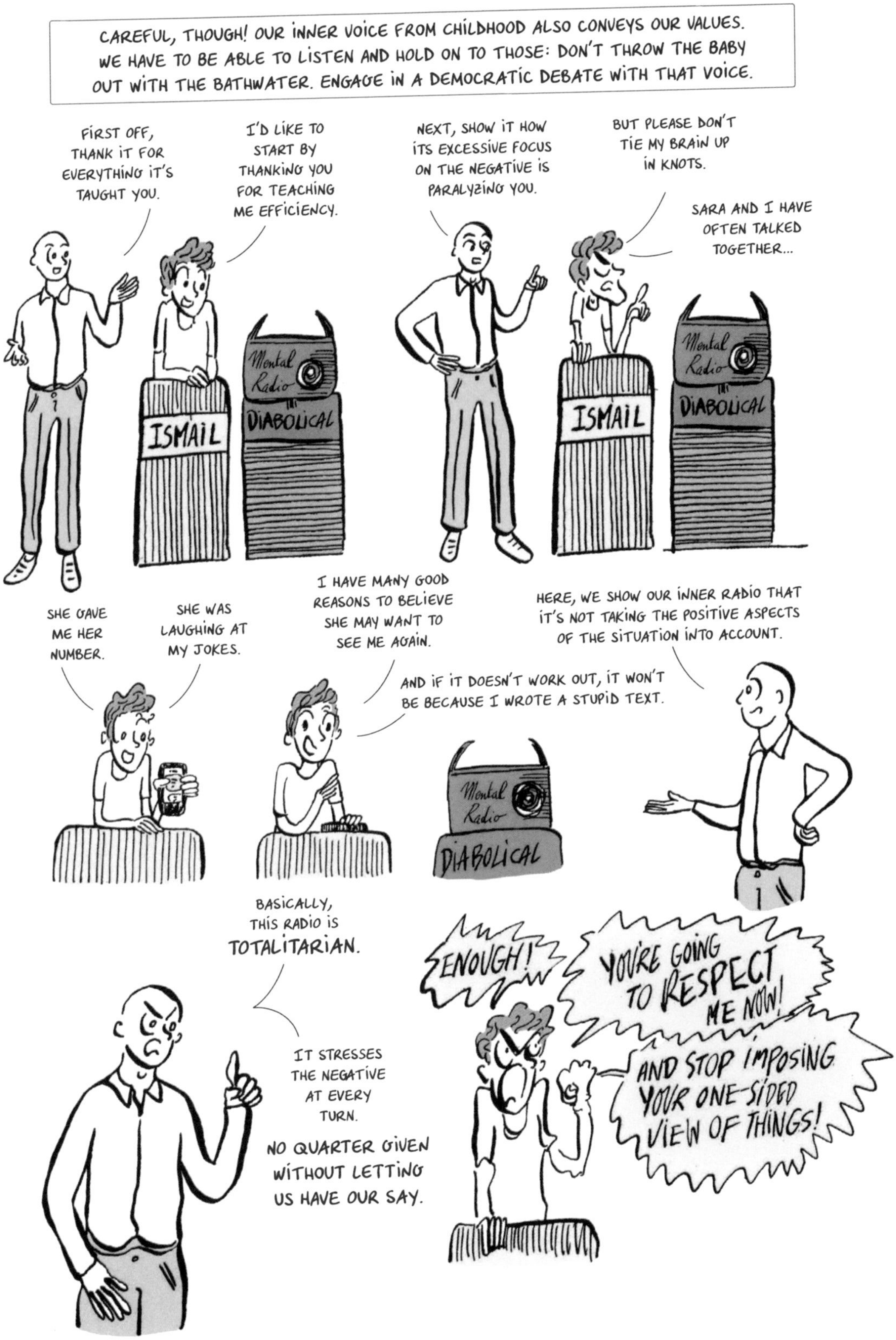
CAREFUL, THOUGH! OUR INNER VOICE FROM CHILDHOOD ALSO CONVEYS OUR VALUES. WE HAVE TO BE ABLE TO LISTEN AND HOLD ON TO THOSE: DON'T THROW THE BABY OUT WITH THE BATHWATER. ENGAGE IN A DEMOCRATIC DEBATE WITH THAT VOICE.
FIRST OFF, THANK IT FOR EVERYTHING IT'S TAUGHT YOU.
I'D LIKE TO START BY THANKING YOU FOR TEACHING ME EFFICIENCY.
ISMAIL
Mental Radio
DIABOLICAL
NEXT, SHOW IT HOW ITS EXCESSIVE FOCUS ON THE NEGATIVE IS PARALYZING YOU.
BUT PLEASE DON'T TIE MY BRAIN UP IN KNOTS.
SARA AND I HAVE OFTEN TALKED TOGETHER...
ISMAIL
Mental Radio
DIABOLICAL
SHE GAVE ME HER NUMBER.
SHE WAS LAUGHING AT MY JOKES.
I HAVE MANY GOOD REASONS TO BELIEVE SHE MAY WANT TO SEE ME AGAIN.
AND IF IT DOESN'T WORK OUT, IT WON'T BE BECAUSE I WROTE A STUPID TEXT.
Mental Radio
DIABOLICAL
HERE, WE SHOW OUR INNER RADIO THAT IT'S NOT TAKING THE POSITIVE ASPECTS OF THE SITUATION INTO ACCOUNT.
BASICALLY, THIS RADIO IS TOTALITARIAN.
IT STRESSES THE NEGATIVE AT EVERY TURN.
NO QUARTER GIVEN WITHOUT LETTING US HAVE OUR SAY.
ENOUGH!
YOU'RE GOING TO RESPECT ME NOW!
AND STOP IMPOSING YOUR ONE-SIDED VIEW OF THINGS!

4. TRY TO BE ITS BEST FRIEND

MANY OF US ARE KINDER TO OUR FRIENDS THAN WE ARE TO OURSELVES. THAT'S WHY I OFTEN USE THE TECHNIQUE OF ASKING YOU WHAT YOU'D SAY TO A FRIEND UNDER THE SAME CIRCUMSTANCES.

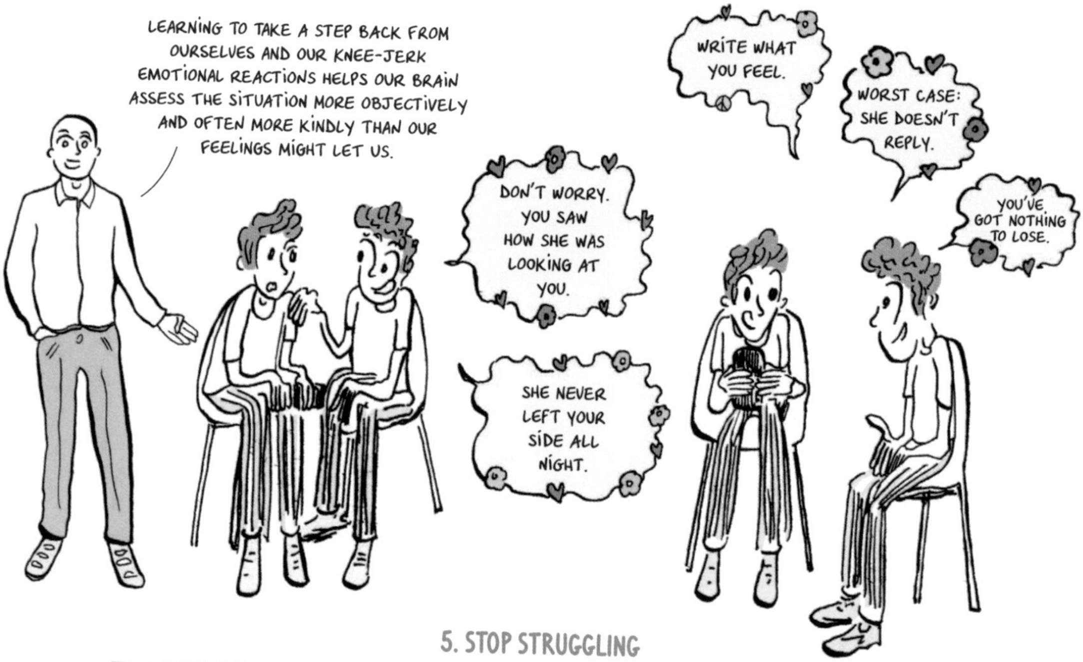
LEARNING TO TAKE A STEP BACK FROM OURSELVES AND OUR KNEE-JERK EMOTIONAL REACTIONS HELPS OUR BRAIN ASSESS THE SITUATION MORE OBJECTIVELY AND OFTEN MORE KINDLY THAN OUR FEELINGS MIGHT LET US.
DON'T WORRY. YOU SAW HOW SHE WAS LOOKING AT YOU.
SHE NEVER LEFT YOUR SIDE ALL NIGHT.
WRITE WHAT YOU FEEL.
WORST CASE: SHE DOESN'T REPLY.
YOU'VE GOT NOTHING TO LOSE.

5. STOP STRUGGLING

TO SOME OF US, ESPECIALLY THOSE WITH LOW SELF-ESTEEM, THE TECHNIQUES I'VE DISCUSSED CAN SEEM LIKE AN ENDLESS, EXHAUSTING STRUGGLE.

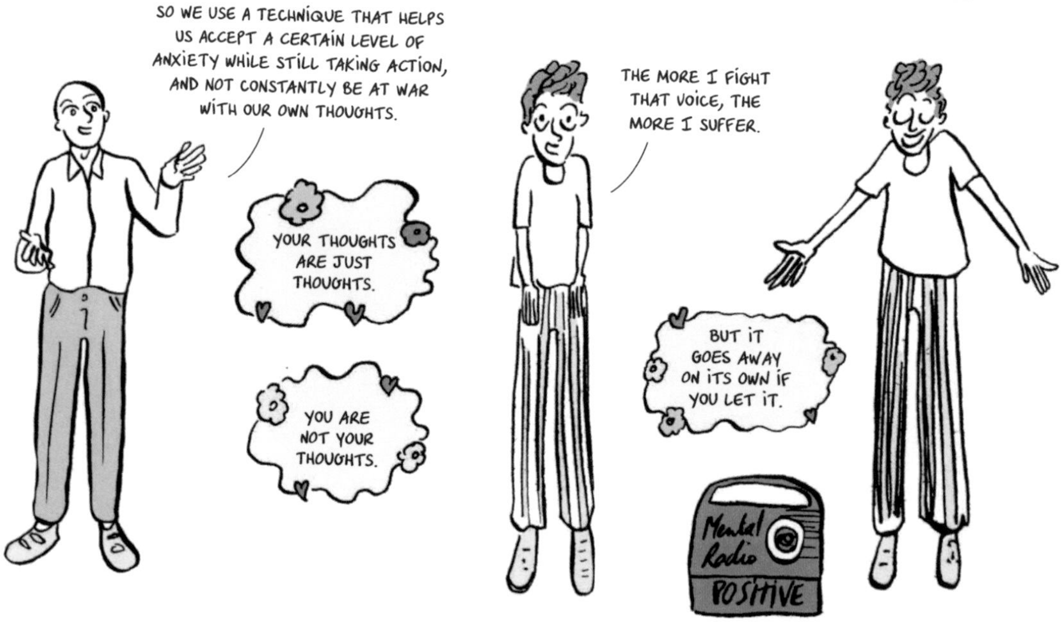
SO WE USE A TECHNIQUE THAT HELPS US ACCEPT A CERTAIN LEVEL OF ANXIETY WHILE STILL TAKING ACTION, AND NOT CONSTANTLY BE AT WAR WITH OUR OWN THOUGHTS.
YOUR THOUGHTS ARE JUST THOUGHTS.
YOU ARE NOT YOUR THOUGHTS.
THE MORE I FIGHT THAT VOICE, THE MORE I SUFFER.
BUT IT GOES AWAY ON ITS OWN IF YOU LET IT.
Mental Radio
POSITIVE

6. DON'T GET TRAPPED ALONE WITH YOUR MENTAL RADIO

WHEN OUR NEGATIVE MENTAL RADIO IS OVERWHELMING, LEADING US TO EXPERIENCE NEGATIVE EMOTIONS, IT MIGHT HELP TO TALK TO KIND AND UPBEAT FRIENDS. THEY'LL HELP US GET DISTANCE FROM OUR MENTAL RADIO.

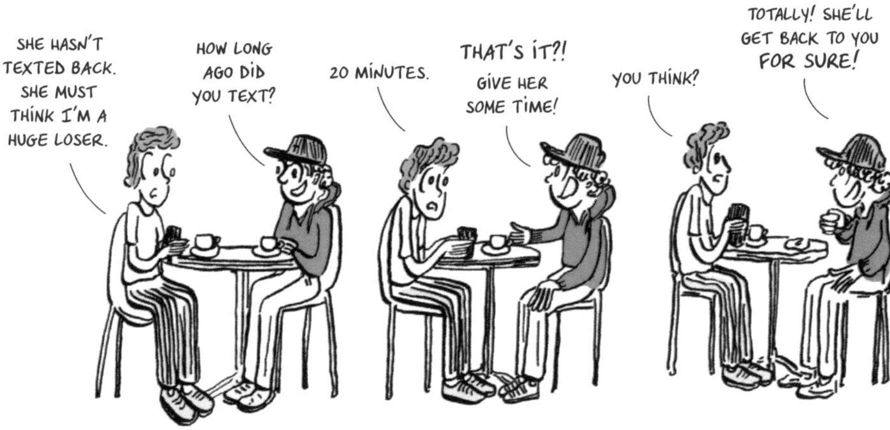
SHE HASN'T TEXTED BACK. SHE MUST THINK I'M A HUGE LOSER.
HOW LONG AGO DID YOU TEXT?
20 MINUTES.
THAT'S IT?! GIVE HER SOME TIME!
YOU THINK?
TOTALLY! SHE'LL GET BACK TO YOU FOR SURE!

7. TRY TO LIVE IN THE MOMENT

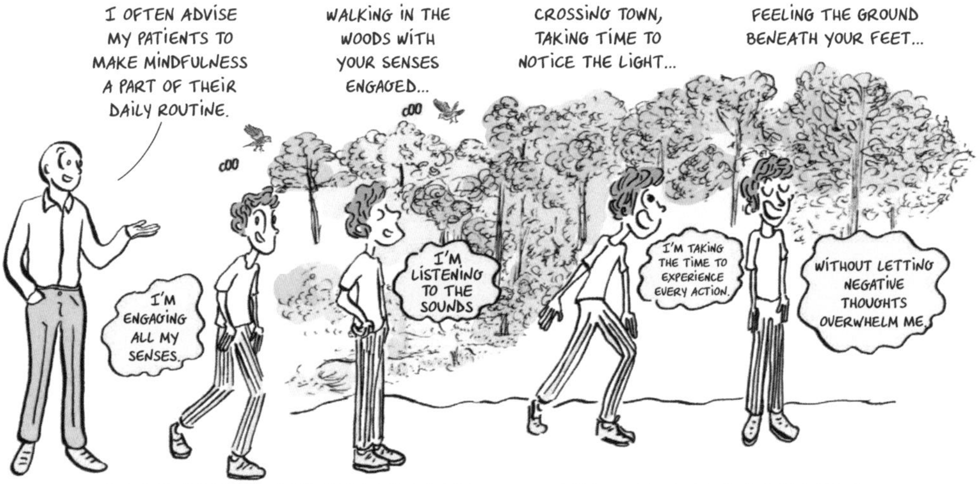
I OFTEN ADVISE MY PATIENTS TO MAKE MINDFULNESS A PART OF THEIR DAILY ROUTINE.
WALKING IN THE WOODS WITH YOUR SENSES ENGAGED...
CROSSING TOWN, TAKING TIME TO NOTICE THE LIGHT...
FEELING THE GROUND BENEATH YOUR FEET...
COO
COO
I'M ENGAGING ALL MY SENSES.
I'M LISTENING TO THE SOUNDS
I'M TAKING THE TIME TO EXPERIENCE EVERY ACTION.
WITHOUT LETTING NEGATIVE THOUGHTS OVERWHELM ME.

TIPS FOR STAYING IN THE MOMENT WON'T WORK FOR EVERYONE.
THE IMPORTANT THING IS FINDING A WAY THAT WORKS FOR YOU.

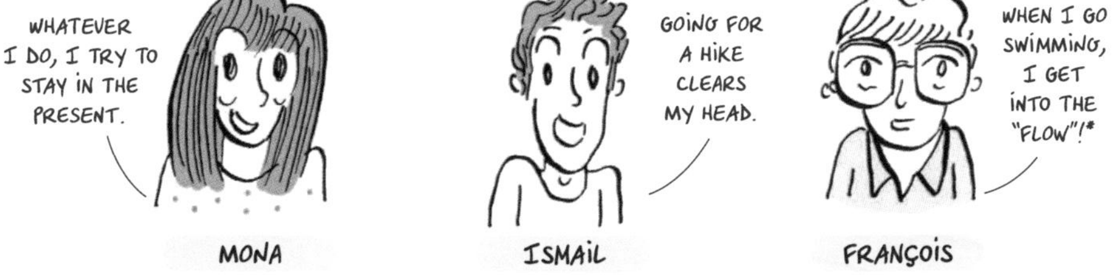
WHATEVER I DO, I TRY TO STAY IN THE PRESENT.
GOING FOR A HIKE CLEARS MY HEAD.
WHEN I GO SWIMMING, I GET INTO THE "FLOW"!*
MONA
ISMAIL
FRANÇOIS

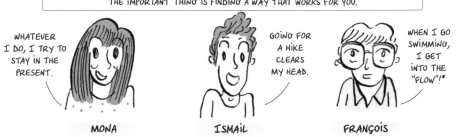

* "FLOW" IS A MENTAL STATE WE ATTAIN WHEN WE ARE DEEPLY ENGAGED IN AND FOCUSED ON AN ACTIVITY.

PANIC ATTACKS
CAN ALSO BE
TREATED!

FOR MONA, THIS MEANS
GOING FROM DEVASTATING,
INCOMPREHENSIBLE EXPERIENCES
WHERE SHE FEELS HER LIFE IS
IN DANGER, TO AN ABILITY TO
GRADUALLY TAME HER FEARS.

SEASON 2 – PANIC DISORDER

In Treatment

WITH MONA

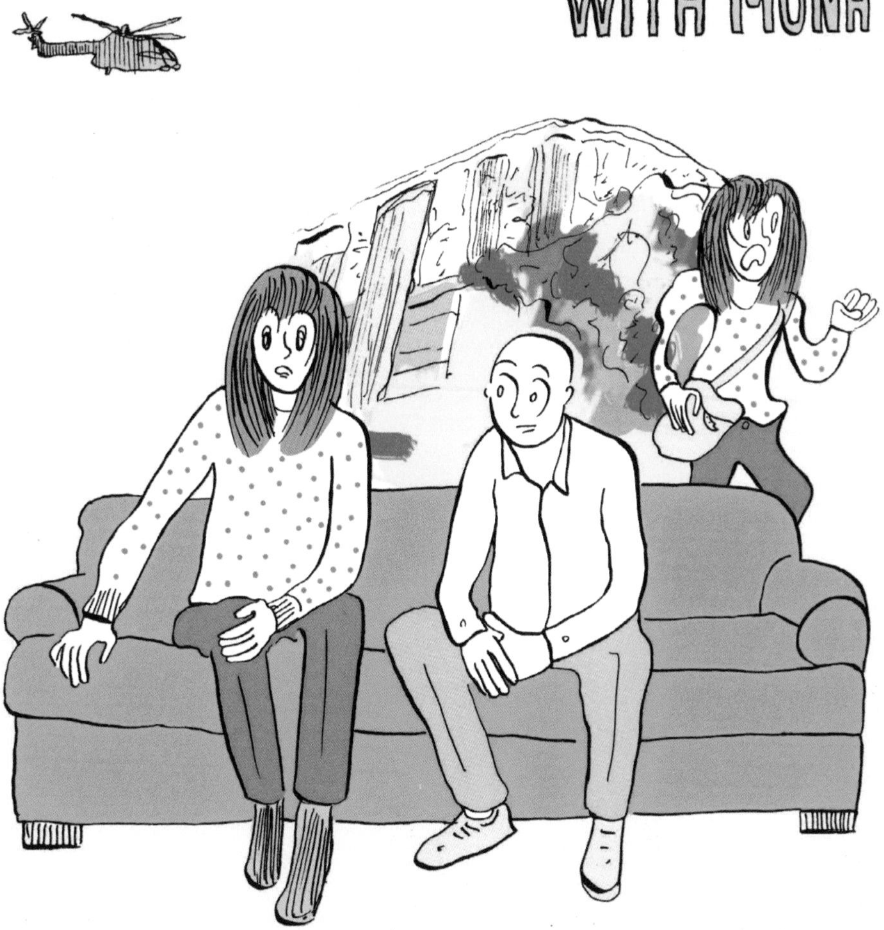

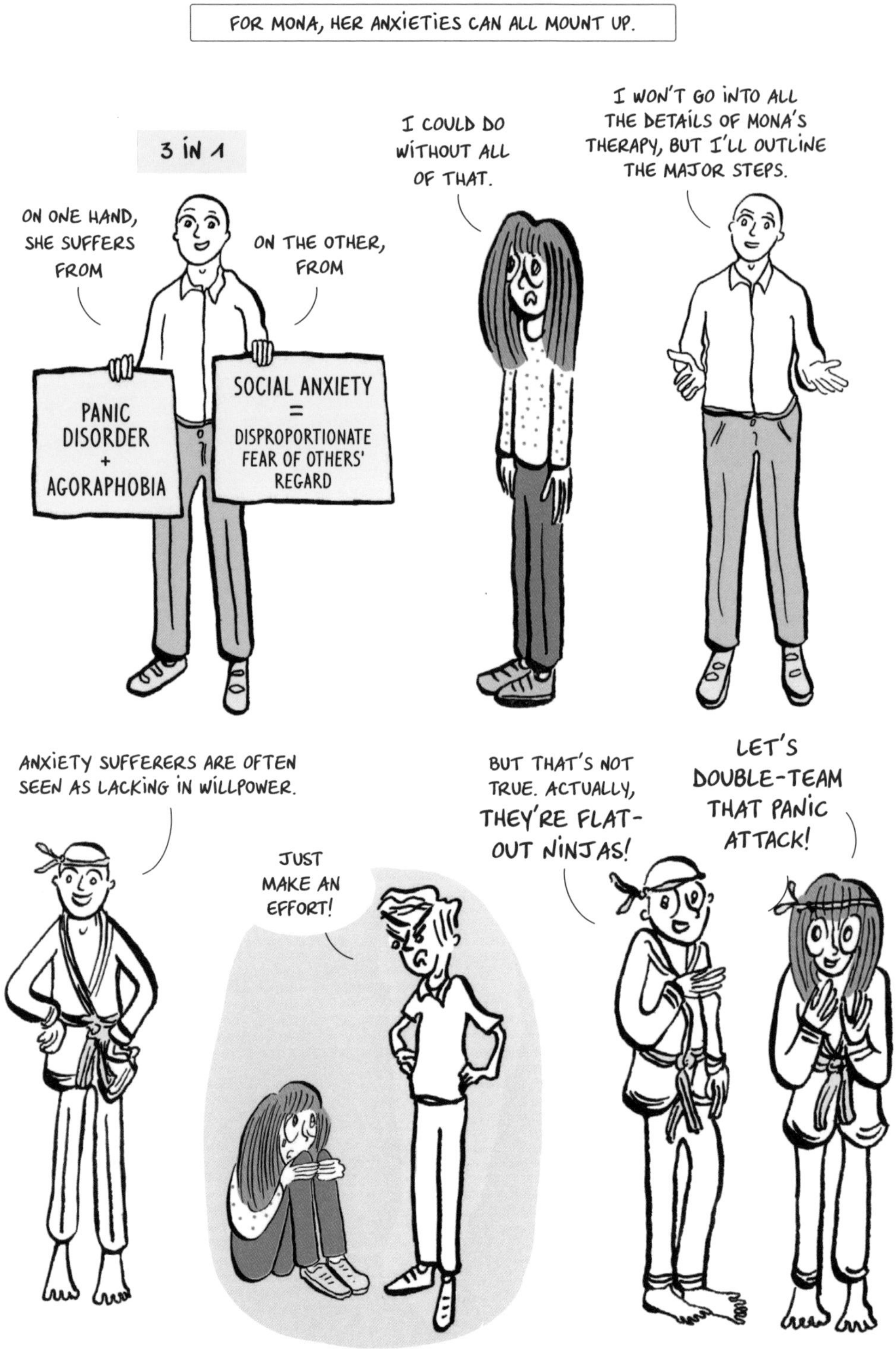
FOR MONA, HER ANXIETIES CAN ALL MOUNT UP.
3 IN 1
ON ONE HAND, SHE SUFFERS FROM
PANIC DISORDER + AGORAPHOBIA
ON THE OTHER, FROM
SOCIAL ANXIETY = DISPROPORTIONATE FEAR OF OTHERS' REGARD
I COULD DO WITHOUT ALL OF THAT.
I WON'T GO INTO ALL THE DETAILS OF MONA'S THERAPY, BUT I'LL OUTLINE THE MAJOR STEPS.
ANXIETY SUFFERERS ARE OFTEN SEEN AS LACKING IN WILLPOWER.
JUST MAKE AN EFFORT!
BUT THAT'S NOT TRUE. ACTUALLY, THEY'RE FLAT-OUT NINJAS!
LET'S DOUBLE-TEAM THAT PANIC ATTACK!

SPEC SHEET: PANIC ATTACK AND HYPERVENTILATION

NOTE:

A PANIC ATTACK CAN HAPPEN:

WITH NO CLEAR CAUSE.	IN PLACES WE DREAD OR HABITUALLY AVOID.	JUST BECAUSE WE'RE FAR FROM HOME.

HELP!

SOMETIMES PANIC IS EVEN TRIGGERED SIMPLY BY PICTURING A SITUATION IN WHICH WE'VE FELT ANXIOUS BEFORE.

IN MOST PANIC ATTACKS, OUR BREATHING SPEEDS UP.

WE CAN ALSO EXPERIENCE ALL SORTS OF DIFFICULTIES REMINISCENT OF MORE SERIOUS CONDITIONS.

THIS IS:

HYPERVENTILATION

CEREBRAL HEMORRHAGE

HEART ATTACK

LOSS OF CONTROL

AN INDIVIDUAL WHO DELIBERATELY SPEEDS UP THEIR BREATHING RATE CAN EXPERIENCE THE SAME SYMPTOMS, EVEN IF THEY'VE NEVER SUFFERED FROM ANXIETY.

I'M GOING CRAZY!

THIS IS, UNFORTUNATELY, FAR FROM WELL-KNOWN.

HYPERVENTILATION
=
METABOLIC ISSUES
=
PANIC ATTACK

STEP 1: DECATASTROPHIZING YOUR THOUGHTS

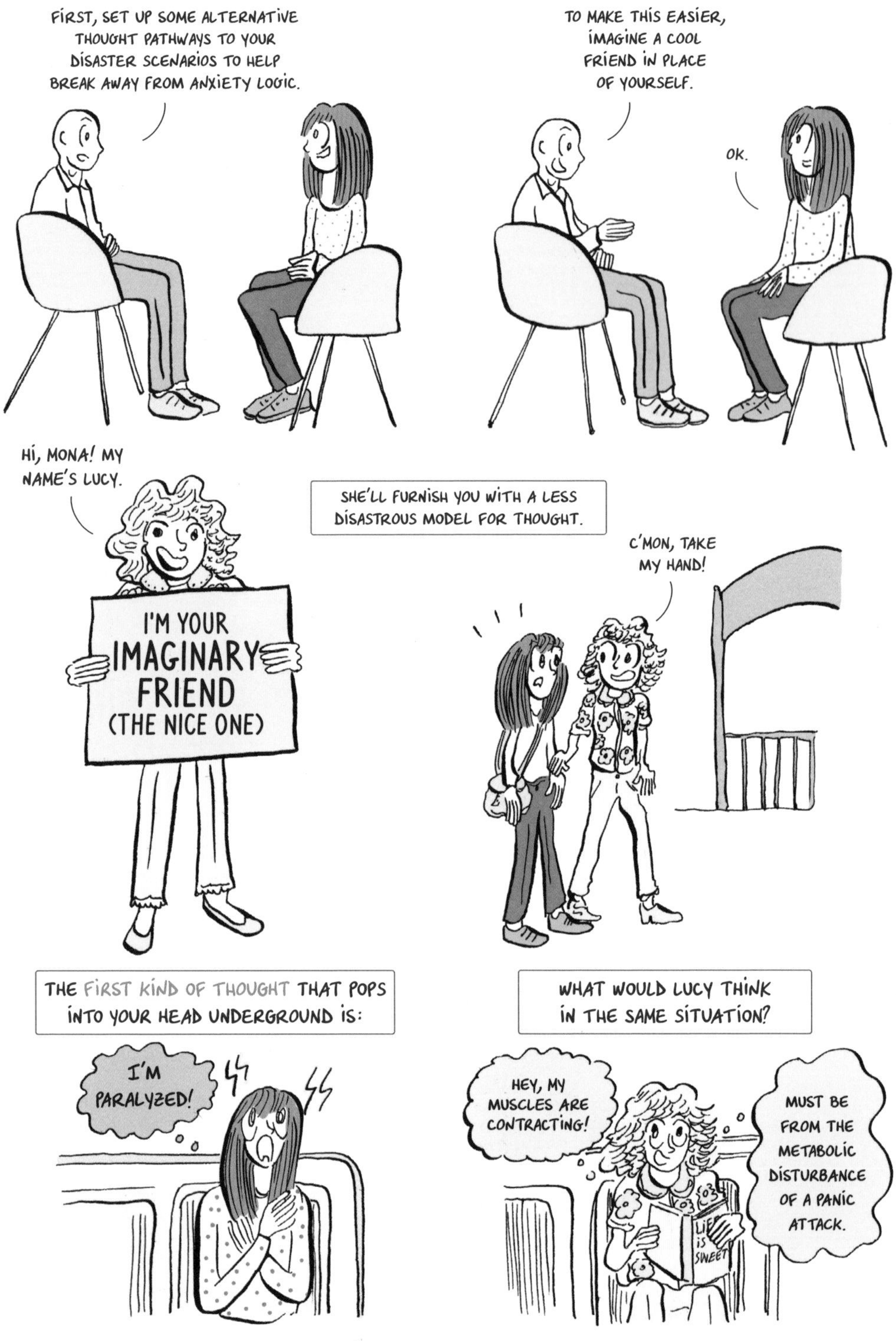
FIRST, SET UP SOME ALTERNATIVE THOUGHT PATHWAYS TO YOUR DISASTER SCENARIOS TO HELP BREAK AWAY FROM ANXIETY LOGIC.
TO MAKE THIS EASIER, IMAGINE A COOL FRIEND IN PLACE OF YOURSELF.
OK.
HI, MONA! MY NAME'S LUCY.
I'M YOUR IMAGINARY FRIEND (THE NICE ONE)
SHE'LL FURNISH YOU WITH A LESS DISASTROUS MODEL FOR THOUGHT.
C'MON, TAKE MY HAND!
THE FIRST KIND OF THOUGHT THAT POPS INTO YOUR HEAD UNDERGROUND IS:
I'M PARALYZED!
WHAT WOULD LUCY THINK IN THE SAME SITUATION?
HEY, MY MUSCLES ARE CONTRACTING!
MUST BE FROM THE METABOLIC DISTURBANCE OF A PANIC ATTACK.
LIFE IS SWEET

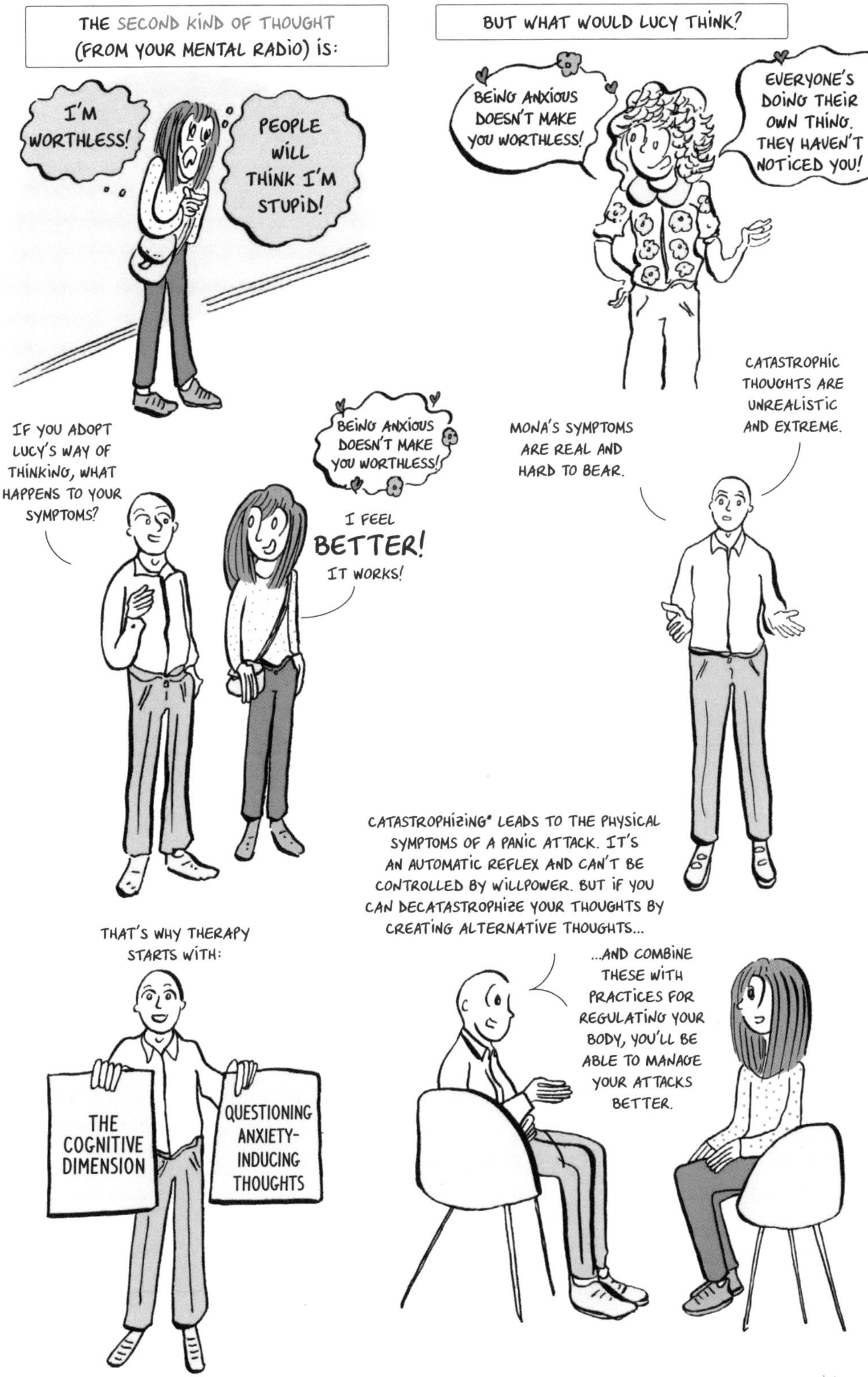
THE SECOND KIND OF THOUGHT (FROM YOUR MENTAL RADIO) IS:
I'M WORTHLESS!
PEOPLE WILL THINK I'M STUPID!
BUT WHAT WOULD LUCY THINK?
BEING ANXIOUS DOESN'T MAKE YOU WORTHLESS!
EVERYONE'S DOING THEIR OWN THING. THEY HAVEN'T NOTICED YOU!
IF YOU ADOPT LUCY'S WAY OF THINKING, WHAT HAPPENS TO YOUR SYMPTOMS?
BEING ANXIOUS DOESN'T MAKE YOU WORTHLESS!
I FEEL BETTER! IT WORKS!
MONA'S SYMPTOMS ARE REAL AND HARD TO BEAR.
CATASTROPHIC THOUGHTS ARE UNREALISTIC AND EXTREME.
THAT'S WHY THERAPY STARTS WITH:
THE COGNITIVE DIMENSION
QUESTIONING ANXIETY-INDUCING THOUGHTS
CATASTROPHIZING* LEADS TO THE PHYSICAL SYMPTOMS OF A PANIC ATTACK. IT'S AN AUTOMATIC REFLEX AND CAN'T BE CONTROLLED BY WILLPOWER. BUT IF YOU CAN DECATASTROPHIZE YOUR THOUGHTS BY CREATING ALTERNATIVE THOUGHTS...
...AND COMBINE THESE WITH PRACTICES FOR REGULATING YOUR BODY, YOU'LL BE ABLE TO MANAGE YOUR ATTACKS BETTER.

*"CATASTROPHIZING" IS A PSYCHIATRIC TERM USED TO DESCRIBE A TENDENCY TO JUMP TO THE WORST POSSIBLE CONCLUSION.

STEP 2: BREATHING AND BODILY REGULATION

THE CANDLE EXERCISE

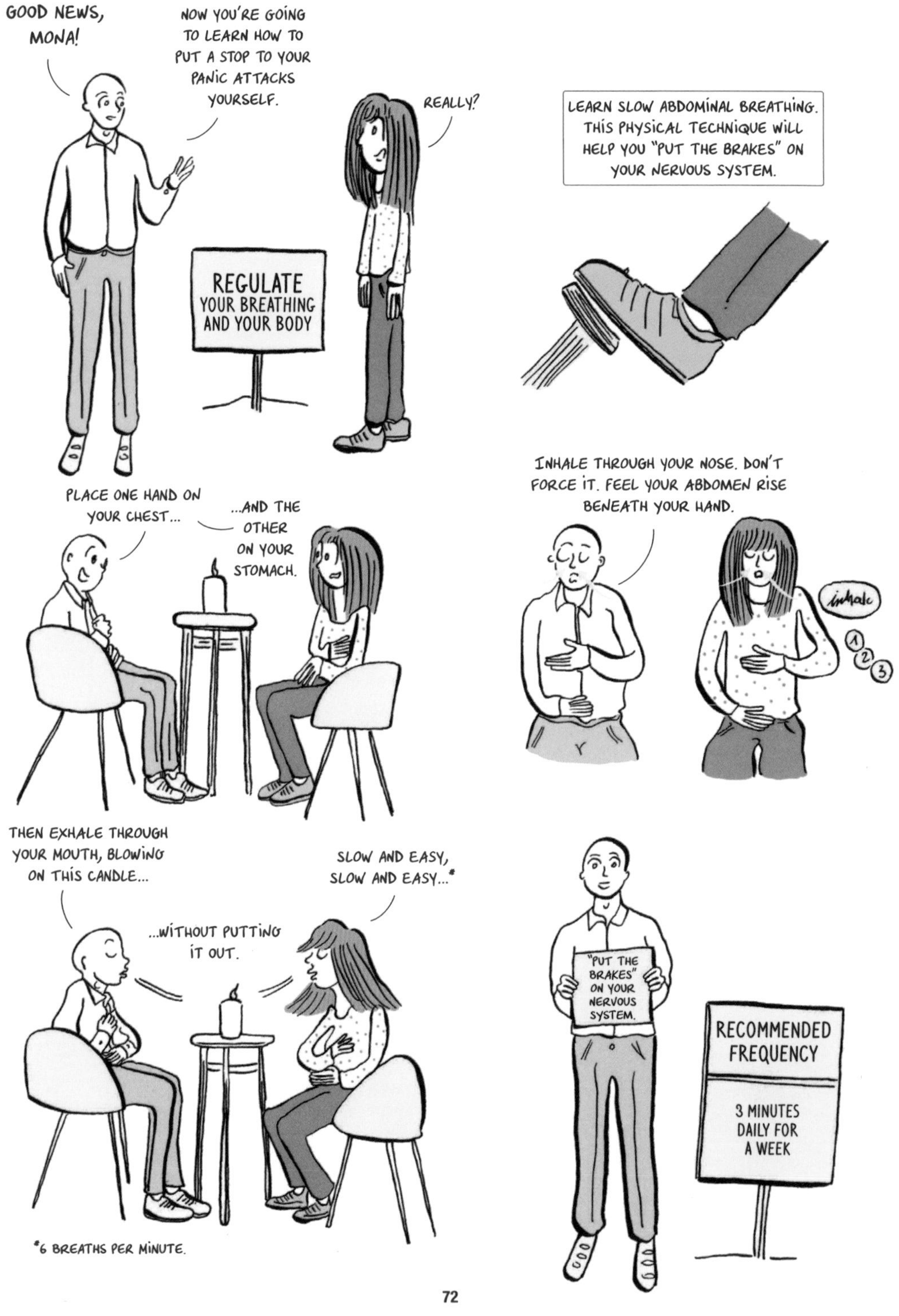
GOOD NEWS, MONA!
NOW YOU'RE GOING TO LEARN HOW TO PUT A STOP TO YOUR PANIC ATTACKS YOURSELF.
REGULATE YOUR BREATHING AND YOUR BODY
REALLY?
LEARN SLOW ABDOMINAL BREATHING. THIS PHYSICAL TECHNIQUE WILL HELP YOU "PUT THE BRAKES" ON YOUR NERVOUS SYSTEM.
PLACE ONE HAND ON YOUR CHEST...
...AND THE OTHER ON YOUR STOMACH.
INHALE THROUGH YOUR NOSE. DON'T FORCE IT. FEEL YOUR ABDOMEN RISE BENEATH YOUR HAND.
inhale
1
2
3
THEN EXHALE THROUGH YOUR MOUTH, BLOWING ON THIS CANDLE...
...WITHOUT PUTTING IT OUT.
SLOW AND EASY, SLOW AND EASY...*
"PUT THE BRAKES" ON YOUR NERVOUS SYSTEM.
RECOMMENDED FREQUENCY
3 MINUTES DAILY FOR A WEEK

*6 BREATHS PER MINUTE.

JACOBSON'S RELAXATION TECHNIQUE

IN 1928, AN AMERICAN PSYCHIATRIST DEMONSTRATED THAT ANXIETY CAUSES OUR MUSCLES TO CONTRACT. HE DEVELOPED A METHOD OF ACTIVE RELAXATION.

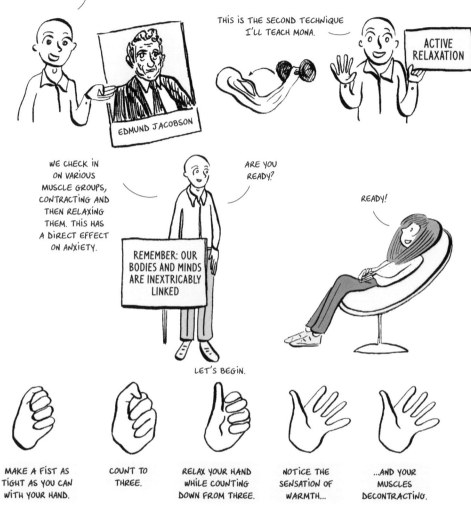

THIS IS THE SECOND TECHNIQUE I'LL TEACH MONA.

EDMUND JACOBSON

ACTIVE RELAXATION

WE CHECK IN ON VARIOUS MUSCLE GROUPS, CONTRACTING AND THEN RELAXING THEM. THIS HAS A DIRECT EFFECT ON ANXIETY.

ARE YOU READY?

READY!

REMEMBER: OUR BODIES AND MINDS ARE INEXTRICABLY LINKED

LET'S BEGIN.

MAKE A FIST AS TIGHT AS YOU CAN WITH YOUR HAND.

COUNT TO THREE.

RELAX YOUR HAND WHILE COUNTING DOWN FROM THREE.

NOTICE THE SENSATION OF WARMTH...

...AND YOUR MUSCLES DECONTRACTING.

WE THEN MOVE ON TO EVERY MUSCLE GROUP IN THE BODY, ONE AFTER ANOTHER.

I RECOMMEND SETTING AN ALARM ON YOUR SMARTPHONE FOR THE SAME TIME EACH DAY.

RECORD YOUR ANXIETY LEVEL IN YOUR SPECIAL THERAPY NOTEBOOK.

YOU TOO CAN TRY THIS TECHNIQUE!

ALARM RELAXATION
18:30

BEFORE
6 / 10
AFTER
3 / 10

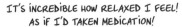

IT'S INCREDIBLE HOW RELAXED I FEEL! AS IF I'D TAKEN MEDICATION!

PRECISELY. RELAXATION CAN ACT JUST LIKE A DRUG.

AND WITHOUT SIDE EFFECTS!

WHAT'S YOUR POISON OF CHOICE?

ALCOHOL

SKUNK

BENZOS

SEDATIVE

WHILE THEY MAY KILL OFF ANXIETY IN THE SHORT TERM, THEY MAY HAVE SIDE EFFECTS OR ADDICTIVE QUALITIES.

ANXIETY 1994-2023

I'LL BE BACK SOON

BEHAVIOURAL ISSUES

PHYSICAL ISSUES

RELATIONSHIP ISSUES

ANGER

VIOLENCE

CIRRHOSIS

ALCOHOLIC NEUROPATHY

KORSAKOFF SYNDROME

DIVORCE

UNEMPLOYMENT

I LOST IT ALL

MONA PRACTISES RELAXATION AT HOME.

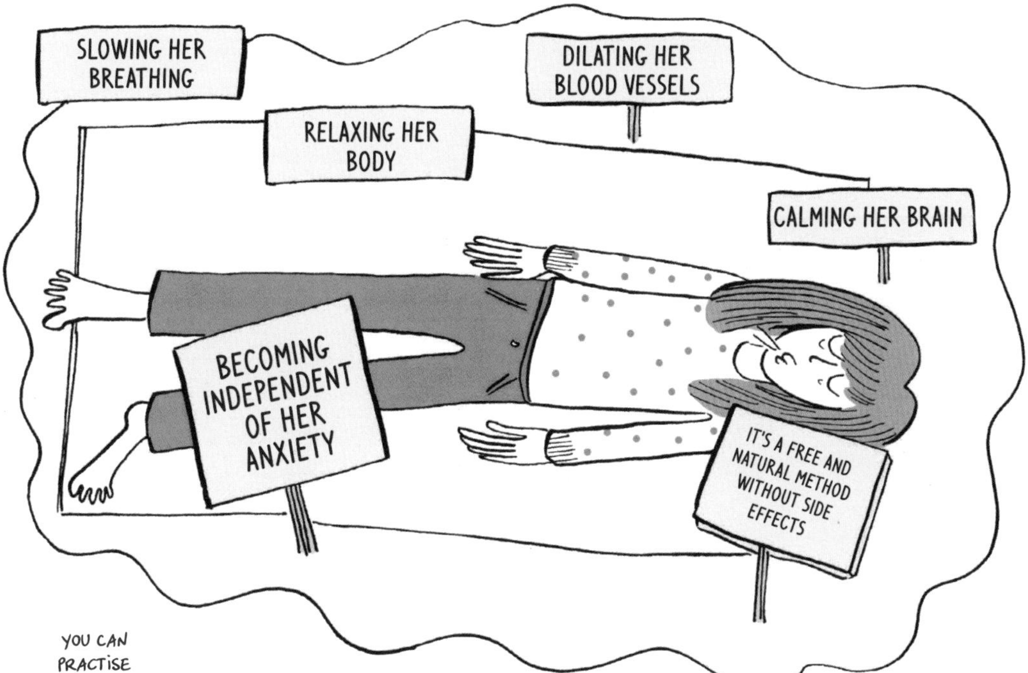

SLOWING HER BREATHING
DILATING HER BLOOD VESSELS
RELAXING HER BODY
CALMING HER BRAIN
BECOMING INDEPENDENT OF HER ANXIETY
IT'S A FREE AND NATURAL METHOD WITHOUT SIDE EFFECTS

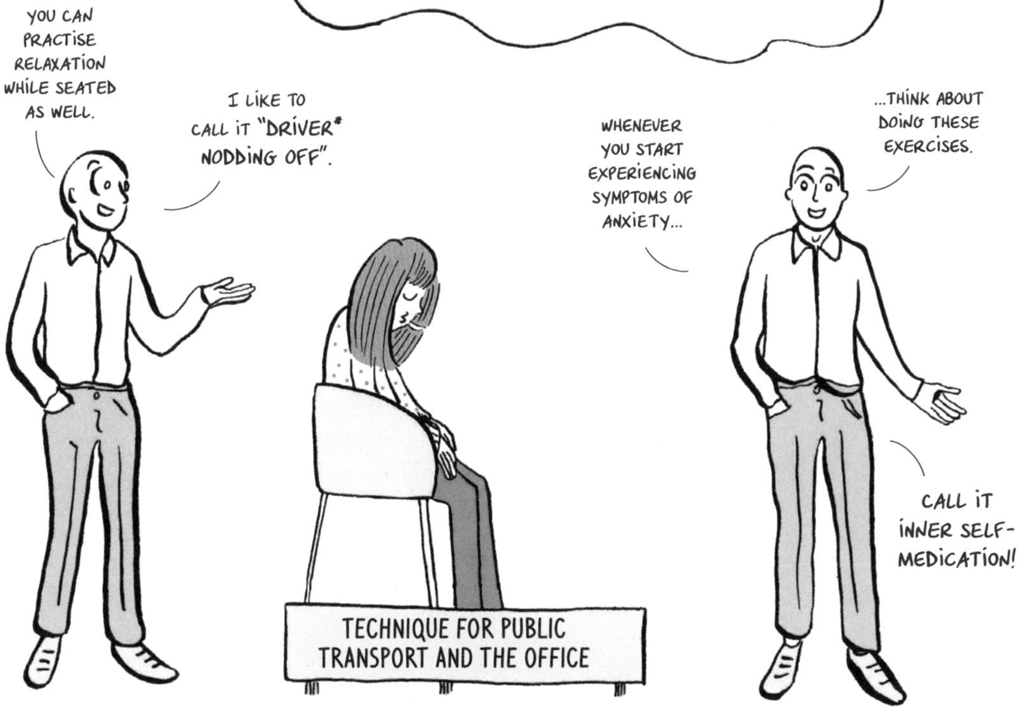

YOU CAN PRACTISE RELAXATION WHILE SEATED AS WELL.
I LIKE TO CALL IT "DRIVER* NODDING OFF".
WHENEVER YOU START EXPERIENCING SYMPTOMS OF ANXIETY...
...THINK ABOUT DOING THESE EXERCISES.
CALL IT INNER SELF-MEDICATION!
TECHNIQUE FOR PUBLIC TRANSPORT AND THE OFFICE

REMEMBER TO ASSIGN YOUR ANXIETY LEVEL A NUMBER FROM 0 TO 10 BEFORE AND AFTER RELAXATION. THIS HELPS REINFORCE THE CONVICTION THAT YOU YOURSELF CAN LOWER YOUR ANXIETY, ASSESS THE EFFECTIVENESS OF THESE EXERCISES, AND MEASURE YOUR PROGRESS.

*DO NOT DO THIS WHILE DRIVING A CAR OR OPERATING ANY MACHINERY.

STEP 3: CONFRONT PHYSICAL SYMPTOMS OF ANXIETY

NOW WE MOVE ON TO "EXPOSURE THERAPY". WE'RE NO LONGER TRYING TO PREVENT PHYSICAL MANIFESTATIONS OF ANXIETY SO MUCH AS CONFRONT THEM, IN ORDER TO DECREASE OUR SUSCEPTIBILITY TO THEM.

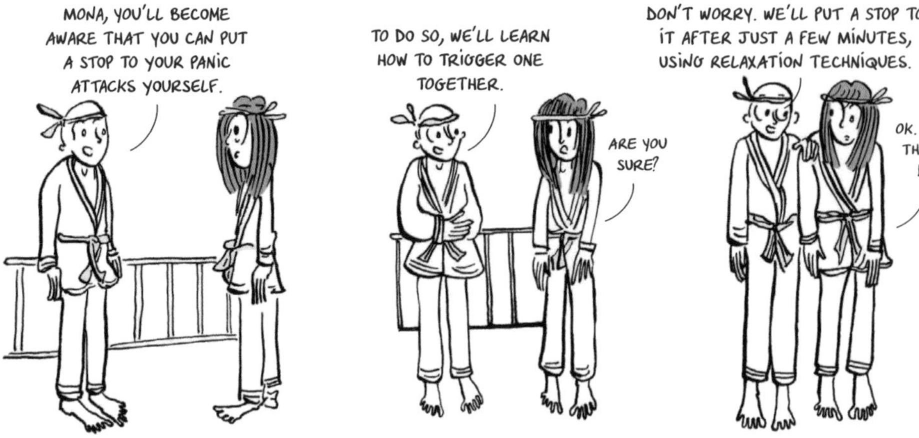
MONA, YOU'LL BECOME AWARE THAT YOU CAN PUT A STOP TO YOUR PANIC ATTACKS YOURSELF.
TO DO SO, WE'LL LEARN HOW TO TRIGGER ONE TOGETHER.
ARE YOU SURE?
DON'T WORRY. WE'LL PUT A STOP TO IT AFTER JUST A FEW MINUTES, USING RELAXATION TECHNIQUES.
OK. YOU'RE THE DOC, DOC!

1. HOW DO YOU TRIGGER A PANIC ATTACK?

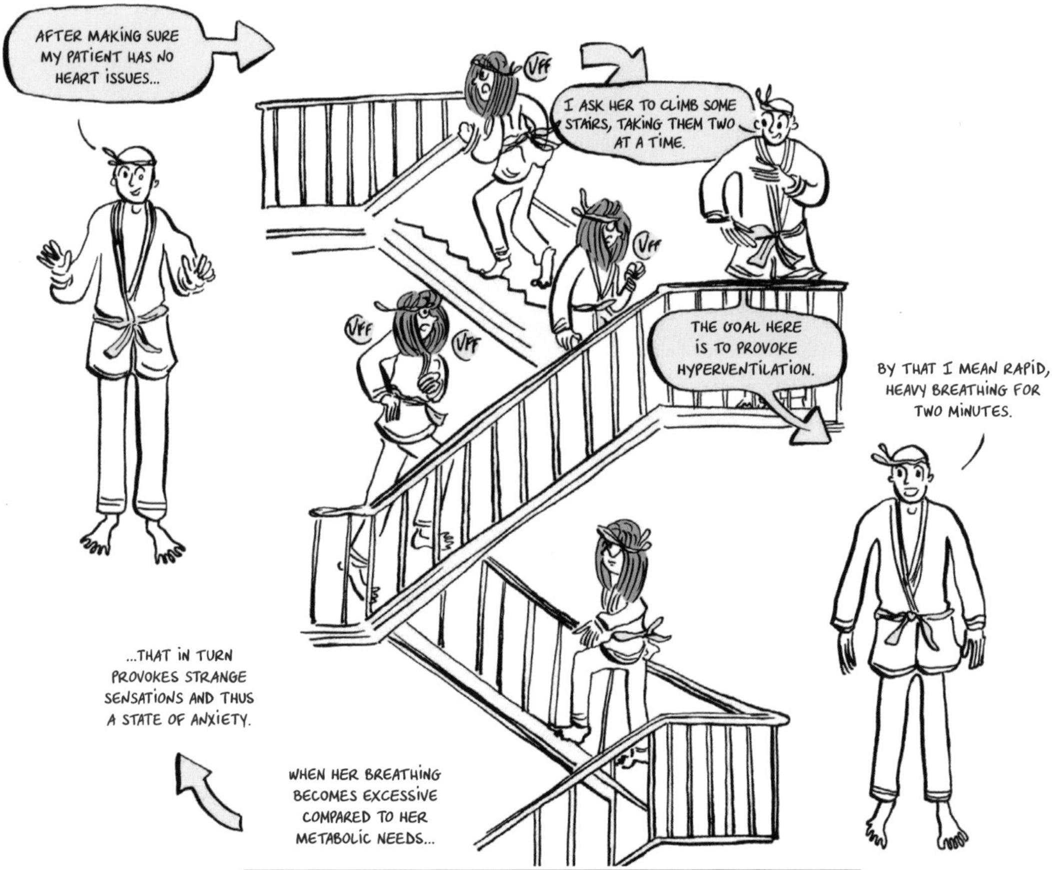
AFTER MAKING SURE MY PATIENT HAS NO HEART ISSUES...
I ASK HER TO CLIMB SOME STAIRS, TAKING THEM TWO AT A TIME.
UFF
UFF
UFF
UFF
THE GOAL HERE IS TO PROVOKE HYPERVENTILATION.
BY THAT I MEAN RAPID, HEAVY BREATHING FOR TWO MINUTES.
WHEN HER BREATHING BECOMES EXCESSIVE COMPARED TO HER METABOLIC NEEDS...
...THAT IN TURN PROVOKES STRANGE SENSATIONS AND THUS A STATE OF ANXIETY.

REMINDER: PANIC ATTACKS ARE IN FACT A BLOOD METABOLISM ISSUE!

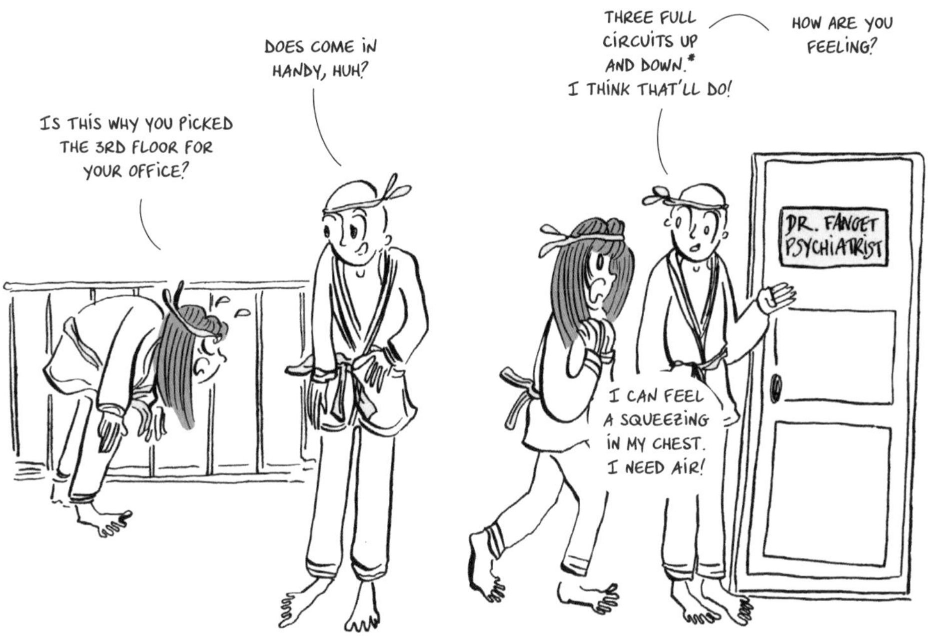
IS THIS WHY YOU PICKED THE 3RD FLOOR FOR YOUR OFFICE?
DOES COME IN HANDY, HUH?
THREE FULL CIRCUITS UP AND DOWN.* I THINK THAT'LL DO!
HOW ARE YOU FEELING?
DR. FANGET PSYCHIATRIST
I CAN FEEL A SQUEEZING IN MY CHEST. I NEED AIR!

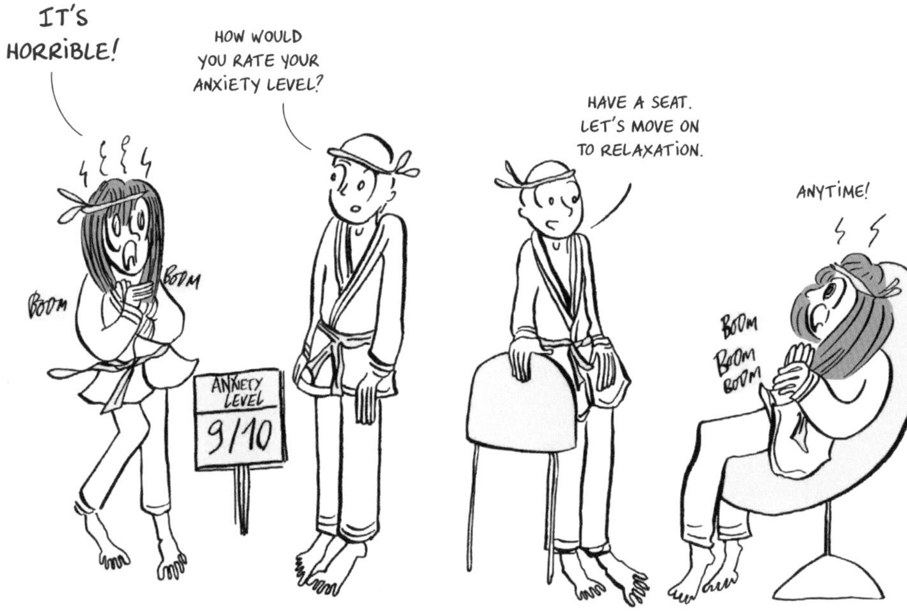
IT'S HORRIBLE!
BOOM
BOOM
HOW WOULD YOU RATE YOUR ANXIETY LEVEL?
ANXIETY LEVEL
9/10
HAVE A SEAT. LET'S MOVE ON TO RELAXATION.
ANYTIME!
BOOM
BOOM
BOOM

CAREFUL!
DON'T TRY THIS TECHNIQUE ON YOUR OWN. A THERAPIST MUST BE PRESENT.

*HIGHLY ATHLETIC PATIENTS MAY NEED MORE FLOORS!

2. HOW DO YOU STOP A PANIC ATTACK?

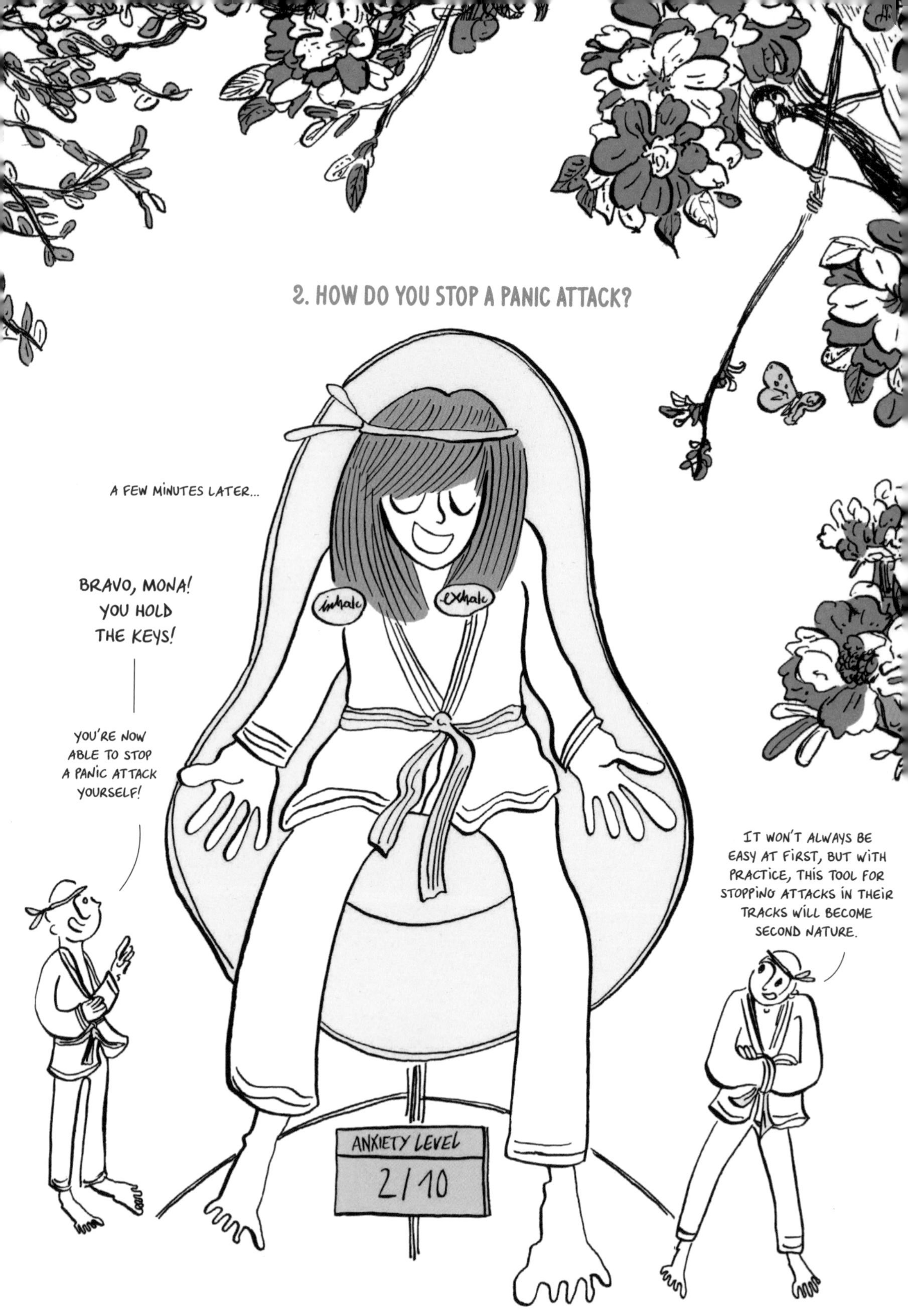
A FEW MINUTES LATER...
inhale
exhale
BRAVO, MONA! YOU HOLD THE KEYS!
YOU'RE NOW ABLE TO STOP A PANIC ATTACK YOURSELF!
IT WON'T ALWAYS BE EASY AT FIRST, BUT WITH PRACTICE, THIS TOOL FOR STOPPING ATTACKS IN THEIR TRACKS WILL BECOME SECOND NATURE.
ANXIETY LEVEL
2/10

STEP 4: CONFRONTING ANXIETY-INDUCING SITUATIONS

NOW THAT MONA IS BETTER ABLE TO HANDLE HER CATASTROPHIC THOUGHTS AND THE PHYSICAL SYMPTOMS OF HER PANIC ATTACKS, WE'LL APPLY ANXIETY MANAGEMENT TO SITUATIONS THAT BOTHER HER IN DAILY LIFE.

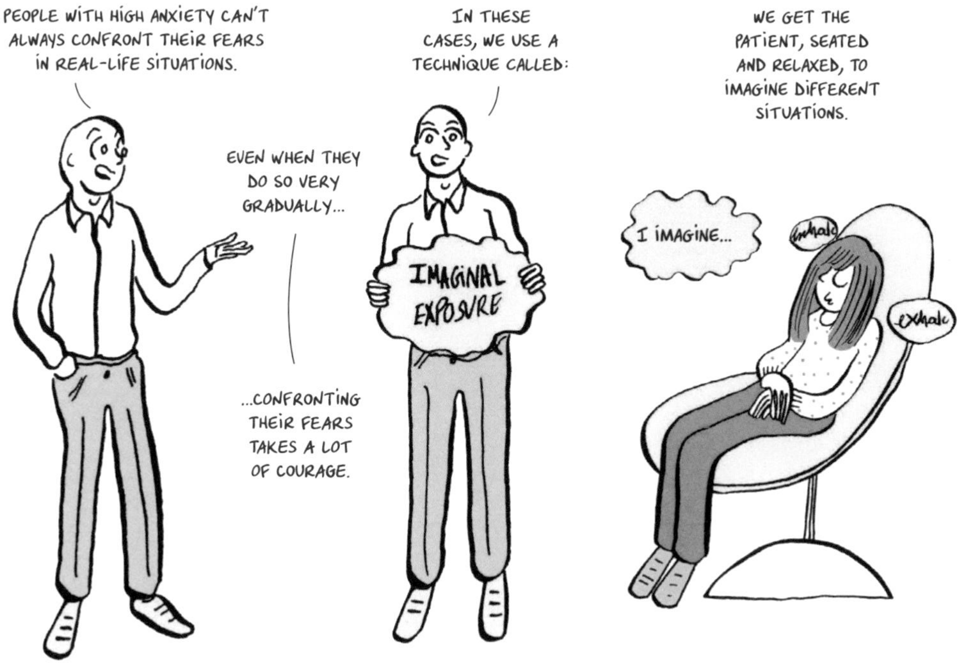

PEOPLE WITH HIGH ANXIETY CAN'T ALWAYS CONFRONT THEIR FEARS IN REAL-LIFE SITUATIONS.
EVEN WHEN THEY DO SO VERY GRADUALLY...
...CONFRONTING THEIR FEARS TAKES A LOT OF COURAGE.
IN THESE CASES, WE USE A TECHNIQUE CALLED:
IMAGINAL EXPOSURE
WE GET THE PATIENT, SEATED AND RELAXED, TO IMAGINE DIFFERENT SITUATIONS.
I IMAGINE...
inhale
exhale

ONCE WE'VE TAKEN ALL THE STEPS IN OUR IMAGINATION, IT'S MUCH EASIER TO TACKLE EXPOSURE IN A REAL-LIFE SETTING. THIS STEP REQUIRES US TO BE GENTLE, GRADUAL, AND CONSISTENT.

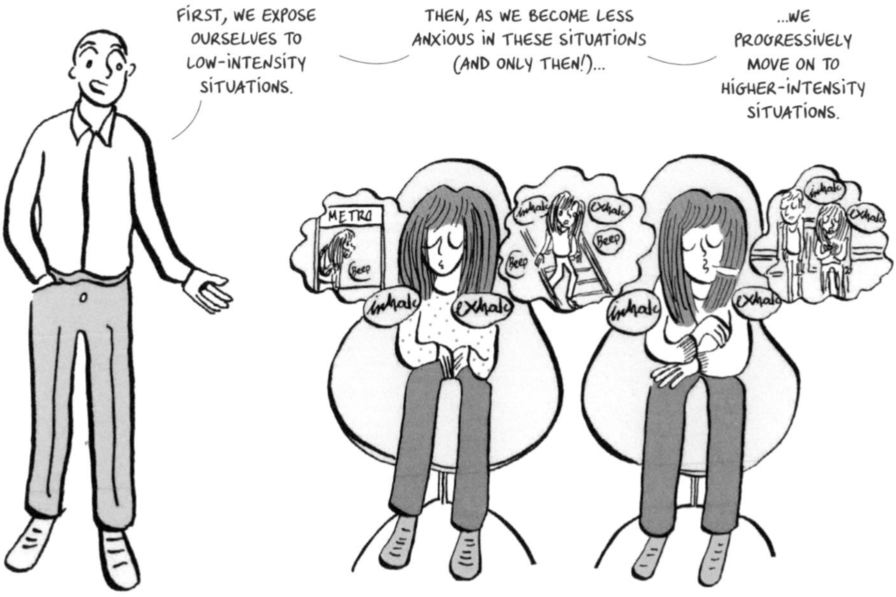

FIRST, WE EXPOSE OURSELVES TO LOW-INTENSITY SITUATIONS.
THEN, AS WE BECOME LESS ANXIOUS IN THESE SITUATIONS (AND ONLY THEN!)...
...WE PROGRESSIVELY MOVE ON TO HIGHER-INTENSITY SITUATIONS.
METRO
Beep
inhale
exhale

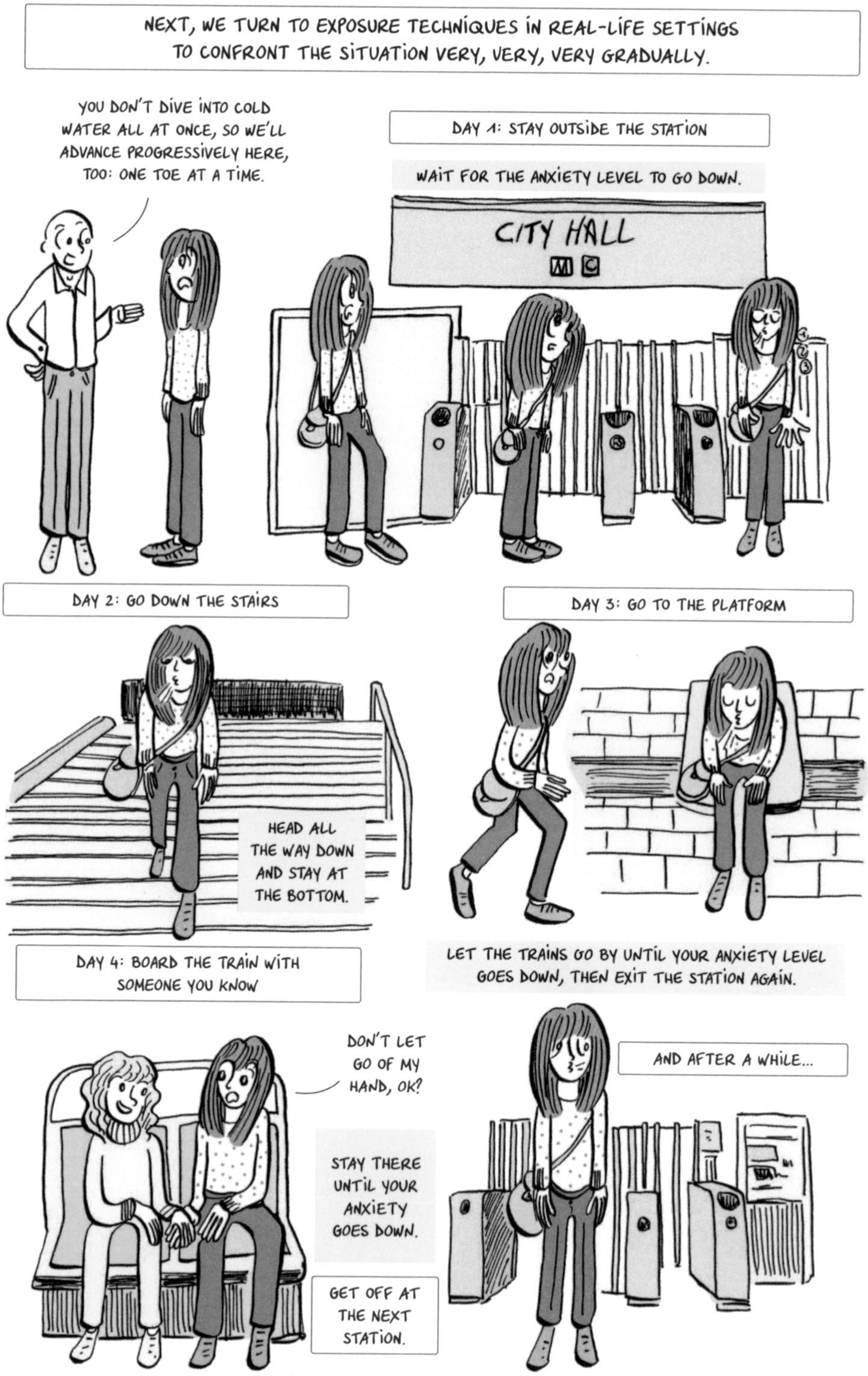
NEXT, WE TURN TO EXPOSURE TECHNIQUES IN REAL-LIFE SETTINGS TO CONFRONT THE SITUATION VERY, VERY, VERY GRADUALLY.
YOU DON'T DIVE INTO COLD WATER ALL AT ONCE, SO WE'LL ADVANCE PROGRESSIVELY HERE, TOO: ONE TOE AT A TIME.
DAY 1: STAY OUTSIDE THE STATION
WAIT FOR THE ANXIETY LEVEL TO GO DOWN.
CITY HALL
DAY 2: GO DOWN THE STAIRS
HEAD ALL THE WAY DOWN AND STAY AT THE BOTTOM.
DAY 3: GO TO THE PLATFORM
LET THE TRAINS GO BY UNTIL YOUR ANXIETY LEVEL GOES DOWN, THEN EXIT THE STATION AGAIN.
DAY 4: BOARD THE TRAIN WITH SOMEONE YOU KNOW
DON'T LET GO OF MY HAND, OK?
STAY THERE UNTIL YOUR ANXIETY GOES DOWN.
GET OFF AT THE NEXT STATION.
AND AFTER A WHILE...

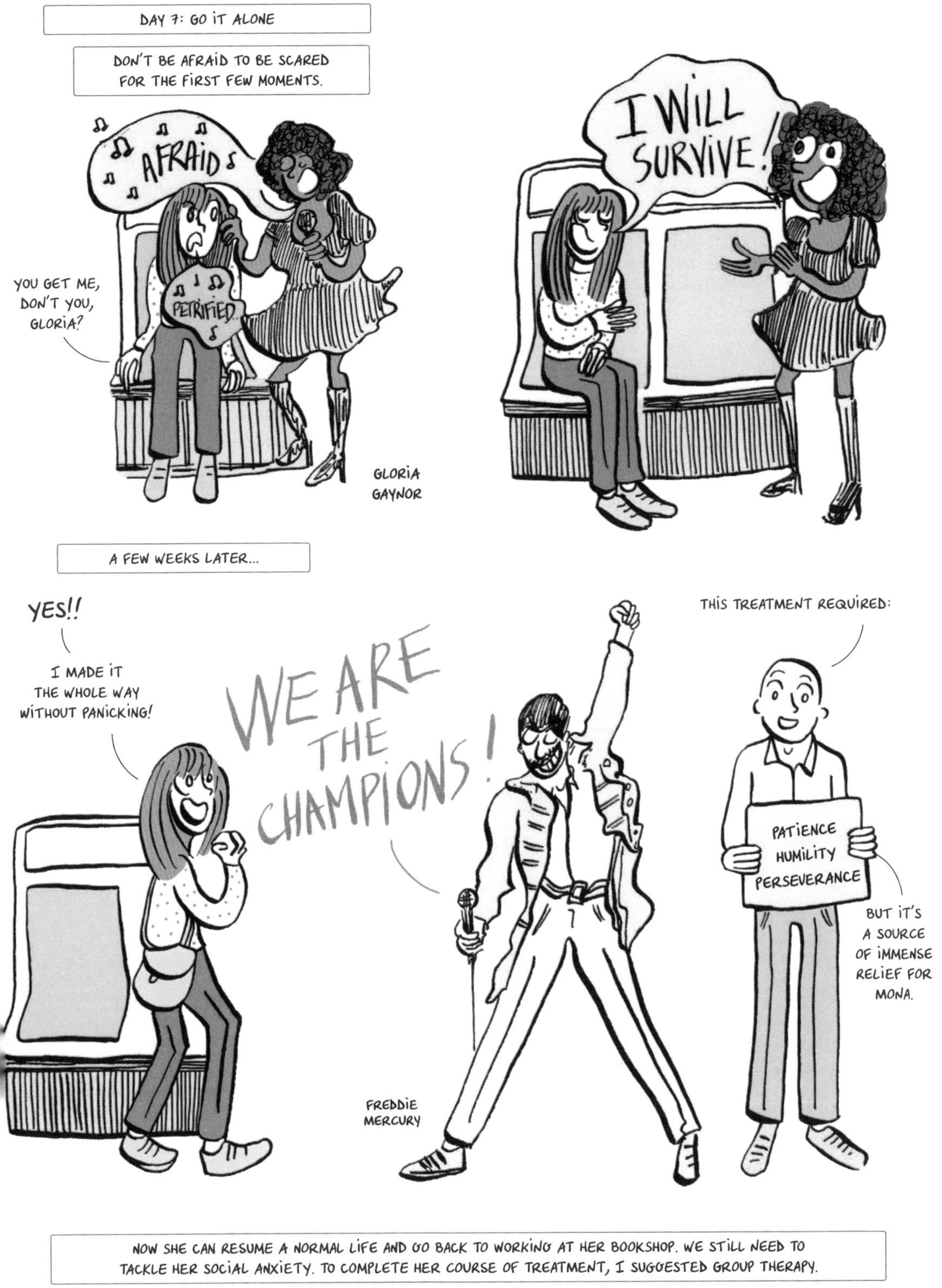
DAY 7: GO IT ALONE
DON'T BE AFRAID TO BE SCARED FOR THE FIRST FEW MOMENTS.
AFRAID
PETRIFIED
YOU GET ME, DON'T YOU, GLORIA?
GLORIA GAYNOR
I WILL SURVIVE!
A FEW WEEKS LATER...
YES!!
I MADE IT THE WHOLE WAY WITHOUT PANICKING!
WE ARE THE CHAMPIONS!
FREDDIE MERCURY
THIS TREATMENT REQUIRED:
PATIENCE
HUMILITY
PERSEVERANCE
BUT IT'S A SOURCE OF IMMENSE RELIEF FOR MONA.
NOW SHE CAN RESUME A NORMAL LIFE AND GO BACK TO WORKING AT HER BOOKSHOP. WE STILL NEED TO TACKLE HER SOCIAL ANXIETY. TO COMPLETE HER COURSE OF TREATMENT, I SUGGESTED GROUP THERAPY.

FOR FRANÇOIS, THE
COURSE OF TREATMENT
WILL BE LONGER, SINCE
ANXIETY IS PERVASIVE
IN HIS LIFE, EVERYWHERE
AND ALL THE TIME.

HIS NEED FOR CONTROL AND
REASSURANCE IS A TRAP, AND
BY STEPPING OUT OF IT, HE'LL
RECOVER HIS INDEPENDENCE AND
FREEDOM. FEAR IS A TYRANT!

SEASON 3 – GAD PATIENTS

In Treatment

WITH FRANÇOIS

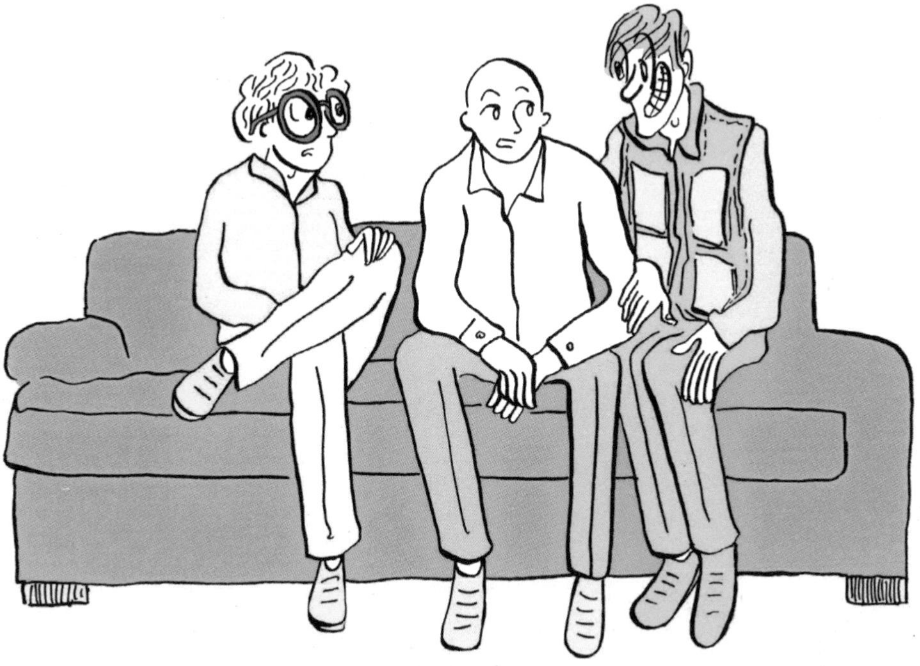

PART 1 — ANALYSIS: LISTENING, UNDERSTANDING

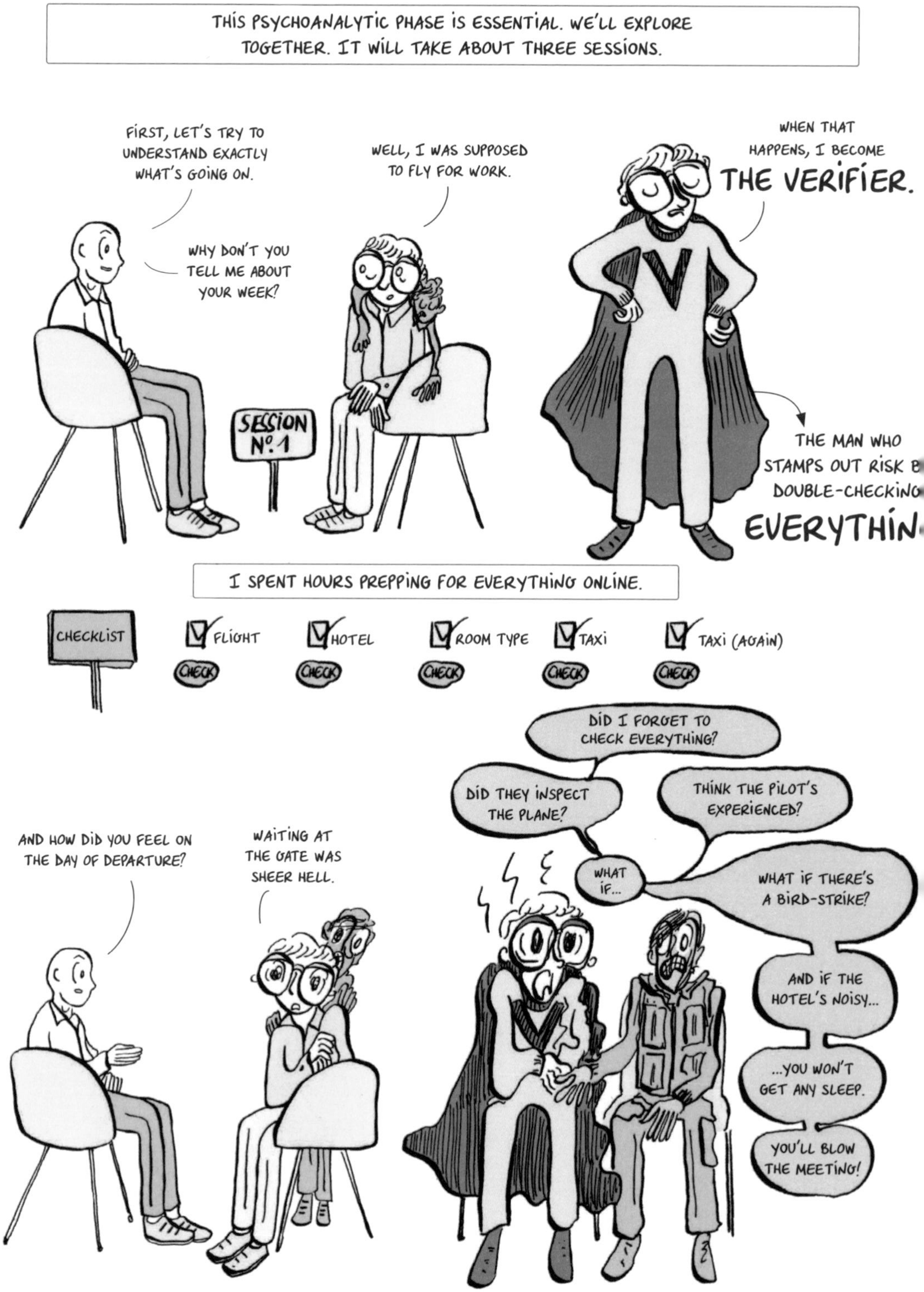

THIS PSYCHOANALYTIC PHASE IS ESSENTIAL. WE'LL EXPLORE TOGETHER. IT WILL TAKE ABOUT THREE SESSIONS.
FIRST, LET'S TRY TO UNDERSTAND EXACTLY WHAT'S GOING ON.
WHY DON'T YOU TELL ME ABOUT YOUR WEEK?
SESSION Nº 1
WELL, I WAS SUPPOSED TO FLY FOR WORK.
WHEN THAT HAPPENS, I BECOME THE VERIFIER.
THE MAN WHO STAMPS OUT RISK B
DOUBLE-CHECKING
EVERYTHIN
I SPENT HOURS PREPPING FOR EVERYTHING ONLINE.
CHECKLIST
FLIGHT
HOTEL
ROOM TYPE
TAXI
TAXI (AGAIN)
CHECK
CHECK
CHECK
CHECK
CHECK
AND HOW DID YOU FEEL ON THE DAY OF DEPARTURE?
WAITING AT THE GATE WAS SHEER HELL.
DID I FORGET TO CHECK EVERYTHING?
DID THEY INSPECT THE PLANE?
THINK THE PILOT'S EXPERIENCED?
WHAT IF...
WHAT IF THERE'S A BIRD-STRIKE?
AND IF THE HOTEL'S NOISY...
...YOU WON'T GET ANY SLEEP.
YOU'LL BLOW THE MEETING!

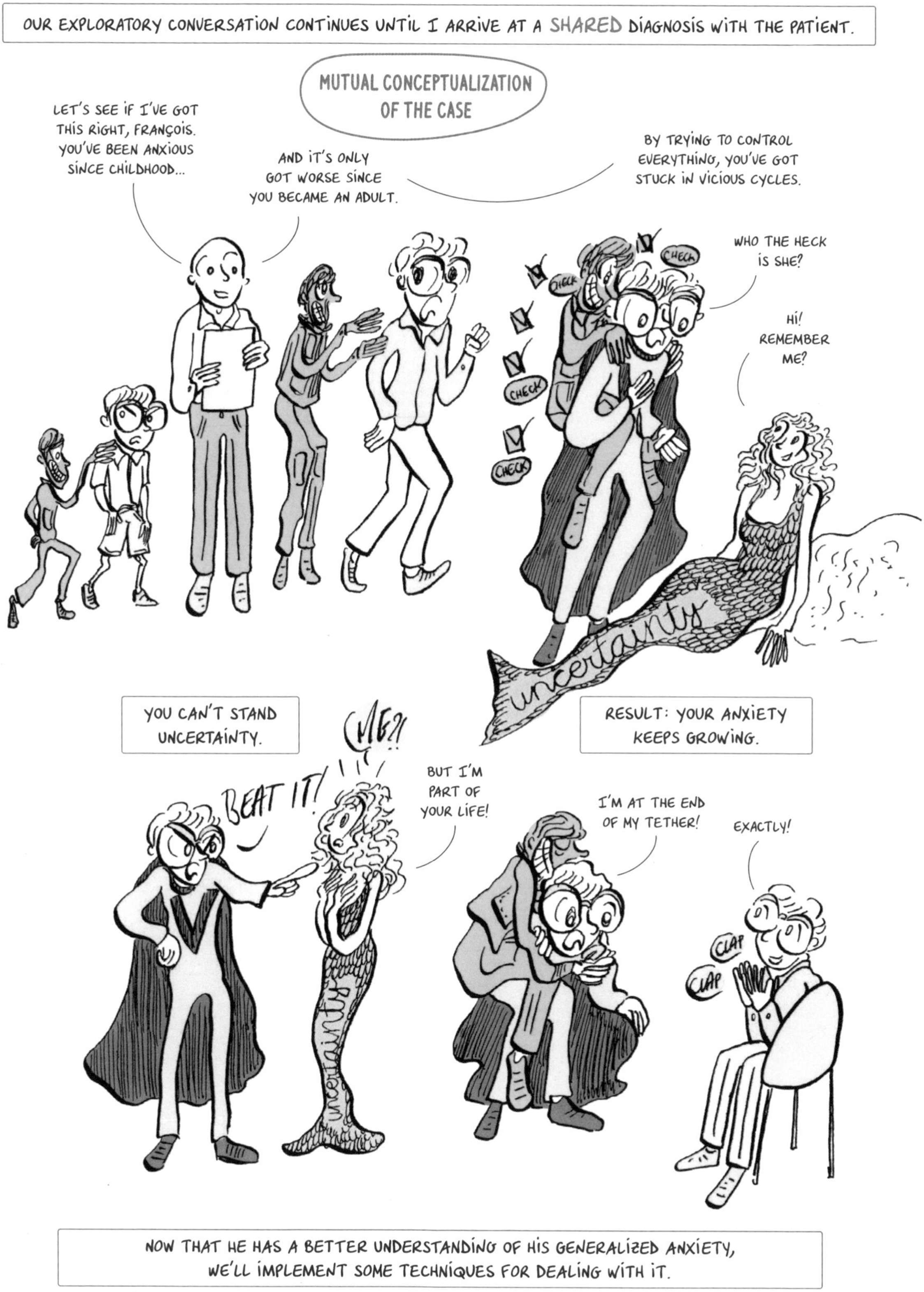
OUR EXPLORATORY CONVERSATION CONTINUES UNTIL I ARRIVE AT A SHARED DIAGNOSIS WITH THE PATIENT.
MUTUAL CONCEPTUALIZATION OF THE CASE
LET'S SEE IF I'VE GOT THIS RIGHT, FRANÇOIS. YOU'VE BEEN ANXIOUS SINCE CHILDHOOD...
AND IT'S ONLY GOT WORSE SINCE YOU BECAME AN ADULT.
BY TRYING TO CONTROL EVERYTHING, YOU'VE GOT STUCK IN VICIOUS CYCLES.
CHECK
CHECK
CHECK
CHECK
WHO THE HECK IS SHE?
HI! REMEMBER ME?
uncertainty
YOU CAN'T STAND UNCERTAINTY.
RESULT: YOUR ANXIETY KEEPS GROWING.
BEAT IT!
ME?!
BUT I'M PART OF YOUR LIFE!
uncertainty
I'M AT THE END OF MY TETHER!
EXACTLY!
CLAP
CLAP
NOW THAT HE HAS A BETTER UNDERSTANDING OF HIS GENERALIZED ANXIETY, WE'LL IMPLEMENT SOME TECHNIQUES FOR DEALING WITH IT.

PART 2 – THE ACTIVE PHASE

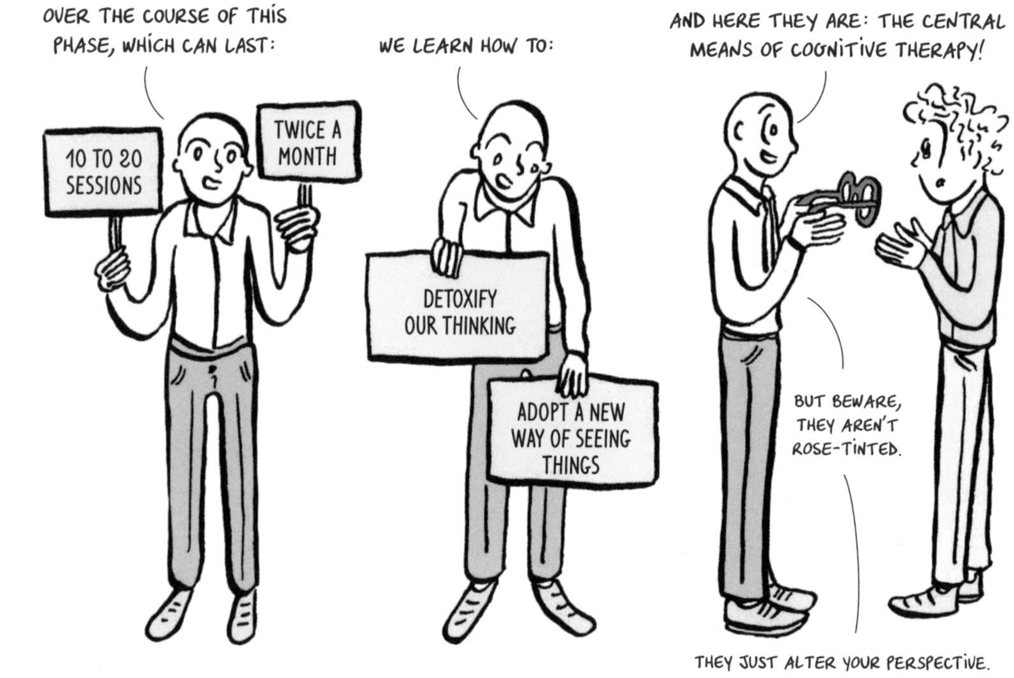

OVER THE COURSE OF THIS PHASE, WHICH CAN LAST:
10 TO 20 SESSIONS
TWICE A MONTH
WE LEARN HOW TO:
DETOXIFY OUR THINKING
ADOPT A NEW WAY OF SEEING THINGS
AND HERE THEY ARE: THE CENTRAL MEANS OF COGNITIVE THERAPY!
BUT BEWARE, THEY AREN'T ROSE-TINTED.
THEY JUST ALTER YOUR PERSPECTIVE.

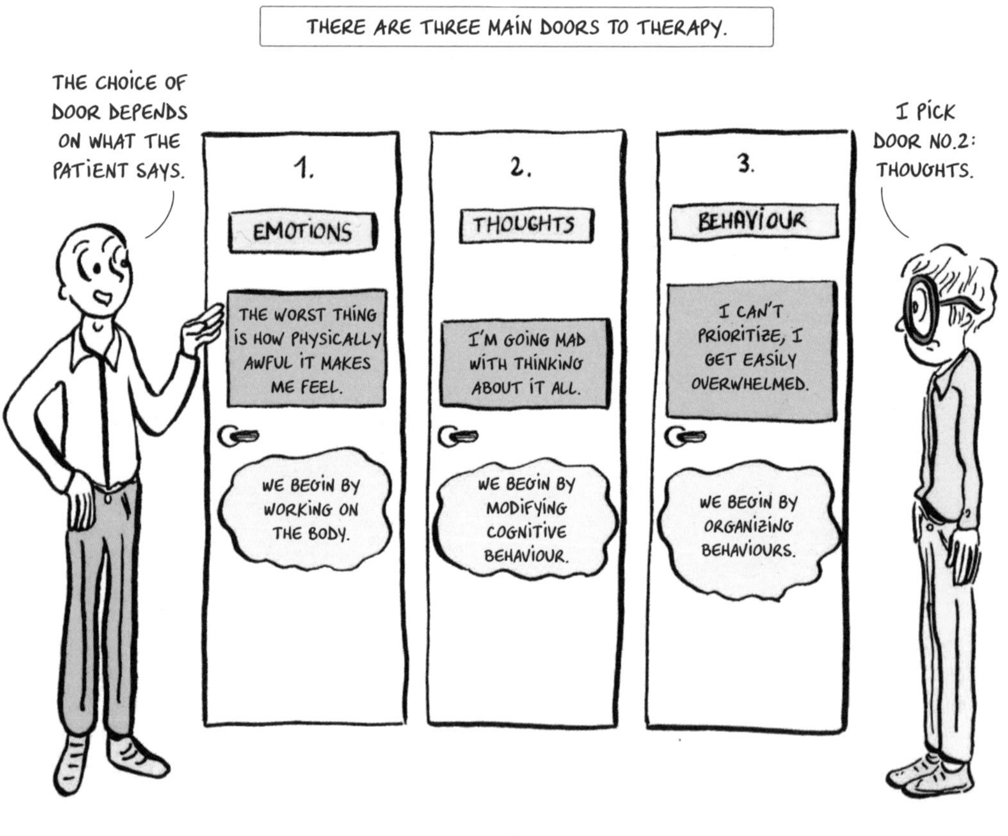

THERE ARE THREE MAIN DOORS TO THERAPY.
THE CHOICE OF DOOR DEPENDS ON WHAT THE PATIENT SAYS.
1.
EMOTIONS
THE WORST THING IS HOW PHYSICALLY AWFUL IT MAKES ME FEEL.
WE BEGIN BY WORKING ON THE BODY.
2.
THOUGHTS
I'M GOING MAD WITH THINKING ABOUT IT ALL.
WE BEGIN BY MODIFYING COGNITIVE BEHAVIOUR.
3.
BEHAVIOUR
I CAN'T PRIORITIZE, I GET EASILY OVERWHELMED.
WE BEGIN BY ORGANIZING BEHAVIOURS.
I PICK DOOR NO.2: THOUGHTS.

1. THREE COLUMNS FOR SEEING MORE CLEARLY

FOR ANXIETY SUFFERERS, EVERYTHING GETS MIXED UP – WHAT GOES ON IN OUR HEADS, OUR BODIES, OUR EMOTIONS, AND OUR BEHAVIOURAL PATTERN.

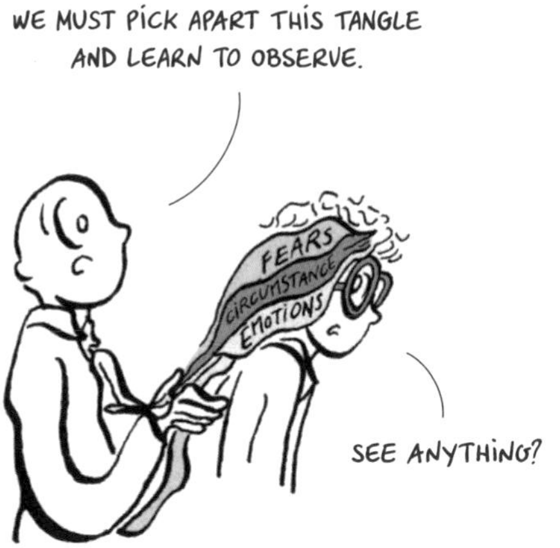
WE MUST PICK APART THIS TANGLE AND LEARN TO OBSERVE.
FEARS
CIRCUMSTANCE
EMOTIONS
SEE ANYTHING?

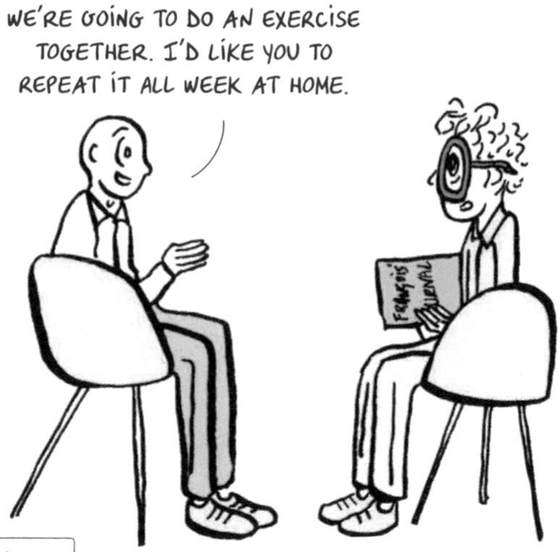
WE'RE GOING TO DO AN EXERCISE TOGETHER. I'D LIKE YOU TO REPEAT IT ALL WEEK AT HOME.
FRANÇOIS' JOURNAL

IT INVOLVES MAKING A NOTE OF EVERY TIME WE FEEL ANXIOUS, IN ONE OF THREE SEPARATE COLUMNS.

SITUATION	EMOTIONS (BODY)	COGNITION (AUTOMATIC THOUGHTS)
My boss asks me to facilitate the next meeting	*– Lump in the throat* *– Confusion* *– Anxiety level: 8/10*	*– I can't pull it off* *– I'll stumble over my words* *– They'll think I suck*

TWO WEEKS LATER.

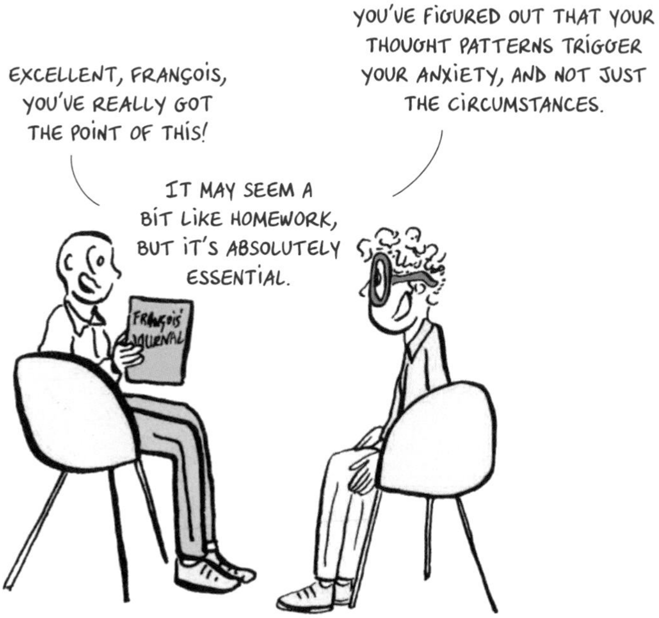
EXCELLENT, FRANÇOIS, YOU'VE REALLY GOT THE POINT OF THIS!
IT MAY SEEM A BIT LIKE HOMEWORK, BUT IT'S ABSOLUTELY ESSENTIAL.
YOU'VE FIGURED OUT THAT YOUR THOUGHT PATTERNS TRIGGER YOUR ANXIETY, AND NOT JUST THE CIRCUMSTANCES.
FRANÇOIS' JOURNAL

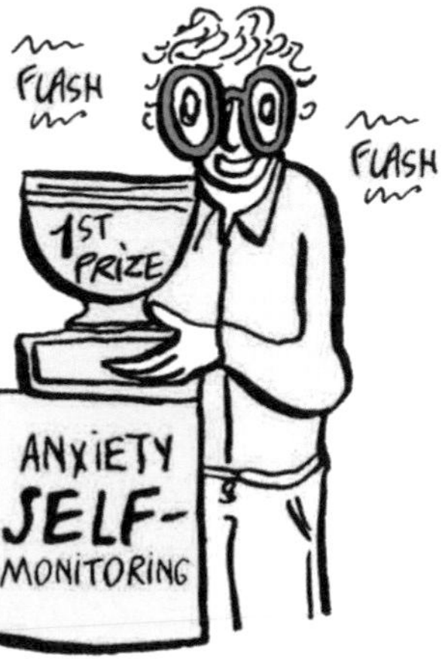
FLASH
FLASH
1ST PRIZE
ANXIETY SELF-MONITORING

2. FIVE COLUMNS FOR LEARNING TO THINK DIFFERENTLY

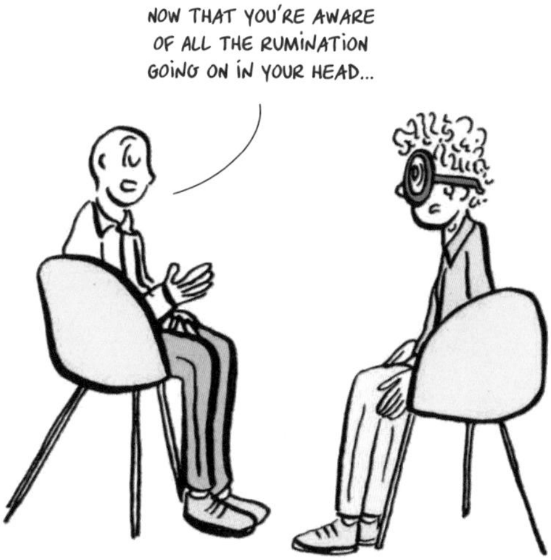
NOW THAT YOU'RE AWARE OF ALL THE RUMINATION GOING ON IN YOUR HEAD...

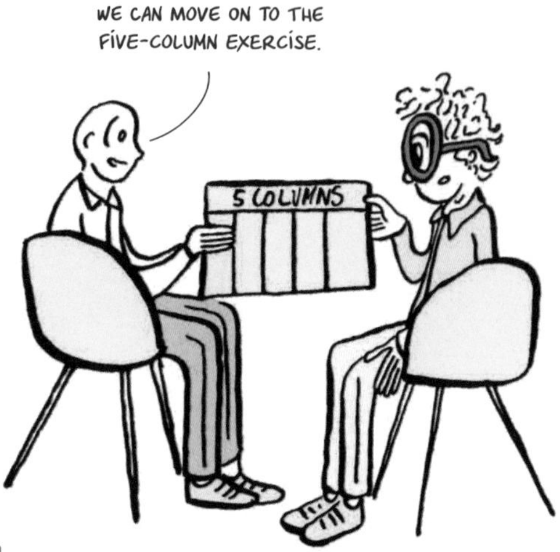
WE CAN MOVE ON TO THE FIVE-COLUMN EXERCISE.
5 COLUMNS

FIRST, YOU'LL ADD A FOURTH COLUMN TO YOUR TABLE FOR RECORDING ALTERNATIVE THOUGHTS.

SITUATION	EMOTIONS (BODY)	COGNITION (AUTOMATIC THOUGHTS)	ALTERNATIVE THOUGHTS

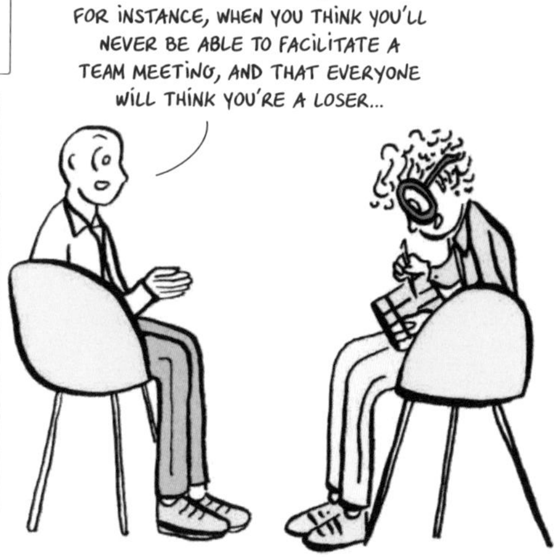
FOR INSTANCE, WHEN YOU THINK YOU'LL NEVER BE ABLE TO FACILITATE A TEAM MEETING, AND THAT EVERYONE WILL THINK YOU'RE A LOSER...

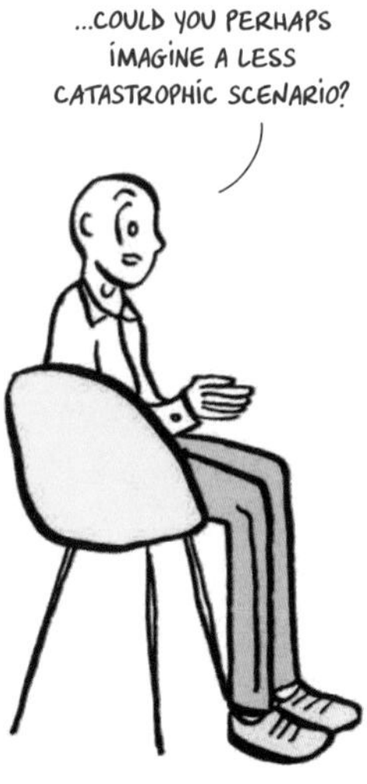
...COULD YOU PERHAPS IMAGINE A LESS CATASTROPHIC SCENARIO?

"MY VOICE WILL TREMBLE, AND PEOPLE WILL THINK I'M NERVOUS BUT NOT A LOSER."

A SLIGHTLY LESS CATASTROPHIC MEETING

François enters the room, trembling because he's so stressed out. His co-workers look at him kindly, as they can plainly see he's nervous.

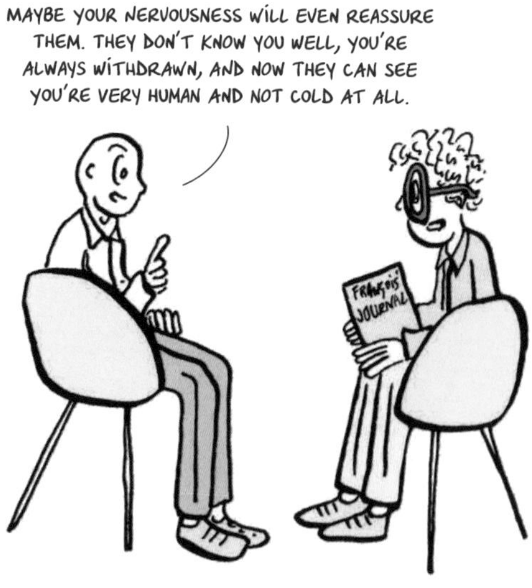
MAYBE YOUR NERVOUSNESS WILL EVEN REASSURE THEM. THEY DON'T KNOW YOU WELL, YOU'RE ALWAYS WITHDRAWN, AND NOW THEY CAN SEE YOU'RE VERY HUMAN AND NOT COLD AT ALL.
FRANÇOIS JOURNAL

FINALLY, YOU ADD A FIFTH COLUMN TO NOTE YOUR ANXIETY LEVEL.

SITUATION	EMOTIONS (BODY)	COGNITION (AUTOMATIC THOUGHTS)	ALTERNATIVE THOUGHTS	ANXIETY LEVEL
My boss asks me to facilitate the next meeting	*– Lump in the throat – Confusion – Anxiety level: 8/10*	*– I can't pull it off – I'll stumble over my words – They'll think I suck*	*– I've had the same thought 100 times, and each time my presentation has gone better than expected – They'll see I'm nervous, that's all*	10 9 8 7 6 5 4 3 2 1

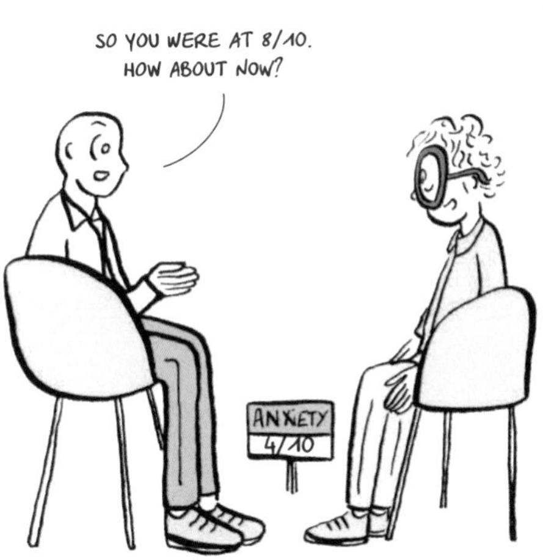
SO YOU WERE AT 8/10. HOW ABOUT NOW?
ANXIETY
4/10

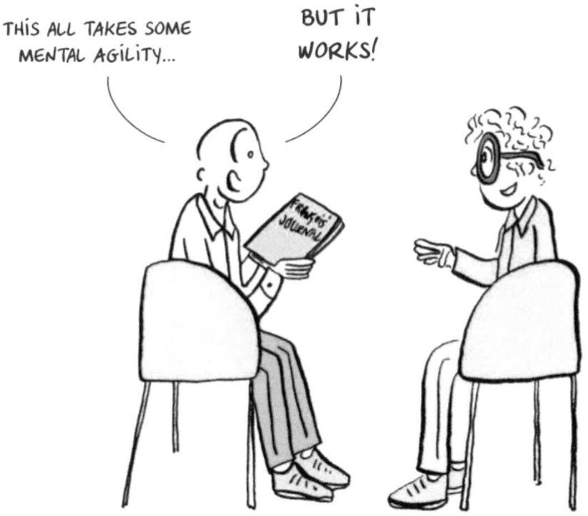
THIS ALL TAKES SOME MENTAL AGILITY...
BUT IT WORKS!

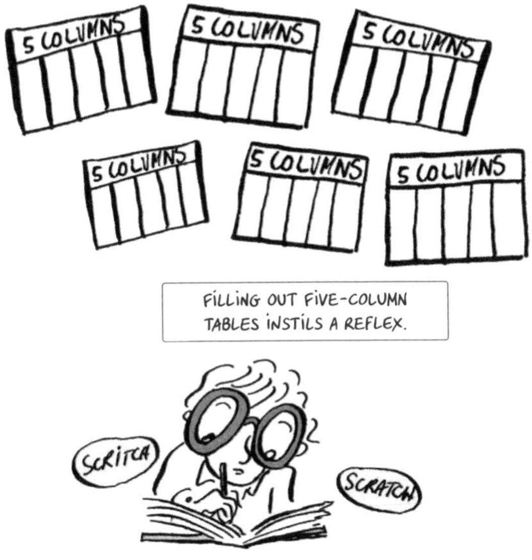
5 COLUMNS
5 COLUMNS
5 COLUMNS
5 COLUMNS
5 COLUMNS
5 COLUMNS
FILLING OUT FIVE-COLUMN TABLES INSTILS A REFLEX.
SCRITCH
SCRATCH

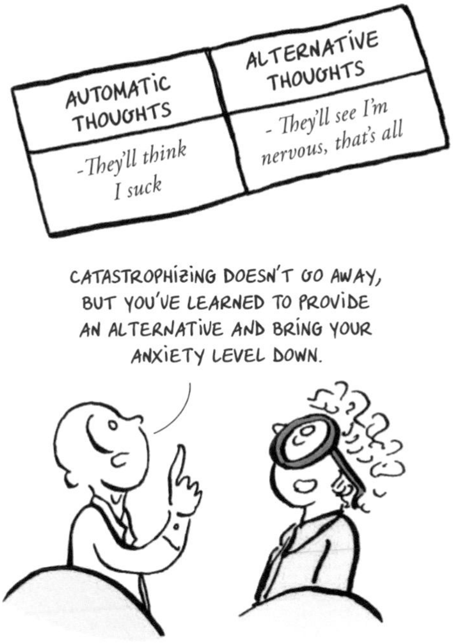
AUTOMATIC THOUGHTS
-They'll think I suck
ALTERNATIVE THOUGHTS
- They'll see I'm nervous, that's all
CATASTROPHIZING DOESN'T GO AWAY, BUT YOU'VE LEARNED TO PROVIDE AN ALTERNATIVE AND BRING YOUR ANXIETY LEVEL DOWN.

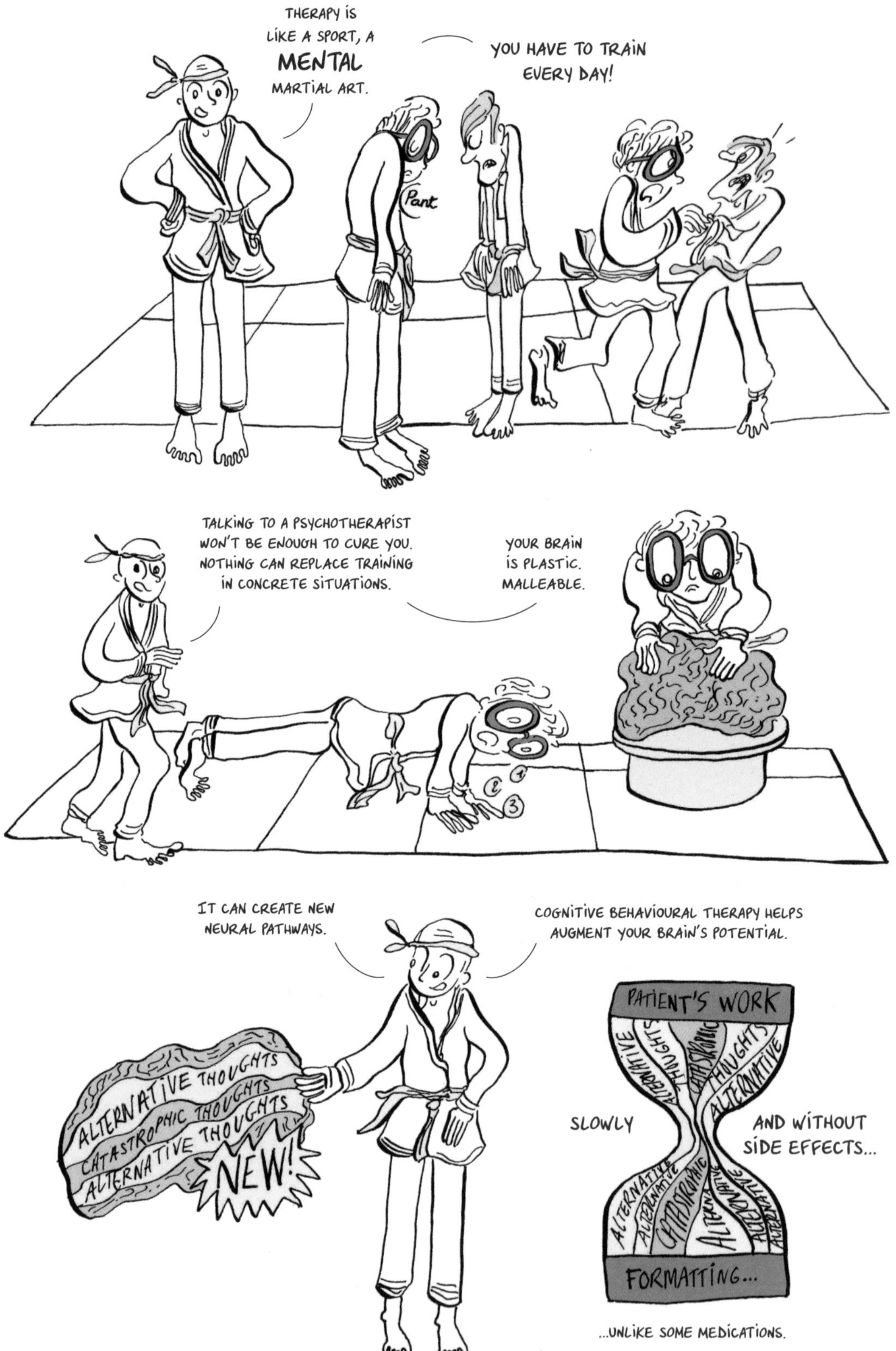
THERAPY IS LIKE A SPORT, A **MENTAL** MARTIAL ART.
YOU HAVE TO TRAIN EVERY DAY!
Pant
TALKING TO A PSYCHOTHERAPIST WON'T BE ENOUGH TO CURE YOU. NOTHING CAN REPLACE TRAINING IN CONCRETE SITUATIONS.
YOUR BRAIN IS PLASTIC. MALLEABLE.
IT CAN CREATE NEW NEURAL PATHWAYS.
COGNITIVE BEHAVIOURAL THERAPY HELPS AUGMENT YOUR BRAIN'S POTENTIAL.
ALTERNATIVE THOUGHTS
CATASTROPHIC THOUGHTS
ALTERNATIVE THOUGHTS
NEW!
PATIENT'S WORK
SLOWLY
AND WITHOUT SIDE EFFECTS...
FORMATTING...
...UNLIKE SOME MEDICATIONS.

3. IMAGINING THE WORST IN ORDER TO ACCEPT UNCERTAINTY

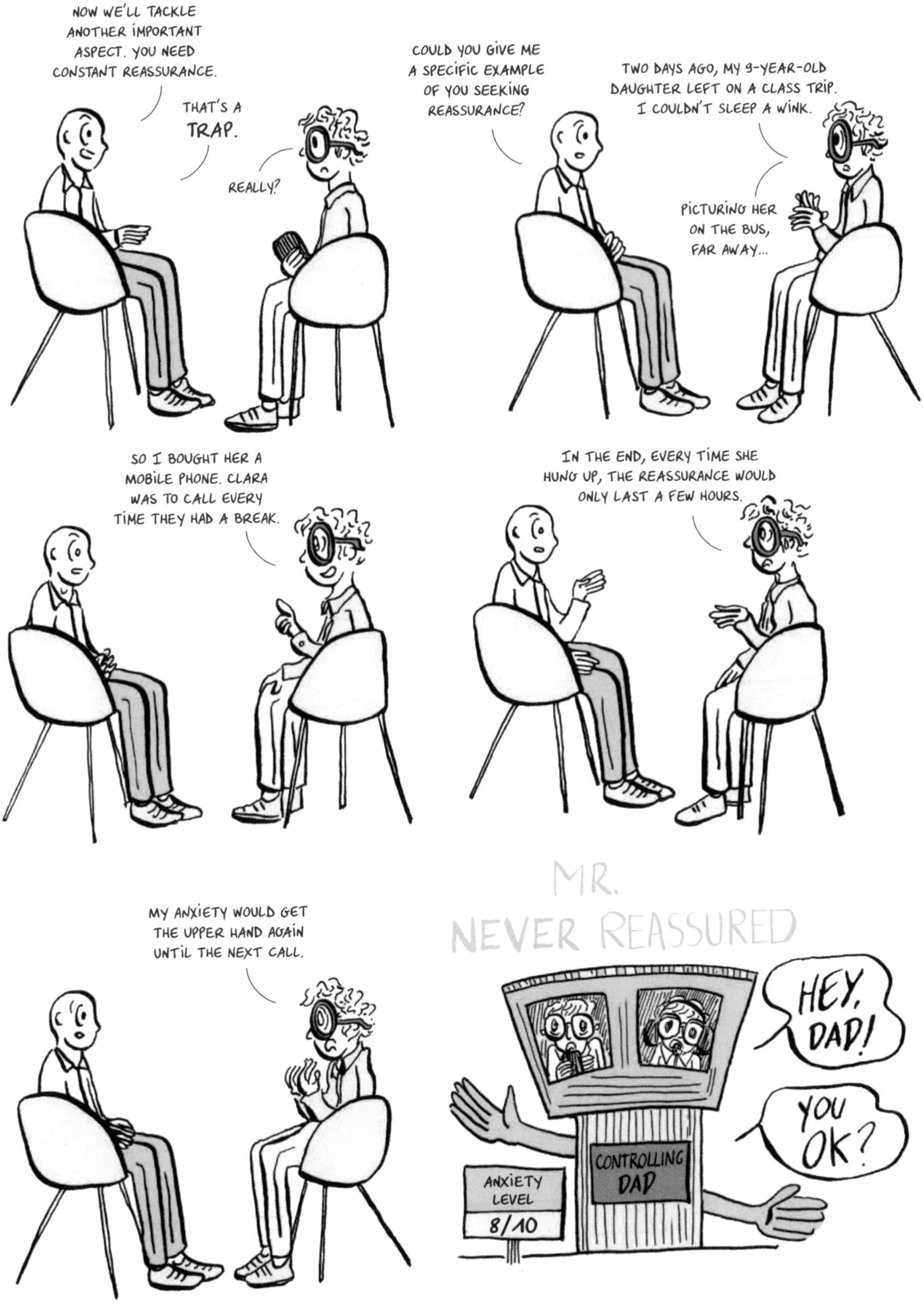

NOW WE'LL TACKLE ANOTHER IMPORTANT ASPECT. YOU NEED CONSTANT REASSURANCE.
THAT'S A TRAP.
REALLY?
COULD YOU GIVE ME A SPECIFIC EXAMPLE OF YOU SEEKING REASSURANCE?
TWO DAYS AGO, MY 9-YEAR-OLD DAUGHTER LEFT ON A CLASS TRIP. I COULDN'T SLEEP A WINK.
PICTURING HER ON THE BUS, FAR AWAY...
SO I BOUGHT HER A MOBILE PHONE. CLARA WAS TO CALL EVERY TIME THEY HAD A BREAK.
IN THE END, EVERY TIME SHE HUNG UP, THE REASSURANCE WOULD ONLY LAST A FEW HOURS.
MY ANXIETY WOULD GET THE UPPER HAND AGAIN UNTIL THE NEXT CALL.
MR. NEVER REASSURED
HEY, DAD!
YOU OK?
ANXIETY LEVEL
8/10
CONTROLLING DAD

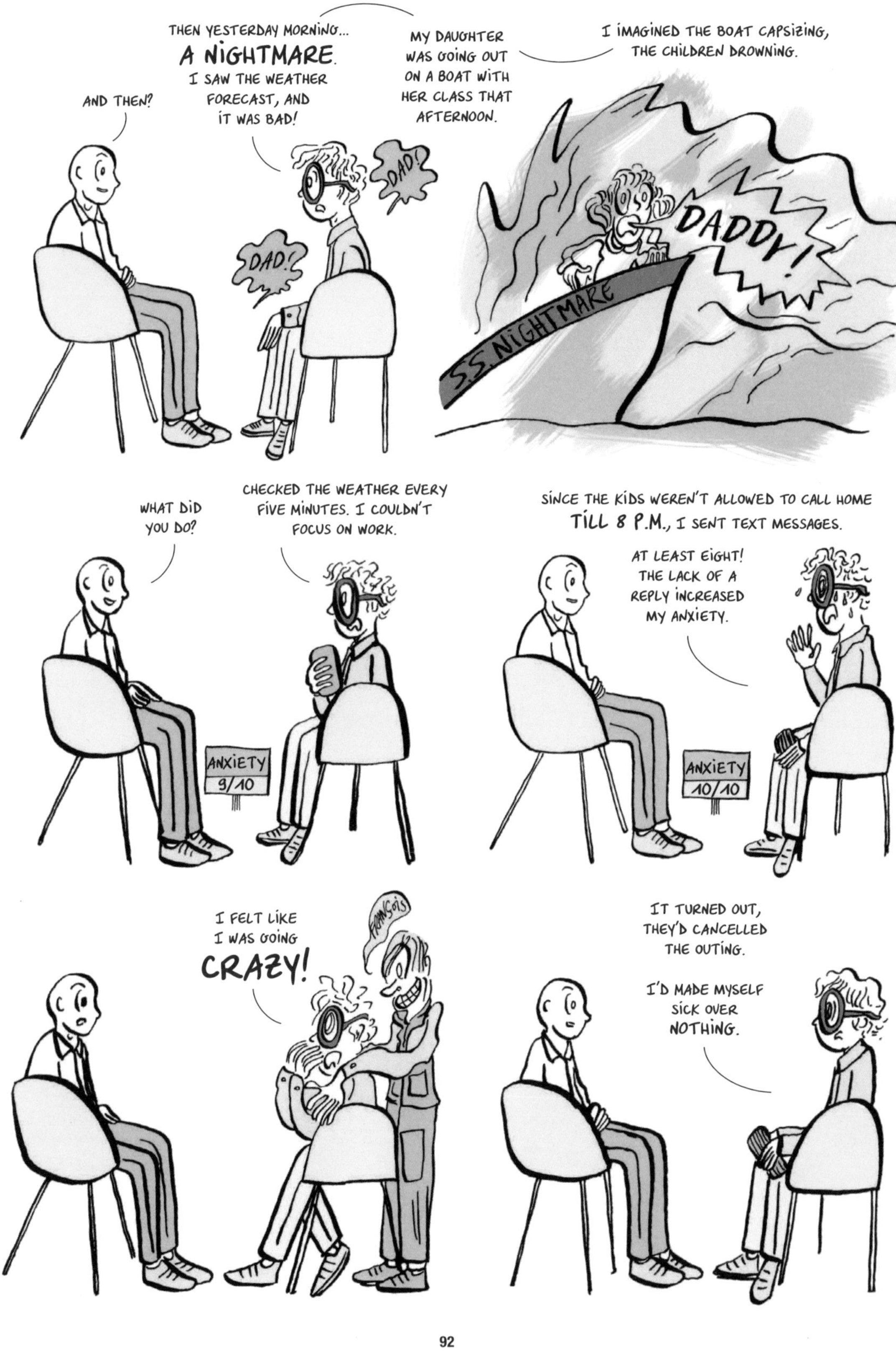
AND THEN?
THEN YESTERDAY MORNING... A NIGHTMARE. I SAW THE WEATHER FORECAST, AND IT WAS BAD!
MY DAUGHTER WAS GOING OUT ON A BOAT WITH HER CLASS THAT AFTERNOON.
DAD?
DAD?
I IMAGINED THE BOAT CAPSIZING, THE CHILDREN DROWNING.
DADDY!
S.S. NIGHTMARE
WHAT DID YOU DO?
CHECKED THE WEATHER EVERY FIVE MINUTES. I COULDN'T FOCUS ON WORK.
ANXIETY 9/10
SINCE THE KIDS WEREN'T ALLOWED TO CALL HOME TILL 8 P.M., I SENT TEXT MESSAGES.
AT LEAST EIGHT! THE LACK OF A REPLY INCREASED MY ANXIETY.
ANXIETY 10/10
I FELT LIKE I WAS GOING CRAZY!
FRANÇOIS
IT TURNED OUT, THEY'D CANCELLED THE OUTING.
I'D MADE MYSELF SICK OVER NOTHING.

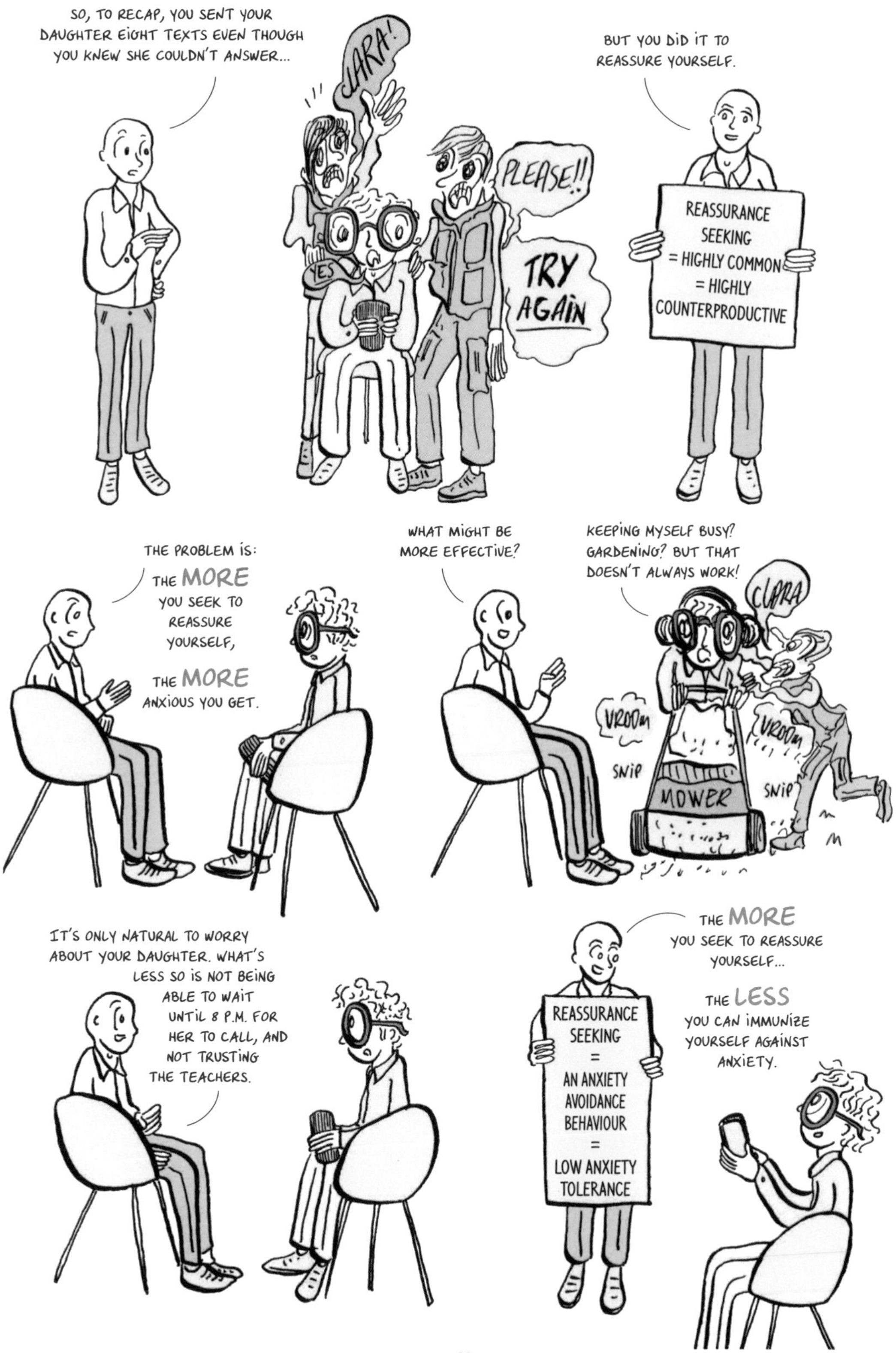

SO, TO RECAP, YOU SENT YOUR DAUGHTER EIGHT TEXTS EVEN THOUGH YOU KNEW SHE COULDN'T ANSWER...
CLARA!
PLEASE!!
YES
TRY AGAIN
BUT YOU DID IT TO REASSURE YOURSELF.
REASSURANCE SEEKING = HIGHLY COMMON = HIGHLY COUNTERPRODUCTIVE
THE PROBLEM IS: THE MORE YOU SEEK TO REASSURE YOURSELF, THE MORE ANXIOUS YOU GET.
WHAT MIGHT BE MORE EFFECTIVE?
KEEPING MYSELF BUSY? GARDENING? BUT THAT DOESN'T ALWAYS WORK!
CLARA
VROOM
SNIP
MOWER
VROOM
SNIP
IT'S ONLY NATURAL TO WORRY ABOUT YOUR DAUGHTER. WHAT'S LESS SO IS NOT BEING ABLE TO WAIT UNTIL 8 P.M. FOR HER TO CALL, AND NOT TRUSTING THE TEACHERS.
THE MORE YOU SEEK TO REASSURE YOURSELF...
THE LESS YOU CAN IMMUNIZE YOURSELF AGAINST ANXIETY.
REASSURANCE SEEKING = AN ANXIETY AVOIDANCE BEHAVIOUR = LOW ANXIETY TOLERANCE

THAT BOAT TRIP SUPPLIES AN EXCELLENT OPPORTUNITY FOR A VERY IMPORTANT EXERCISE. YOU'LL LEARN TO LET YOUR ANXIETY LIVE, DOING NOTHING TO STOP IT.

YOU SAY CLARA CAN CALL YOU AT 8 P.M.? WHAT TIME DO YOU START WORRYING?

6 P.M., MAYBE EARLIER.

FROM 6 TO 8, YOU'RE GOING TO OBSERVE ALL THE SCENARIOS THAT POP INTO YOUR HEAD.

RECORD THEM IN YOUR NOTEBOOK OR ON YOUR PHONE AND ASSIGN EACH AN ANXIETY LEVEL FROM 0 TO 10.

STORM	TRUCK	SPIDER	ACCIDENT
4/10	7/10	9/10	8/10

WHATEVER YOU DO, DON'T TRY TO ALLEVIATE YOUR ANXIETY, KEEP YOURSELF OCCUPIED, RELAX, OR MEDITATE.

BUT... THAT'LL BE AWFUL!

YES, BECAUSE YOU'VE LOST THE **HABIT OF** PROCESSING ANXIETY.

BUT YOU'LL COME TO REALIZE THAT JUST BECAUSE YOU CAN THINK OF HORRIBLE THINGS, IT DOESN'T MEAN THEY'RE GOING TO HAPPEN.

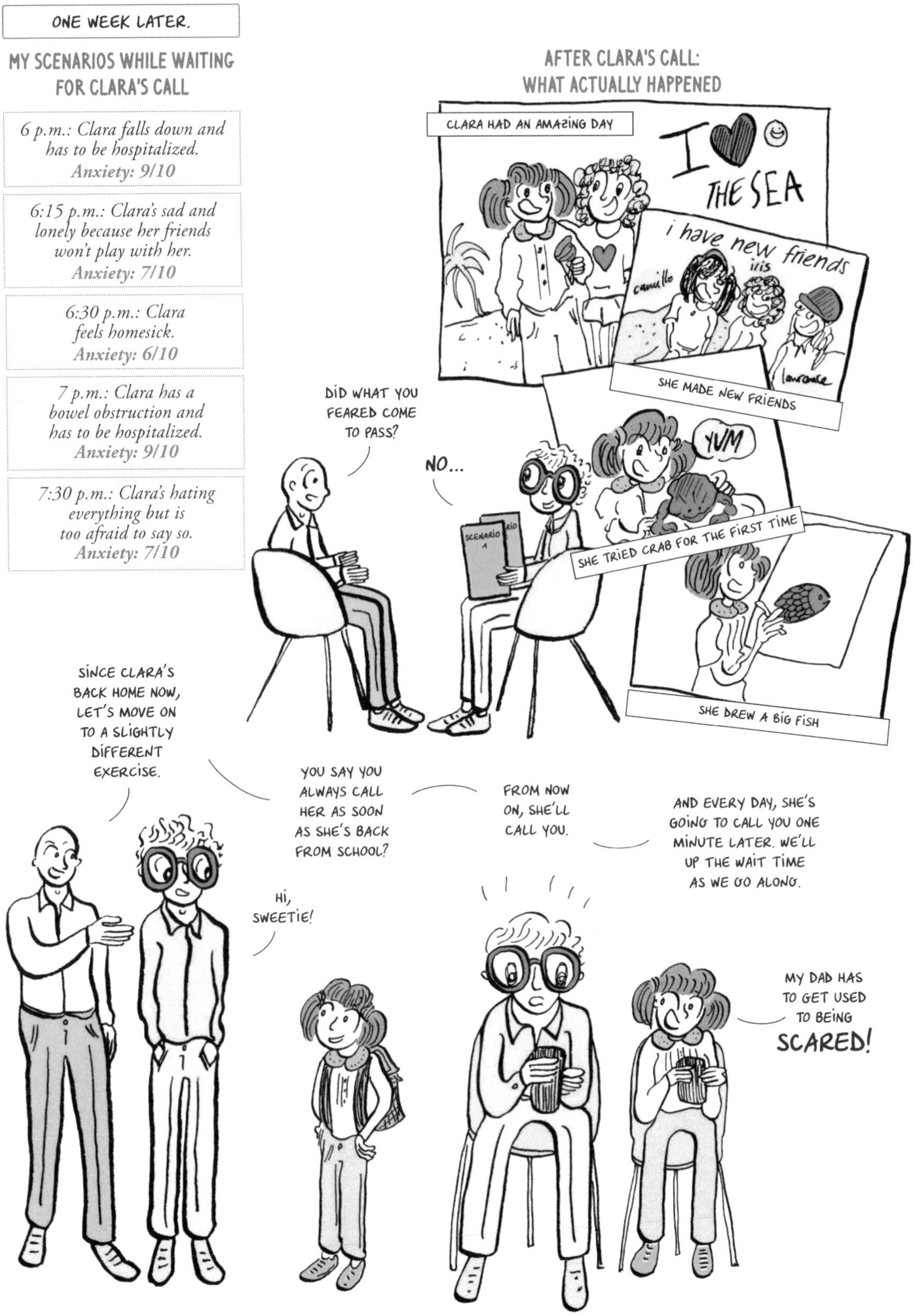
ONE WEEK LATER.
MY SCENARIOS WHILE WAITING FOR CLARA'S CALL
6 p.m.: Clara falls down and has to be hospitalized. Anxiety: 9/10
6:15 p.m.: Clara's sad and lonely because her friends won't play with her. Anxiety: 7/10
6:30 p.m.: Clara feels homesick. Anxiety: 6/10
7 p.m.: Clara has a bowel obstruction and has to be hospitalized. Anxiety: 9/10
7:30 p.m.: Clara's hating everything but is too afraid to say so. Anxiety: 7/10
AFTER CLARA'S CALL: WHAT ACTUALLY HAPPENED
CLARA HAD AN AMAZING DAY
I ♥ THE SEA
i have new friends
camillo
iris
lawrence
SHE MADE NEW FRIENDS
YUM
SHE TRIED CRAB FOR THE FIRST TIME
SHE DREW A BIG FISH
DID WHAT YOU FEARED COME TO PASS?
NO...
SCENARIO A
SINCE CLARA'S BACK HOME NOW, LET'S MOVE ON TO A SLIGHTLY DIFFERENT EXERCISE.
YOU SAY YOU ALWAYS CALL HER AS SOON AS SHE'S BACK FROM SCHOOL?
FROM NOW ON, SHE'LL CALL YOU.
AND EVERY DAY, SHE'S GOING TO CALL YOU ONE MINUTE LATER. WE'LL UP THE WAIT TIME AS WE GO ALONG.
HI, SWEETIE!
MY DAD HAS TO GET USED TO BEING SCARED!

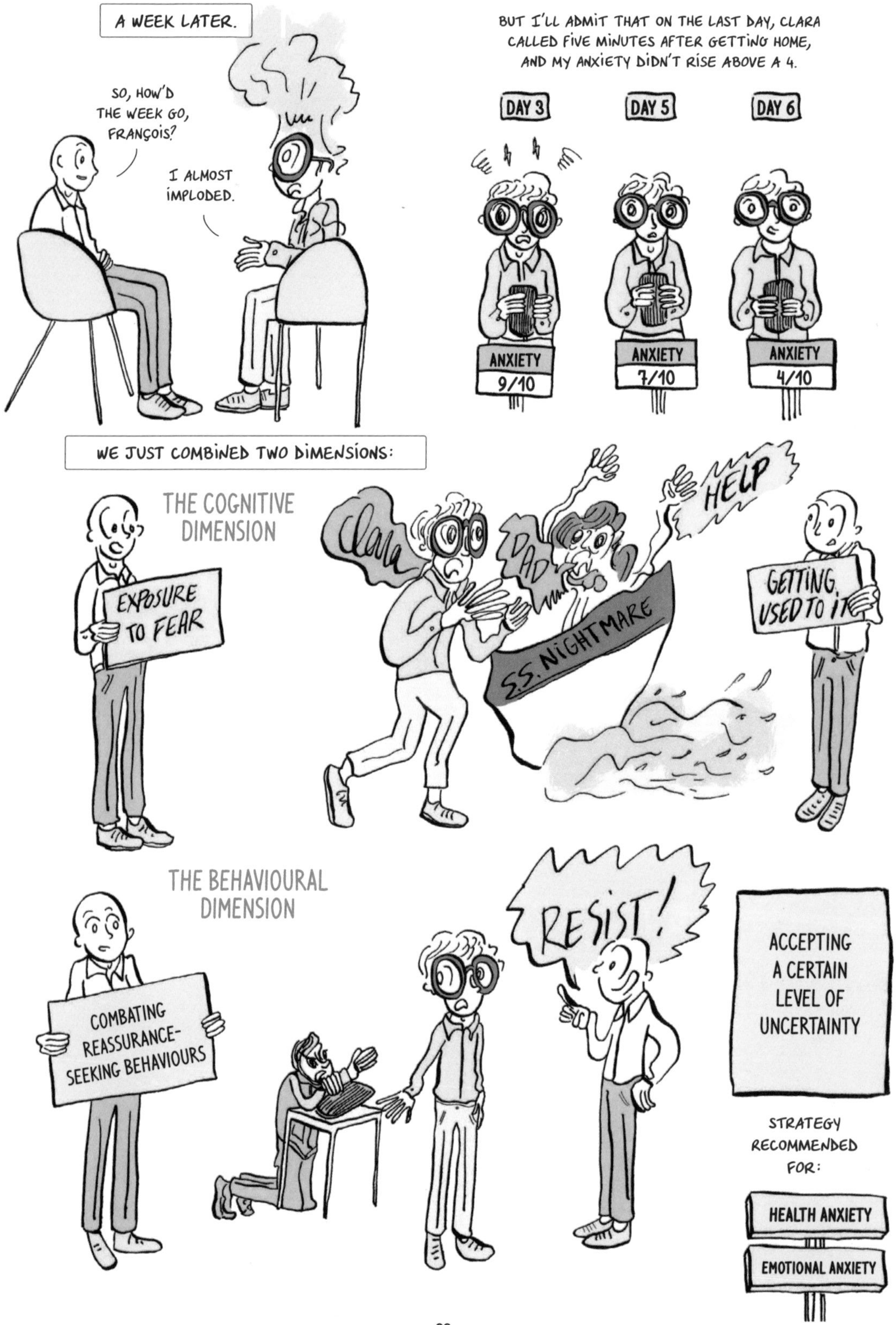
A WEEK LATER.
SO, HOW'D THE WEEK GO, FRANÇOIS?
I ALMOST IMPLODED.
BUT I'LL ADMIT THAT ON THE LAST DAY, CLARA CALLED FIVE MINUTES AFTER GETTING HOME, AND MY ANXIETY DIDN'T RISE ABOVE A 4.
DAY 3
DAY 5
DAY 6
ANXIETY 9/10
ANXIETY 7/10
ANXIETY 4/10
WE JUST COMBINED TWO DIMENSIONS:
THE COGNITIVE DIMENSION
EXPOSURE TO FEAR
Clara
DAD
HELP
S.S. NIGHTMARE
GETTING USED TO IT
THE BEHAVIOURAL DIMENSION
COMBATING REASSURANCE-SEEKING BEHAVIOURS
RESIST!
ACCEPTING A CERTAIN LEVEL OF UNCERTAINTY
STRATEGY RECOMMENDED FOR:
HEALTH ANXIETY
EMOTIONAL ANXIETY

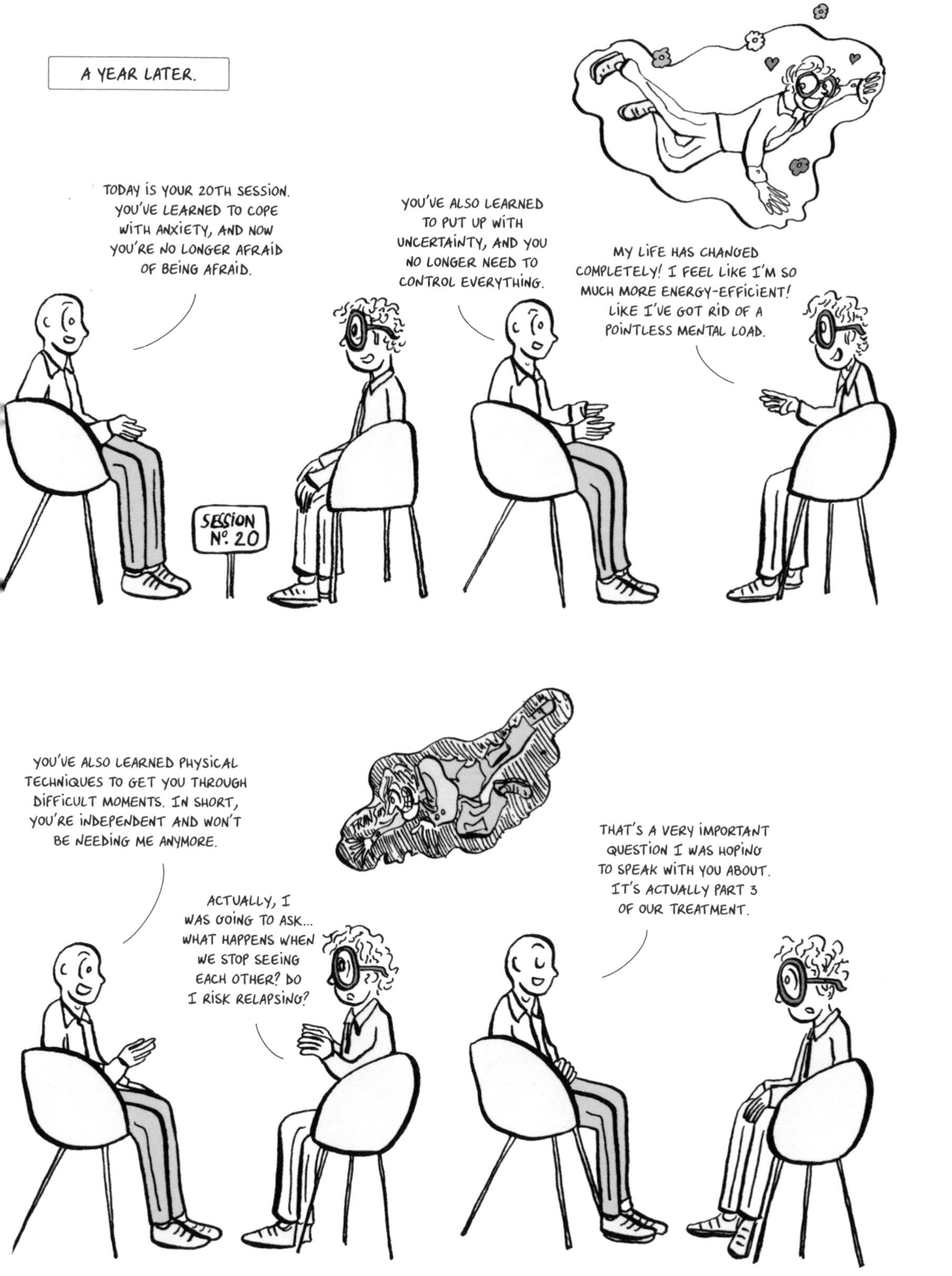
A YEAR LATER.
TODAY IS YOUR 20TH SESSION. YOU'VE LEARNED TO COPE WITH ANXIETY, AND NOW YOU'RE NO LONGER AFRAID OF BEING AFRAID.
SESSION Nº. 20
YOU'VE ALSO LEARNED TO PUT UP WITH UNCERTAINTY, AND YOU NO LONGER NEED TO CONTROL EVERYTHING.
MY LIFE HAS CHANGED COMPLETELY! I FEEL LIKE I'M SO MUCH MORE ENERGY-EFFICIENT! LIKE I'VE GOT RID OF A POINTLESS MENTAL LOAD.
YOU'VE ALSO LEARNED PHYSICAL TECHNIQUES TO GET YOU THROUGH DIFFICULT MOMENTS. IN SHORT, YOU'RE INDEPENDENT AND WON'T BE NEEDING ME ANYMORE.
ACTUALLY, I WAS GOING TO ASK... WHAT HAPPENS WHEN WE STOP SEEING EACH OTHER? DO I RISK RELAPSING?
THAT'S A VERY IMPORTANT QUESTION I WAS HOPING TO SPEAK WITH YOU ABOUT. IT'S ACTUALLY PART 3 OF OUR TREATMENT.

PART 3 — CONSOLIDATION PHASE

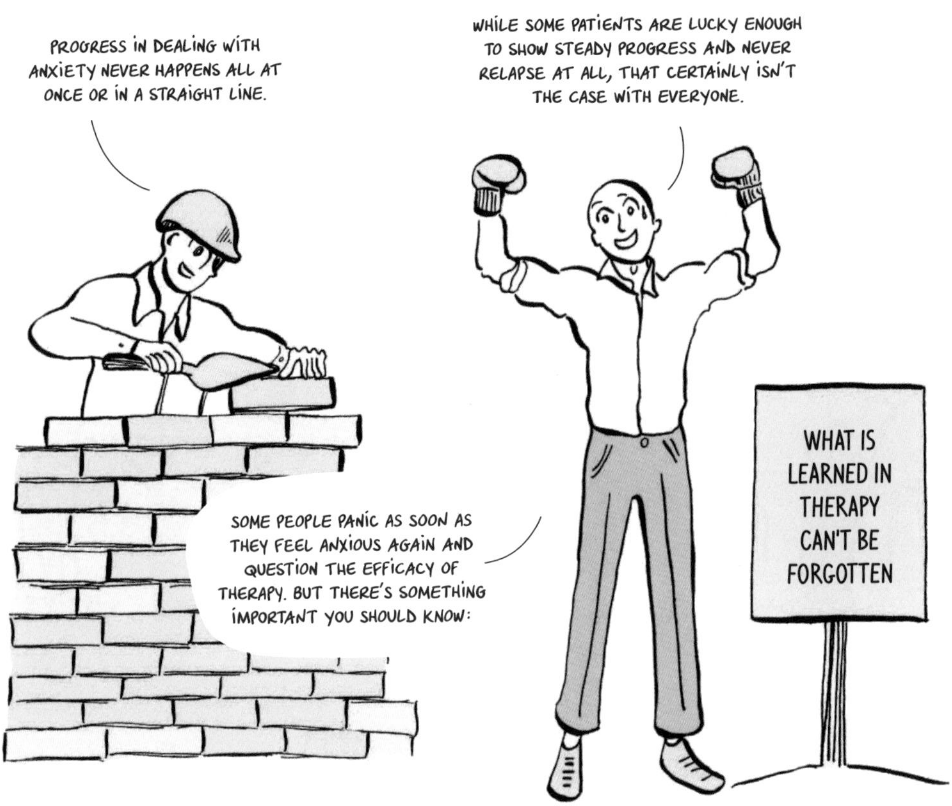
PROGRESS IN DEALING WITH ANXIETY NEVER HAPPENS ALL AT ONCE OR IN A STRAIGHT LINE.
WHILE SOME PATIENTS ARE LUCKY ENOUGH TO SHOW STEADY PROGRESS AND NEVER RELAPSE AT ALL, THAT CERTAINLY ISN'T THE CASE WITH EVERYONE.
SOME PEOPLE PANIC AS SOON AS THEY FEEL ANXIOUS AGAIN AND QUESTION THE EFFICACY OF THERAPY. BUT THERE'S SOMETHING IMPORTANT YOU SHOULD KNOW:
WHAT IS LEARNED IN THERAPY CAN'T BE FORGOTTEN

HERE'S WHAT'S HAPPENING:

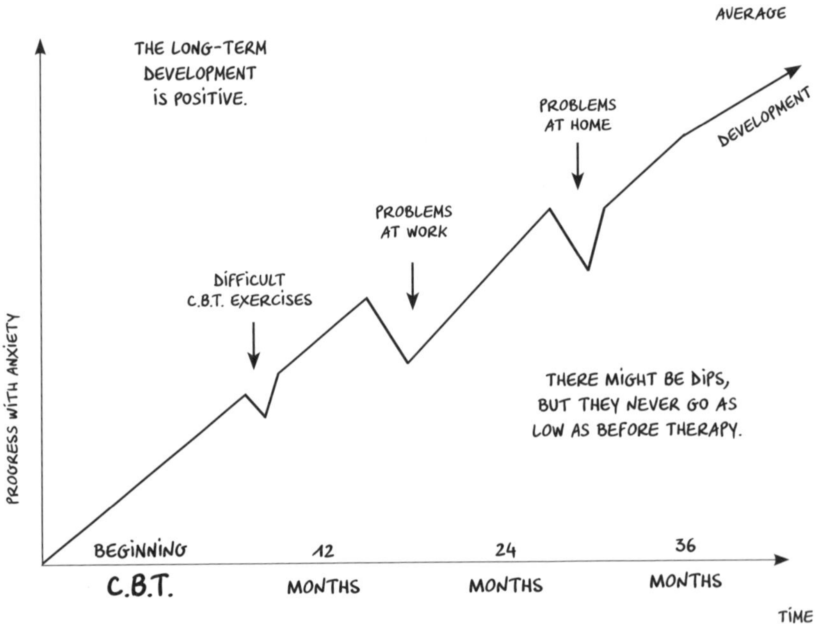
AVERAGE
THE LONG-TERM DEVELOPMENT IS POSITIVE.
PROBLEMS AT HOME
DEVELOPMENT
PROBLEMS AT WORK
DIFFICULT C.B.T. EXERCISES
THERE MIGHT BE DIPS, BUT THEY NEVER GO AS LOW AS BEFORE THERAPY.
PROGRESS WITH ANXIETY
BEGINNING
C.B.T.
12
MONTHS
24
MONTHS
36
MONTHS
TIME

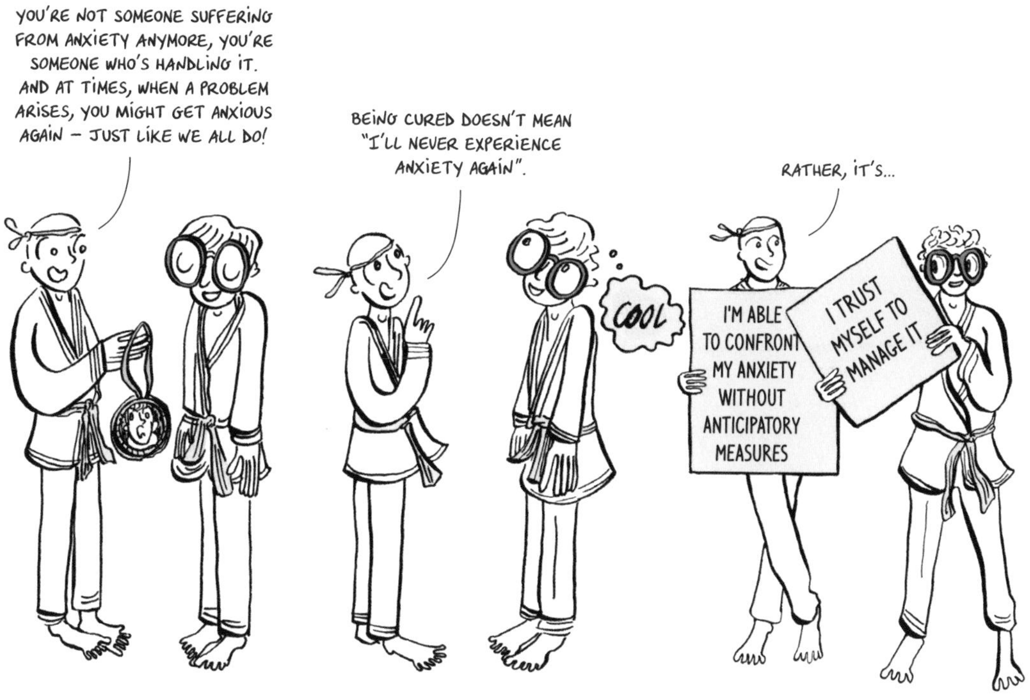
YOU'RE NOT SOMEONE SUFFERING FROM ANXIETY ANYMORE, YOU'RE SOMEONE WHO'S HANDLING IT. AND AT TIMES, WHEN A PROBLEM ARISES, YOU MIGHT GET ANXIOUS AGAIN – JUST LIKE WE ALL DO!
BEING CURED DOESN'T MEAN "I'LL NEVER EXPERIENCE ANXIETY AGAIN".
COOL
RATHER, IT'S...
I'M ABLE TO CONFRONT MY ANXIETY WITHOUT ANTICIPATORY MEASURES
I TRUST MYSELF TO MANAGE IT

AFTER TREATMENT, EVERY CASE IS DIFFERENT. SOME PEOPLE NEED TOP-UP SESSIONS ONCE OR TWICE A YEAR.

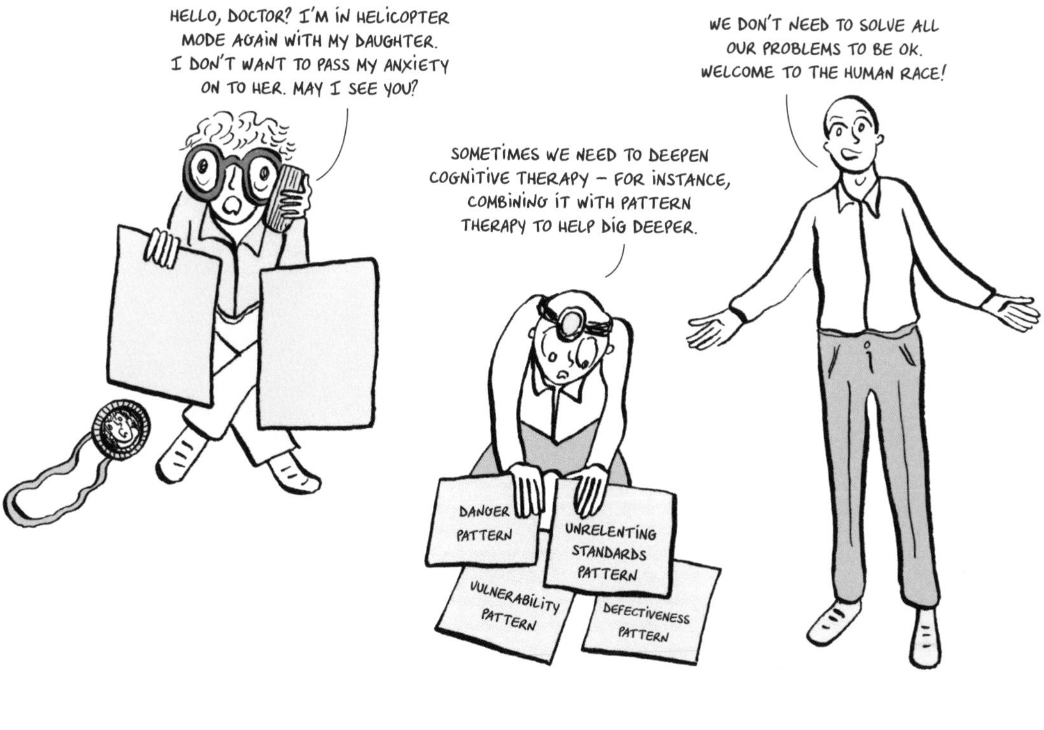
HELLO, DOCTOR? I'M IN HELICOPTER MODE AGAIN WITH MY DAUGHTER. I DON'T WANT TO PASS MY ANXIETY ON TO HER. MAY I SEE YOU?
SOMETIMES WE NEED TO DEEPEN COGNITIVE THERAPY – FOR INSTANCE, COMBINING IT WITH PATTERN THERAPY TO HELP DIG DEEPER.
DANGER PATTERN
UNRELENTING STANDARDS PATTERN
VULNERABILITY PATTERN
DEFECTIVENESS PATTERN
WE DON'T NEED TO SOLVE ALL OUR PROBLEMS TO BE OK. WELCOME TO THE HUMAN RACE!

EPILOGUE

THE ANXIETY CLUB

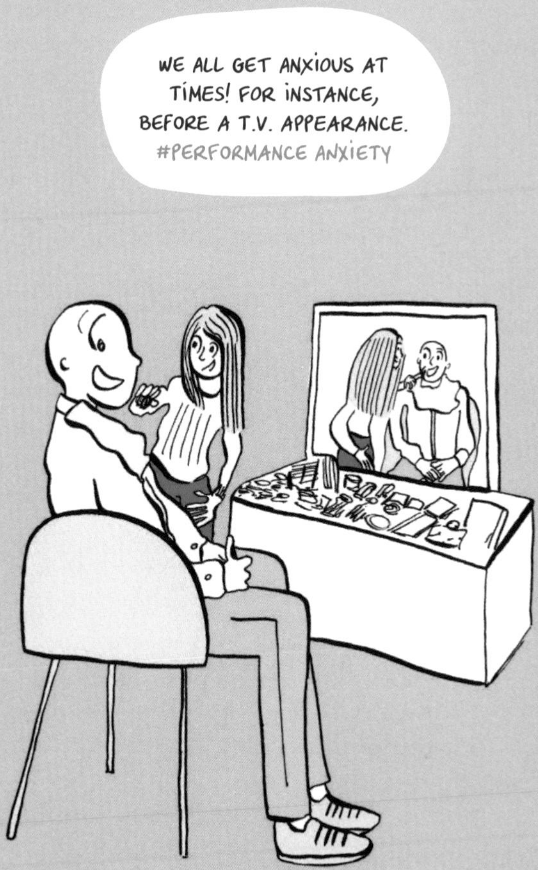
WE ALL GET ANXIOUS AT TIMES! FOR INSTANCE, BEFORE A T.V. APPEARANCE.
#PERFORMANCE ANXIETY

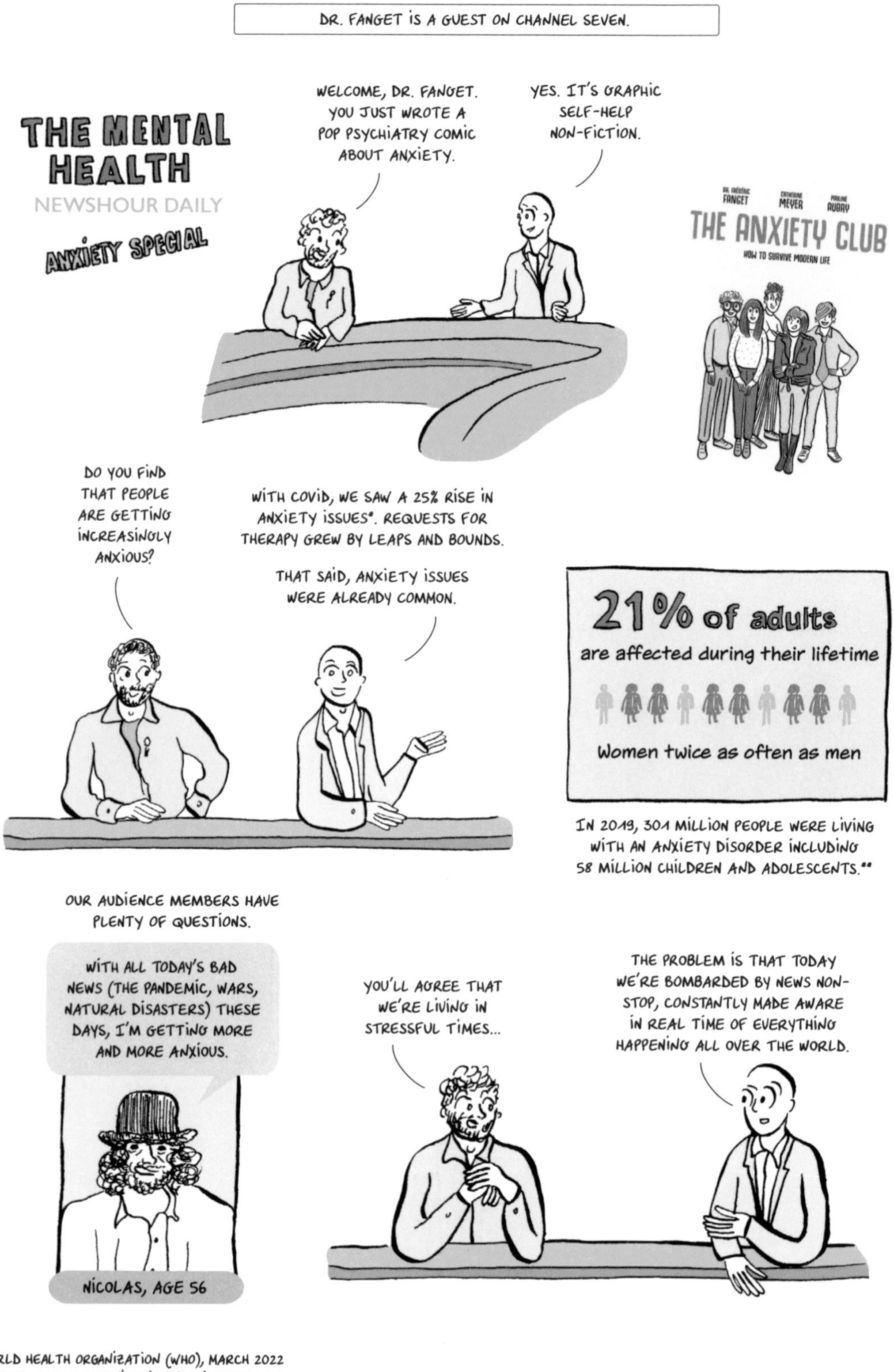
DR. FANGET IS A GUEST ON CHANNEL SEVEN.
THE MENTAL HEALTH
NEWSHOUR DAILY
ANXIETY SPECIAL
WELCOME, DR. FANGET. YOU JUST WROTE A POP PSYCHIATRY COMIC ABOUT ANXIETY.
YES. IT'S GRAPHIC SELF-HELP NON-FICTION.
FANGET
MEYER
AUBRY
THE ANXIETY CLUB
HOW TO SURVIVE MODERN LIFE
DO YOU FIND THAT PEOPLE ARE GETTING INCREASINGLY ANXIOUS?
WITH COVID, WE SAW A 25% RISE IN ANXIETY ISSUES*. REQUESTS FOR THERAPY GREW BY LEAPS AND BOUNDS.
THAT SAID, ANXIETY ISSUES WERE ALREADY COMMON.
21% of adults
are affected during their lifetime
Women twice as often as men
IN 2019, 301 MILLION PEOPLE WERE LIVING WITH AN ANXIETY DISORDER INCLUDING 58 MILLION CHILDREN AND ADOLESCENTS.**
OUR AUDIENCE MEMBERS HAVE PLENTY OF QUESTIONS.
WITH ALL TODAY'S BAD NEWS (THE PANDEMIC, WARS, NATURAL DISASTERS) THESE DAYS, I'M GETTING MORE AND MORE ANXIOUS.
NICOLAS, AGE 56
YOU'LL AGREE THAT WE'RE LIVING IN STRESSFUL TIMES...
THE PROBLEM IS THAT TODAY WE'RE BOMBARDED BY NEWS NON-STOP, CONSTANTLY MADE AWARE IN REAL TIME OF EVERYTHING HAPPENING ALL OVER THE WORLD.

*WORLD HEALTH ORGANIZATION (WHO), MARCH 2022
**WORLD HEALTH ORGANIZATION (WHO), JUNE 2022

BUT TO MANAGE ANXIETY, IT'S IMPORTANT THAT WE LEARN TO PUT UP WITH WAITING AND AVOID "RIGHT AWAY".

YOU SEE, IMAGES SPEAK DIRECTLY TO THE BRAIN'S EMOTION CENTRES. WE CAN'T GET ANY DISTANCE.

WE HAVE TO LEARN HOW TO TURN OFF OUR SCREENS AND GIVE OUR BRAIN TIME TO IMPLEMENT ITS TOOLS FOR PROCESSING AND ANALYZING THE NEWS.

MY WIFE'S SCARED OF EVERYTHING. I ALWAYS TRY TO REASSURE HER BUT, ON A DAILY BASIS, IT CAN BE A BIT MUCH.

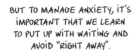

ANTOINE, AGE 40

THANKS FOR RAISING THAT VERY IMPORTANT POINT, ANTOINE. ANXIETY SUFFERERS KNOW WE CAN WEAR OUT OUR LOVED ONES WITH OUR CONSTANT WORRYING.

MANY END UP IN RELATIONSHIPS WITH REASSURING PARTNERS.

THE RIGHT ATTITUDE IS TO BE PRESENT AND UNDERSTANDING, WILLING TO LISTEN — BUT WITHIN REASON.

BUT THAT'S OFTEN DIFFICULT.

KNOW WHEN TO GENTLY TELL AN ANXIOUS PERSON TO **STOP** IF THEY'RE REPEATING THE SAME FEARS

REORIENT THEM TOWARD **FACTS**

CAREFUL: TWO BEHAVIOURS TO AVOID

GETTING ANGRY INSTEAD OF BEING UNDERSTANDING

BEING TOO UNDERSTANDING

DON'T WORRY. I'LL SEE TO **EVERYTHING**

THANKS. I'M SORRY... I'M TOO ANXIOUS, MY STOMACH HURTS, I GET DIZZY — IT'S ALL BECAUSE I'M TOO ANXIOUS. I'M SORRY.

I'VE HAD ENOUGH! FOR YEARS NOW, YOU'VE BEEN WORRYING **OVER NOTHING!**

BUT IT'S NOT AN ACT!

LISTENING AT LENGTH EVEN WHEN THEY'RE REPEATING THEMSELVES AND NOT GETTING ANYWHERE ONLY TENDS TO FEED THE PHENOMENON.

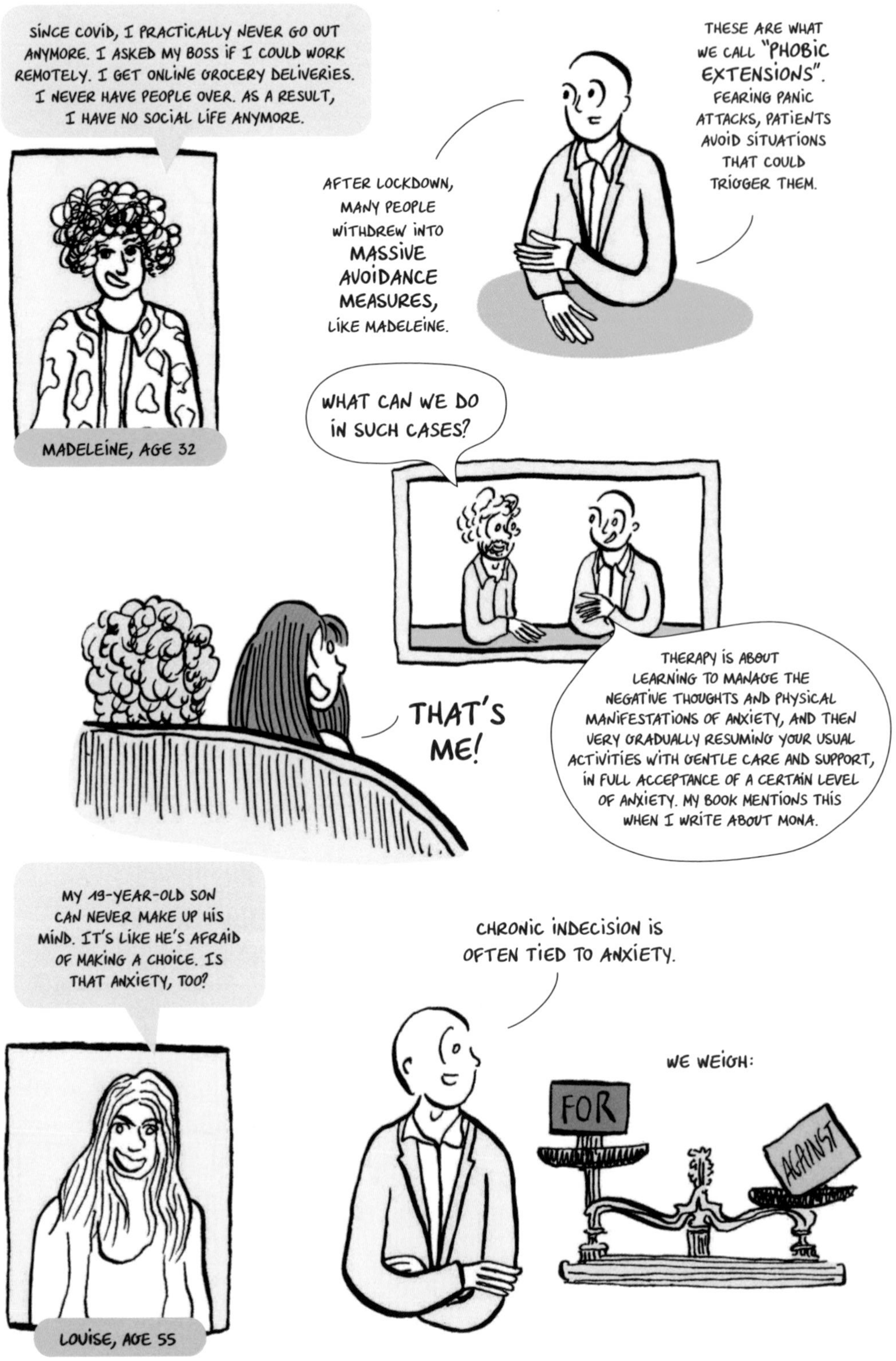
SINCE COVID, I PRACTICALLY NEVER GO OUT ANYMORE. I ASKED MY BOSS IF I COULD WORK REMOTELY. I GET ONLINE GROCERY DELIVERIES. I NEVER HAVE PEOPLE OVER. AS A RESULT, I HAVE NO SOCIAL LIFE ANYMORE.
MADELEINE, AGE 32
AFTER LOCKDOWN, MANY PEOPLE WITHDREW INTO MASSIVE AVOIDANCE MEASURES, LIKE MADELEINE.
THESE ARE WHAT WE CALL "PHOBIC EXTENSIONS". FEARING PANIC ATTACKS, PATIENTS AVOID SITUATIONS THAT COULD TRIGGER THEM.
WHAT CAN WE DO IN SUCH CASES?
THAT'S ME!
THERAPY IS ABOUT LEARNING TO MANAGE THE NEGATIVE THOUGHTS AND PHYSICAL MANIFESTATIONS OF ANXIETY, AND THEN VERY GRADUALLY RESUMING YOUR USUAL ACTIVITIES WITH GENTLE CARE AND SUPPORT, IN FULL ACCEPTANCE OF A CERTAIN LEVEL OF ANXIETY. MY BOOK MENTIONS THIS WHEN I WRITE ABOUT MONA.
MY 19-YEAR-OLD SON CAN NEVER MAKE UP HIS MIND. IT'S LIKE HE'S AFRAID OF MAKING A CHOICE. IS THAT ANXIETY, TOO?
LOUISE, AGE 55
CHRONIC INDECISION IS OFTEN TIED TO ANXIETY.
WE WEIGH:
FOR
AGAINST

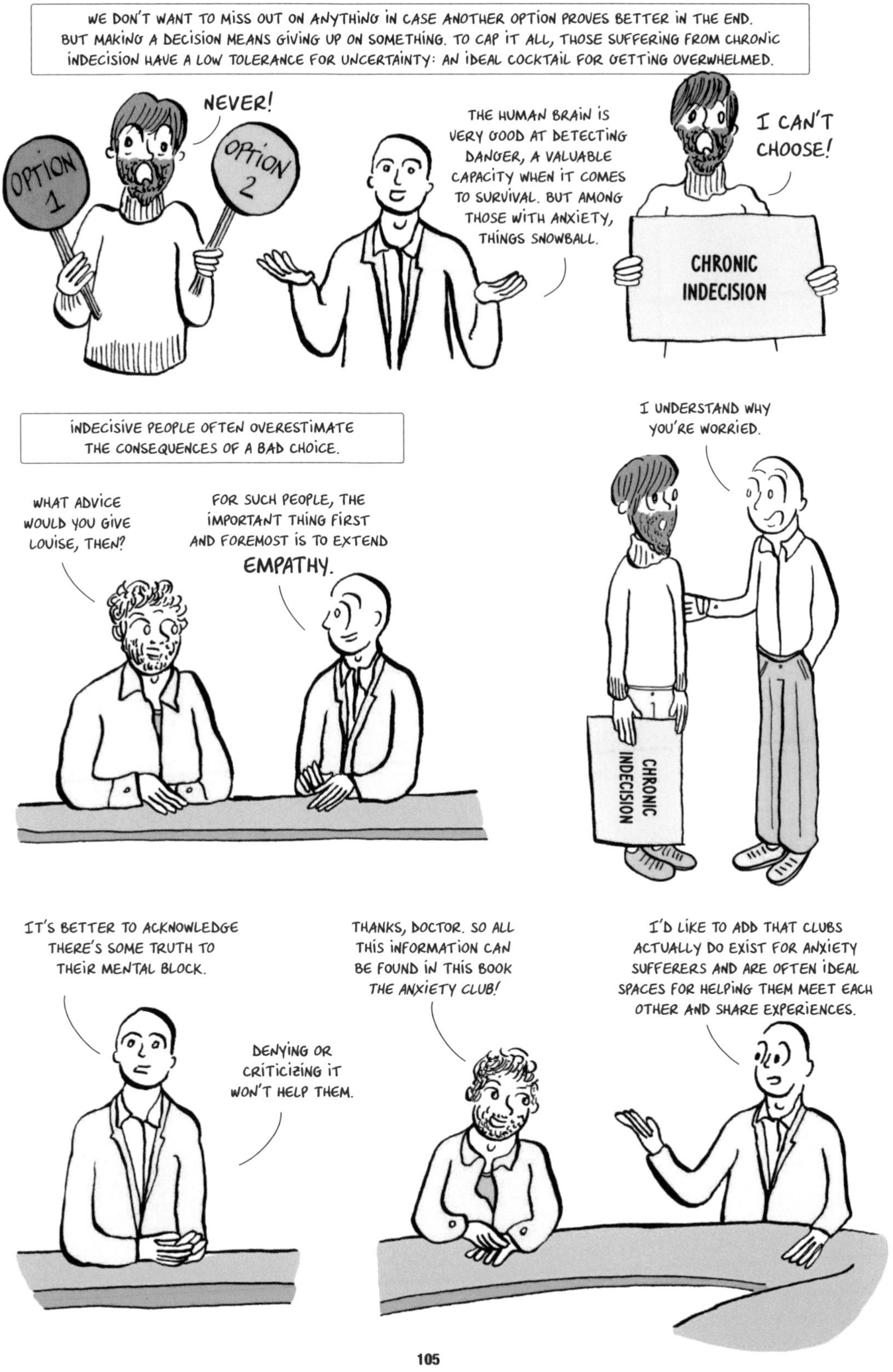
WE DON'T WANT TO MISS OUT ON ANYTHING IN CASE ANOTHER OPTION PROVES BETTER IN THE END. BUT MAKING A DECISION MEANS GIVING UP ON SOMETHING. TO CAP IT ALL, THOSE SUFFERING FROM CHRONIC INDECISION HAVE A LOW TOLERANCE FOR UNCERTAINTY: AN IDEAL COCKTAIL FOR GETTING OVERWHELMED.
OPTION 1
NEVER!
OPTION 2
THE HUMAN BRAIN IS VERY GOOD AT DETECTING DANGER, A VALUABLE CAPACITY WHEN IT COMES TO SURVIVAL. BUT AMONG THOSE WITH ANXIETY, THINGS SNOWBALL.
I CAN'T CHOOSE!
CHRONIC INDECISION
INDECISIVE PEOPLE OFTEN OVERESTIMATE THE CONSEQUENCES OF A BAD CHOICE.
WHAT ADVICE WOULD YOU GIVE LOUISE, THEN?
FOR SUCH PEOPLE, THE IMPORTANT THING FIRST AND FOREMOST IS TO EXTEND EMPATHY.
I UNDERSTAND WHY YOU'RE WORRIED.
CHRONIC INDECISION
IT'S BETTER TO ACKNOWLEDGE THERE'S SOME TRUTH TO THEIR MENTAL BLOCK.
DENYING OR CRITICIZING IT WON'T HELP THEM.
THANKS, DOCTOR. SO ALL THIS INFORMATION CAN BE FOUND IN THIS BOOK THE ANXIETY CLUB!
I'D LIKE TO ADD THAT CLUBS ACTUALLY DO EXIST FOR ANXIETY SUFFERERS AND ARE OFTEN IDEAL SPACES FOR HELPING THEM MEET EACH OTHER AND SHARE EXPERIENCES.

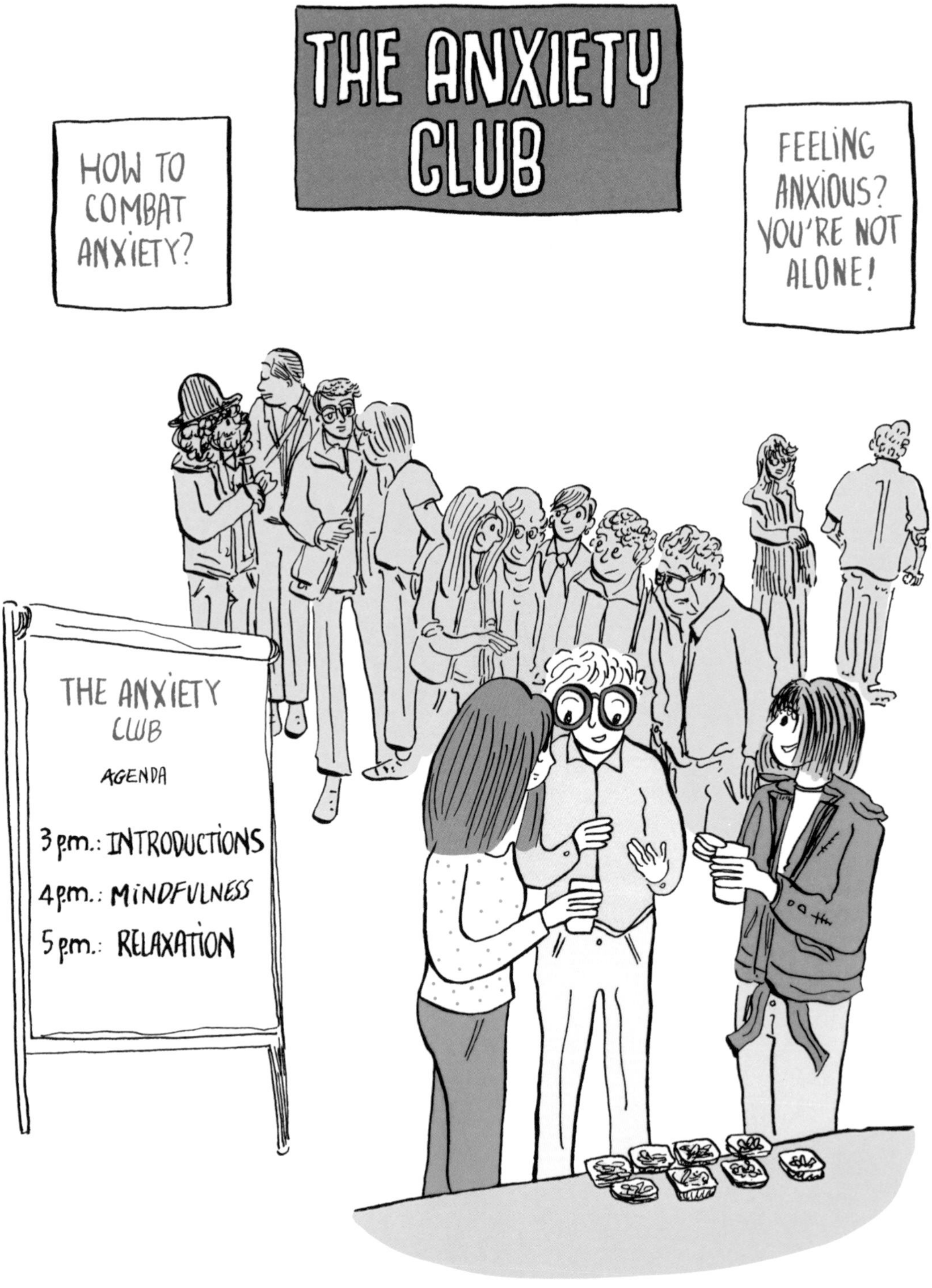
THE ANXIETY CLUB
HOW TO COMBAT ANXIETY?
FEELING ANXIOUS? YOU'RE NOT ALONE!
THE ANXIETY CLUB
AGENDA
3 p.m.: INTRODUCTIONS
4 p.m.: MINDFULNESS
5 p.m.: RELAXATION

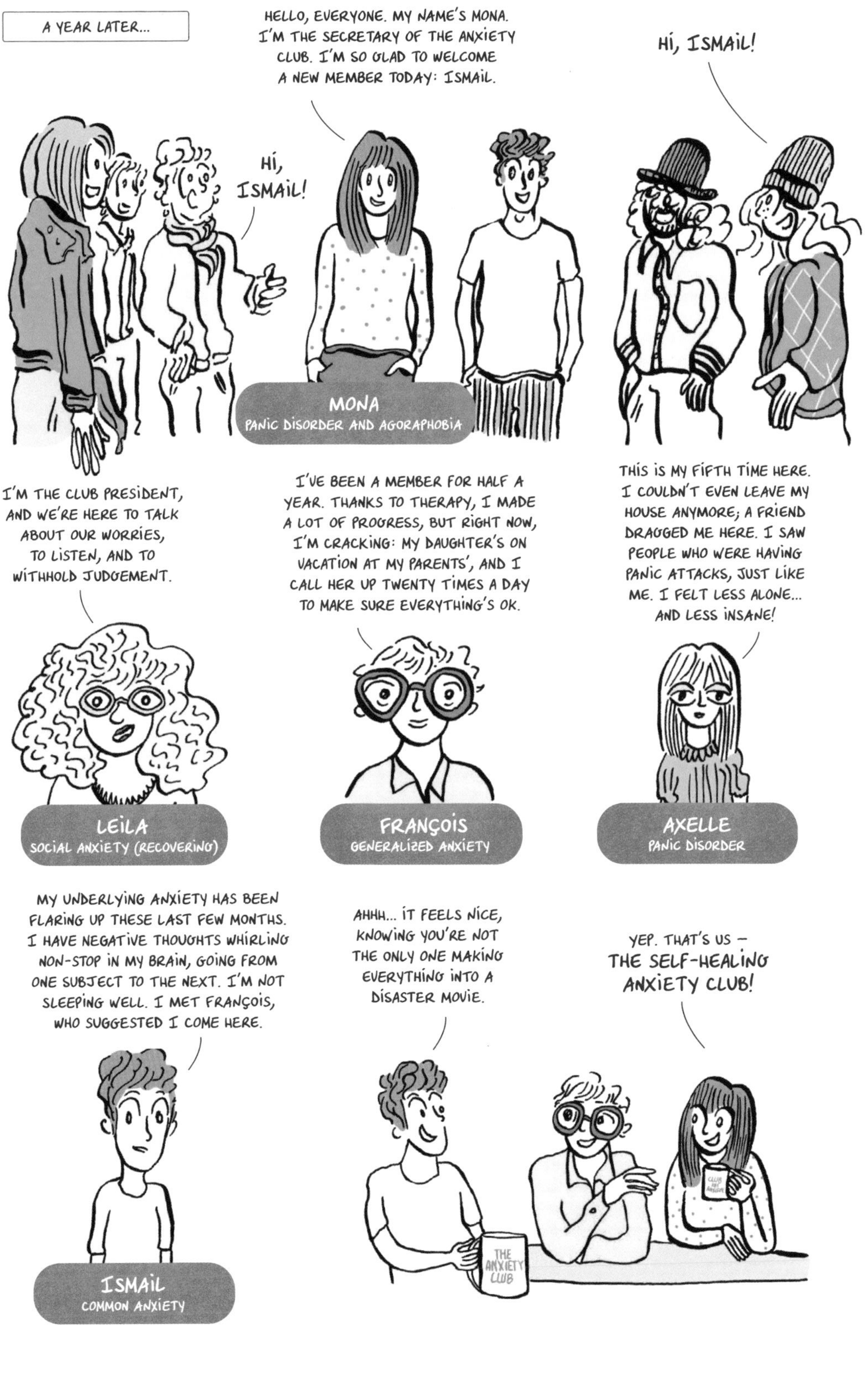
A YEAR LATER...
HELLO, EVERYONE. MY NAME'S MONA. I'M THE SECRETARY OF THE ANXIETY CLUB. I'M SO GLAD TO WELCOME A NEW MEMBER TODAY: ISMAIL.
HI, ISMAIL!
HI, ISMAIL!
MONA
PANIC DISORDER AND AGORAPHOBIA
I'M THE CLUB PRESIDENT, AND WE'RE HERE TO TALK ABOUT OUR WORRIES, TO LISTEN, AND TO WITHHOLD JUDGEMENT.
LEILA
SOCIAL ANXIETY (RECOVERING)
I'VE BEEN A MEMBER FOR HALF A YEAR. THANKS TO THERAPY, I MADE A LOT OF PROGRESS, BUT RIGHT NOW, I'M CRACKING: MY DAUGHTER'S ON VACATION AT MY PARENTS', AND I CALL HER UP TWENTY TIMES A DAY TO MAKE SURE EVERYTHING'S OK.
FRANÇOIS
GENERALIZED ANXIETY
THIS IS MY FIFTH TIME HERE. I COULDN'T EVEN LEAVE MY HOUSE ANYMORE; A FRIEND DRAGGED ME HERE. I SAW PEOPLE WHO WERE HAVING PANIC ATTACKS, JUST LIKE ME. I FELT LESS ALONE... AND LESS INSANE!
AXELLE
PANIC DISORDER
MY UNDERLYING ANXIETY HAS BEEN FLARING UP THESE LAST FEW MONTHS. I HAVE NEGATIVE THOUGHTS WHIRLING NON-STOP IN MY BRAIN, GOING FROM ONE SUBJECT TO THE NEXT. I'M NOT SLEEPING WELL. I MET FRANÇOIS, WHO SUGGESTED I COME HERE.
ISMAIL
COMMON ANXIETY
AHHH... IT FEELS NICE, KNOWING YOU'RE NOT THE ONLY ONE MAKING EVERYTHING INTO A DISASTER MOVIE.
YEP. THAT'S US — THE SELF-HEALING ANXIETY CLUB!
THE ANXIETY CLUB

FURTHER READING

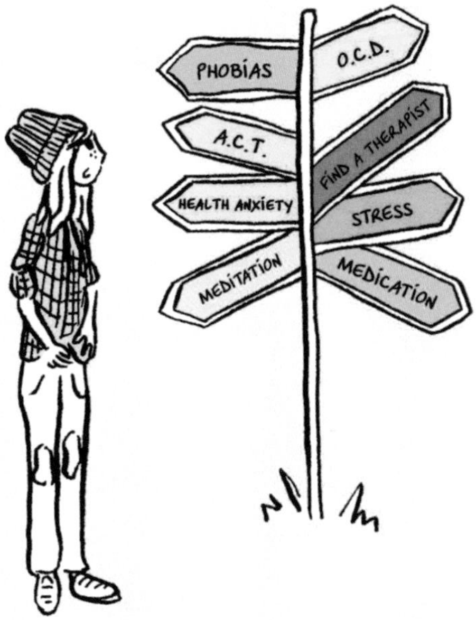
PHOBIAS
O.C.D.
A.C.T.
FIND A THERAPIST
HEALTH ANXIETY
STRESS
MEDITATION
MEDICATION

WHAT ARE THE TAKEAWAYS?

If we were to walk away from this book retaining only, as Rabelais put it, "the substantial marrow", what would that be?

1. Anxiety is a normal phenomenon, useful to human survival.
2. It is the result of physiological, psychological, and behavioural mechanisms. Understanding these is the first step to getting better.
3. Anxiety can be treated! But treatment isn't about getting rid of anxiety; rather, it's about being in greater control of the situation.
4. The goals of therapy are:
   - learning how to manage uncertainty;
   - becoming more confident in facing the unforeseen;
   - incrementally confronting our fears;
   - better managing our emotions; and
   - living a more tranquil life.
5. One final point: self-care is a matter of practice. Contrary to what gurus would have us believe, there's no magical solution. We must take what we need from therapy and make it our own.

FINDING OUT MORE ABOUT ANXIETY

WHAT ARE THE DIFFERENT ANXIETY DISORDERS?

In this comic, we used our three characters – Ismail, Mona, and François – to examine three kinds of anxiety. There are many other kinds of disorders, from social anxiety to separation anxiety, that we had neither space nor time to delve into in these pages. What follows is a fuller presentation of the family of pathological anxieties.

Generalized anxiety disorder, or GAD, which we dwelled on at length with François, is characterized by excessive worry, an almost constant feeling of anxiety, and may be accompanied by physical symptoms: fatigue, muscle tension, sleep issues, difficulty concentrating, irritable bowel syndrome (IBS), and more. Often, this "fear of everything" feeds on events from everyday life: the health or safety of loved ones, household chores (various repairs, scheduling), and professional responsibilities.

Panic disorder, characterized by panic attacks, shows up as sudden, intense panic, a feeling of imminent death or disaster, and fear of losing all self-control. Symptoms – heart palpitations, trembling, dizziness, etc – are described on page 36. In most cases, the incident never happens again. In order to be diagnosed with a "panic disorder", a person would have to suffer many recurrent and unexpected attacks, followed by several months of fear of having more attacks (fear of fear) and behavioural changes tied to anxiety.

Agoraphobia is defined as a pathological fear of finding oneself in an unfamiliar place from which it would be difficult to escape or be rescued. This gives rise to a fear of leaving one's house or home, entering a shop and being in the middle of a crowd or in a public space, the train or undergound, and so on. As we saw with Mona, this disorder is frequently associated with panic attacks.

Separation anxiety is characterized by a fear or excessive and inappropriate anxiety that arises at a developmental stage when the patient must separate themselves from people they are close to. This pathology is common among children, but I have encountered it more than once in adult patients. It was never a part of the initial diagnosis, and only targeted questions on the full scope of a patient's normal activities enabled me to detect this disorder first arising in childhood.

Social anxiety disorder is much more than mere shyness. We are talking here about individuals who fear other people's judgement so much that they can barely bring themselves to have coffee with a co-worker, for example. The very thought of speaking up in a meeting terrifies them, and their personal lives are empty because of their fear of confessing to others their feelings for them. Social anxiety is common, and quite often tied to difficulties with assertiveness and self-esteem.

Post-traumatic stress disorder (PTSD) can manifest if we have been exposed to situations of extreme stress involving the possibility of death or the threat of bodily harm: war, natural disaster, assault, terrorism, rape, etc. It may also result from

witnessing such situations. Typically, we will mentally relive the traumatizing event (memories, nightmares, flashbacks, etc.) and avoid anything even faintly reminiscent of it. PTSD is common and leads to very intense states of anxiety that often require therapy.

We don't cover PTSD in this book because the latest edition of the Diagnostic and Statistical Manual of Mental Disorders (DSM-5) classifies it not as an Anxiety Disorder but rather in its own new category of Trauma and Stressor-Related Disorders, which require a different therapeutic approach.

#Phobias are fears of specific objects or situations disproportionate to the actual danger involved. The most commonly encountered simple phobias involve animals, but there are far more phobias in the world. I'll let you learn about them in a little test below.

Test your knowledge of vocabulary

Match the name of each phobia with the correct definition by drawing lines from the letters to the numbers.

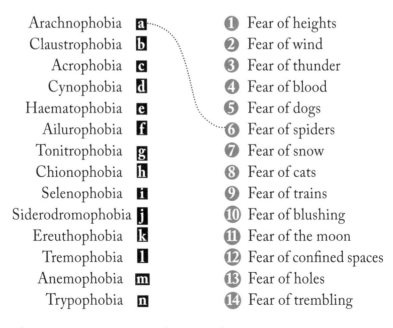

Arachnophobia	**a**	❶ Fear of heights
Claustrophobia	**b**	❷ Fear of wind
Acrophobia	**c**	❸ Fear of thunder
Cynophobia	**d**	❹ Fear of blood
Haematophobia	**e**	❺ Fear of dogs
Ailurophobia	**f**	❻ Fear of spiders
Tonitrophobia	**g**	❼ Fear of snow
Chionophobia	**h**	❽ Fear of cats
Selenophobia	**i**	❾ Fear of trains
Siderodromophobia	**j**	❿ Fear of blushing
Ereuthophobia	**k**	⓫ Fear of the moon
Tremophobia	**l**	⓬ Fear of confined spaces
Anemophobia	**m**	⓭ Fear of holes
Trypophobia	**n**	⓮ Fear of trembling

Answers: a/6; b/12; c/1; d/5; e/4; f/8; g/3; h/7; i/11; j/9; k/10; l/14; m/2; n/13

Health anxiety is the excessive and recurring fear of a serious illness. The slightest physical symptom provokes a feeling of mortal danger: a headache makes you suspect a brain tumour, a cough lung cancer, etc.

Selective mutism is characterized by a child's regularly occurring inability to speak in specific social situations where they are meant to, such as school, while being perfectly able to speak in other situations.

Anxiety disorders induced by a substance or medication are common. Doctors must consider this possibility and look for causes. Also of note is how commonly withdrawal from various medications can cause severe anxiety. To avoid such symptoms, I strongly advise gradually reducing medications under a doctor's care. Do not hesitate to consult your GP / Medical Practitioner: they are aware of all the medications you may be taking for other conditions.

Anxiety disorders caused by another medical condition are also far from rare. Again, your GP's / Medical Practitioner's opinion may be of great help.

OCD, or Obsessive-Compulsive Disorder, is characterized by recurring obsessions that lead to intense anxiety. To reduce this anxiety, people with OCD adopt behaviours that make them feel safe and often take the form of compulsions. DSM-5 moved OCD out from under the Anxiety Disorder section into a new category: Obsessive-Compulsive and Related Disorders. In this category, we should also note the fear of acting out, or of committing an aggressive act against a loved one. This is a factor driving a great many people to seek help.

The thought of wanting to harm another is neither healthy nor reasonable, and leads to intense anxiety and feelings of shame. Patients keep such thoughts secret, but fortunately they do not often follow them up with action.

NOTE:
An anxiety disorder may be related to another mental disorder. That's why seeing a doctor is essential before any treatment, so as to discover any other disorders that might themselves require different handling.

WHEN DOES ANXIETY BECOME PATHOLOGICAL?

A healthy lifestyle is the first-line defence against anxiety disorders. What is a healthy lifestyle? Making sure we eat well, get good sleep, and engage in regular physical activity. But sometimes, this is sadly not enough.

→ What warning signs should I be looking out for?

If your anxiety is intense and non-stop, or if it is accompanied by significant difficulty in functioning (you can no longer work or get around in a normal fashion), you must seek help. Any anxiety that is accompanied by avoidance of important activities (errands, appointments) and has major repercussions on your social, personal, and professional life is considered pathological.

→ What will happen if I don't get help?

When anxiety is as intense as it was with Mona and François in this comic, it will not go away without help. And if you do not get treatment, it may lead to complications such as addiction, depression, and other related anxiety disorders. Consequences for your personal and home life are another risk: many patients seek treatment in order not to pass their anxiety on to their children.

MEDICATION: WHEN SHOULD I TAKE IT, WHAT SHOULD I TAKE, AND WHAT ARE THE RISKS?

In this section, I'll only be discussing medications whose effectiveness has been scientifically proven. You may hear talk of other available products (such as magnesium or essential oils), but their usefulness has not been scientifically established. You should also know that only medical professionals are authorized to prescribe medication.

➜ Sedatives, anxiolytics, benzodiazepines: are they useful?

Speaking for myself, I avoid prescribing benzodiazepine-type anxiolytics over the long term whenever possible. While these products are sometimes indispensable in the short term (a finite prescription for a few weeks or months) for patients suffering intensely, long-term use must be avoided due to the risk of increased tolerance and other undesirable effects, including respiratory depression and memory issues. In fact, the maximum recommended prescription duration for an anxiolytic is twelve weeks, and for a sedative-hypnotic (sleeping pill) is four weeks.*

➜ Why should long-term use be avoided?

Admittedly, anxiolytics produce an immediate calming effect. They dispel fears for a while, but they do not allow us to carry out the learning that will enable us to confront anxiety-inducing situations. If you're taking an anxiolytic, as soon as you're confronted with a stressful event, you are feeding the "all-or-nothing" mindset ("I'll only act if I have no fear") that therapy tries to get you out of. It is counterproductive to anaesthetize your fears. You can learn to face them and not freeze up when you feel afraid. That's the whole point of this book and the treatments I've explored.

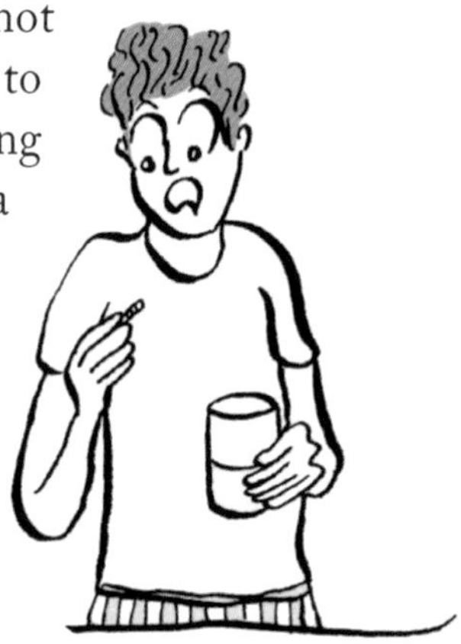

➜ What are some recommended medications, then?

Anxiolytics do not address the cause of the problem, only its symptoms. I often use a bacterial throat infection as an example. Your doctor prescribes you a painkiller and an antibiotic. You feel the effects of the analgesic, which relieves pain at once, but the antibiotic is what's working on the root cause of the infection over the course of several days. And yet you're not aware of it affecting the bacteria. In much the same way, a

* Different medications will vary. Always consult your doctor/medical practitioner.

psychiatrist can prescribe an anxiolytic and an antidepressant. In other words, the anxiolytic is analogous to the analgesic, and the antidepressant to the antibiotic.

That's why, for long-term treatment, we prefer selective serotonin reuptake inhibitors (SSRIs). These are antidepressants, and there is less chance of building up a tolerance to them. Above all, they address the biological factor involved in severe anxiety disorders – namely, the uptake of serotonin, a neurotransmitter essential to regulating anxiety.

NOTE:
People often confuse antidepressants and anxiolytics. The side effects of tolerance and habituation so often attributed to antidepressants actually belong to benzodiazepine-type anxiolytics. These two classes of medications are utterly unrelated and share neither application nor side effects. Never hesitate to ask your doctor questions, and always beware of false information.

→ What are SSRIs, or selective serotonin reuptake inhibitors?

In the most serious cases, when anxiety is so pervasive it makes living a normal life impossible – as was the case with François, who suffered from severe GAD – we must sometimes resort to selective serotonin reuptake inhibitors. Unlike with benzodiazepines, there is less risk of building up a tolerance to SSRIs (as far as we know). They are a long-term treatment that regularizes the normal cerebral secretion of serotonin. In practice, after a consultation with a doctor to make sure there are no contraindications, these medications are recommended when anxiety is too intense for therapy alone, or when patients present with another psychological disorder – for instance, depression. To date, there are no known toxic effects associated with long-term use, which is not the case with benzodiazepines. But be careful: if these medications do not sufficiently improve your anxiety issues, it is often essential to seek out behavioural and cognitive therapy. These will complement and round out the effects of medication, and in many cases will enable you to stop taking them.

IMPORTANT

Treatment with medication should be left to specialists. Everyone is different, and what helps someone you know might not be suited to you. There is a great deal of false and distorted information circulating about these substances. I can only urge you to consult a doctor well-versed in anxiety disorders. They will be able to tell you if medications are needed, with or without psychotherapy.

→ Stress, anxiety, fear: what's the difference?

These words often get mixed up, so it seems useful to redefine them here.

STRESS: An environmental adaptation mechanism, it was first theorized by Quebecois doctor Hans Selye, who coined the word. In *Le Stress de la vie* (*The Stress of Life*, 1956), Hans Selye defined stress as "the ensemble of physiological and psychological means that a person makes use of to adapt to a given event". It is, then, a physiological response to being confronted by a disturbance in our surroundings, whether a real danger, a physical threat, or a psychological one.

Qualitatively speaking, there are two types of stress:
- **good stress** is stimulating and helps us succeed. It can provide motivation and assist us in making good decisions;
- **bad stress** occurs when we have a hard time managing our difficulties, especially over a longer period of time. It is harmful and can make us lose our composure.

From a temporal standpoint, there are two very different kinds of stress:

- **acute stress,** in reaction to an isolated event. It may sometimes be sudden (PTSD).
- **chronic stress,** which indicates a poor adaptation on the part of an individual to environmental disturbances.

ANXIETY (STATE): An emotion experienced inside ourselves, it is defined as "normal" when it constitutes a response to a stressor from daily life, but can prove psychopathological when it becomes the cause of pain or an inability to function. This book has discussed it a great deal.

ANXIETY (TRAIT): These are physical manifestations of anxiety in all its varieties (fear, dread, worry, apprehension, anguish, unease). These are often considered anxiety disorders and trigger:

- **cognitive mental manifestations,** including the catastrophizing we discussed at length, especially in François' case.
- **physical manifestations,** with numerous bodily symptoms, especially in Mona's case.

Physical symptoms can manifest in an ongoing way, as in the case of GAD, or in an abrupt and isolated way, as with panic attacks.

→ How long does a panic attack last?
A panic attack can last up to 90 minutes. No matter what happens, it stops by itself after describing a bell curve. While it may be extremely, even horrifically, painful, you should know that it won't last.

→ **If we cure one symptom (e.g. fear of bridges), is there a risk it will re-emerge somewhere else?**

This is a myth left over from psychoanalysis, which refers to "symptom substitution". This stems from the idea that if the deep psychological cause (lurking in the unconscious) has not been taken into account, the symptom will resurface in another form. This vision of psychology as a pressure cooker is merely a hypothesis that has never been verified by facts or scientific study. Most people who have learned to develop effective strategies to get rid of one or more phobias with a therapist continue, on their own, to free themselves from others. In the event of relapse, we must return to psychotherapy for a deeper exploration (which isn't always necessary for everyone).

→ Sometimes, during panic attacks, I feel like I'm becoming schizophrenic. Can panic attacks lead to psychosis?

Some panic attacks feel so truly terrifying that people in the grip of them feel like they're losing their mind: "The world is different, my body's changing, I'm not me anymore!" Or "It's like my life's playing out and I'm just watching. I feel like I'm becoming schizophrenic." They speak of "depersonalization" and "derealization". It is important to know that if such symptoms, experienced during a panic attack that lasts a few minutes, vanish afterwards, they are in no way related to schizophrenia. In order to diagnose schizophrenia, please consult a practising psychiatrist.

→ What is the difference between panic disorder and GAD?

If your anxiety is constant, like a background noise that never goes away, then you are suffering from GAD. If it comes and goes, sometimes even suddenly, it is more likely a panic disorder. You should know that these two disorders can coexist.

BEEP
BEEP
BEEP
BEEP
BEEP

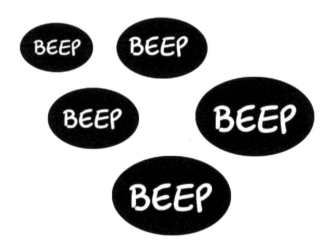

HOW DO WE PICK A GOOD THERAPIST?

First of all, what exactly is psychotherapy? Psychotherapy literally means "healing (*therapeia*) for the mind (*psyche*)". Taking good care of ourself means recognizing that something isn't going right, knowing when to say "Enough!" to suffering, and taking charge when it comes to feeling better. A therapist can help us get a better handle on the problem, provide tools for resolving it, and accompany us on the journey towards improvement.

WHAT ARE THE DIFFERENT KINDS OF THERAPISTS?

It is often assumed that "therapist" means "psychoanalyst". In reality, psychoanalysts are in the minority among mental health practitioners worldwide. Therapy covers a great many more modes of treatment. Let's try to clear away some of the misunderstandings that can arise from the various titles and labels associated with different caregivers.

PSYCHOLOGIST
→ A holder of master's or doctoral degree in psychology. Some are clinicians (they have a practice and see patients), while others are not. Industrial or organizational psychologists, for instance, carry out skills assessments or studies of the workplace environment, but do not see patients.

PSYCHIATRIST
→ A doctor specializing in mental health. The title is conferred after years of medical study and specialization in psychiatry. Psychiatrists alone among the various mental health professionals can prescribe medication: anxiolytics, antidepressants, etc. They can also perform psychotherapy. Training in general psychotherapy is part of their curriculum. But in order to treat severe anxiety disorders and practice cognitive or behavioural therapy, they must first obtain a professional

training degree or licence in that field to complement their training in psychotherapy.

PSYCHOANALYST

→ An heir – whether close or distant – to Sigmund Freud (1856–1939), the psychoanalyst employs an approach founded on analysis of the unconscious as theorized in early 20th-century Vienna. (Other, entirely unrelated conceptions of the unconscious exist – for instance, in neuroscience.) Qualifying as a psychoanalyst involves years of training and self-analysis, as well as a detailed observation of practical cases.

There are a great many schools of psychoanalysis, with differing degrees of compatibility. As the name implies, the purpose of psychoanalysis is analysis: well-being may result, but it is not the discipline's primary goal.

PSYCHOTHERAPIST

→ The titles of "clinical psychologist", "psychiatrist", and "psychoanalyst" give practitioners the right to call themselves psychotherapists, on the condition that they have undergone the necessary training and are registered with the relevant governing body.

These four labels – psychologist, psychiatrist, psychoanalyst, and psychotherapist – are not mutually exclusive. It is possible to be both a psychiatrist and a psychoanalyst, for example.

"ALTERNATIVE" COUNSELLORS

→ The terms "counsellor" and "advisor" are not protected by law. They refer to people who cannot or do not wish to make use of one of the titles we have previously defined. There are, in fact, a large number of self-proclaimed life coaches and spiritual advisors who employ highly diverse and occasionally sectarian methods. These should in no way be considered psychology. If you're interested in seeking help from such counsellors, be sure to check that they are affiliated with the relevant governing body in your country.

NOTE:
The titles of psychologist, psychiatrist, psychoanalyst, and psychotherapist are protected by law. Those of advisor and counsellor are not: anyone can put up a plaque and claim them.

WHAT ARE THE MOST EFFECTIVE TREATMENTS FOR ANXIETY DISORDERS?

At the time of writing, the only treatment recognized by international scientific consensus for severe anxiety disorders is **cognitive behavioural therapy (CBT)**.

The advice and techniques I propose in this book belong to this approach. CBT aims to identify and correct reflexes (whether of thought or behaviour) that we engage in without thinking and cause us difficulty (anxiety, phobias, panic attacks, self-denigration, excessive and unfounded pessimism, etc.).

In a certain number of cases, **schema therapy** (see Bibliography) includes elements of CBT.

The CBT movement has evolved a great deal in the last few years. There is talk of a "third wave" that places emphasis on emotions, which is why CBET (the "E" is for "emotional") has begun to take off. New methods are making their appearance. Some of the main ones are:

- **ACT, or acceptance and commitment therapy,** (Steven Hayes), focuses on distancing ourselves from unpleasant emotions and recentring our values in life, by way of mindfulness meditation practices.
- **MBSR, or mindfulness-based stress reduction**, (Jon Kabat-Zinn et al.), proposes a stress-reduction programme based on intensive mindfulness training.
- **MBCT, or mindfulness-based cognitive therapy**, (Zindel Segal et al.), is a kind of psychotherapy drawing on both mindfulness meditation practices and cognitive therapy.

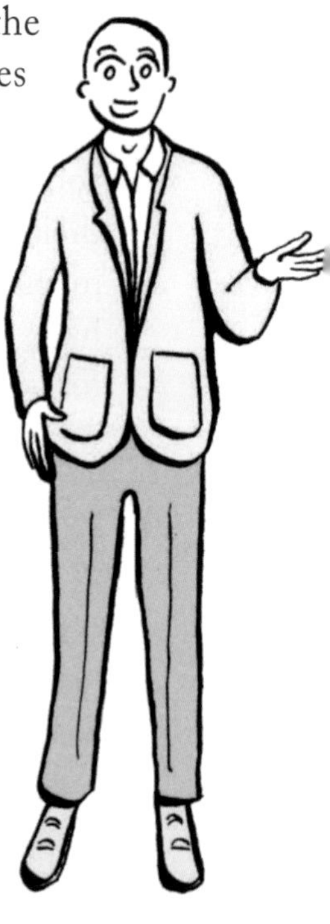

Of course, many other schools of therapy exist, such as systemic therapy, humanist therapy, etc… but none have secured enough proof of effectiveness in treating severe anxiety disorders, although they may be of interest for other mental health issues.

HOW DO I FIND THE RIGHT THERAPIST?

Look into their training and qualifications

Are they licensed or certified? What is their official title? Don't hesitate to verify their experience online. If someone is a psychologist, psychiatrist, or psychotherapist, their titles are regulated by governing bodies.

Various databases list professionals who have undergone specialized training that is officially recognized by their peers.

Have you noticed any improvement?

If, after several months, your issues remain unaffected and you see no improvement, speak with your psychotherapist before changing caregivers. This way, you will be able to take stock of your treatment, evaluating what's working for you, and what isn't. You might be surprised, when speaking with your therapist, to notice that they understand you better than you think. They will be able to hear your misgivings, and adapt their treatment to make it more effective. Switching therapists involves a significant loss of time. I've met many patients who have prolonged severe anxiety issues by changing therapists too soon and too often. Do not rely on your first impression: wait at least until the third session to get an idea of what your relationship with your therapist will look like, and expect no results until after at least a dozen sessions. If you have a good relationship with your therapist, the two of you will be able to discuss your dissatisfactions, asking questions and discussing possible solutions.

→ Does psychotherapy have to take a lot of time?

With anxiety disorders, treatment usually lasts anything between six months and two years, at a rate of two to four sessions per month. Several studies have shown that there is no point in dragging therapy on for years if it yields no results.

→ Does therapy have to cost a lot to be effective?

Absolutely not. The cost depends on your insurance, your healthcare system, and your practitioner's title.

→ Is psychotherapy ever covered by insurance?

If you're seeing a psychiatrist, psychotherapy is usually partly covered by national and individual health insurance—but how much of the latter can vary from country to country. With certified psychologists, some insurance companies will require a copayment, or a fixed amount that you are required to pay for individual sessions. This, too, depends on your insurance coverage. Here's a tip: do your research before starting therapy, and don't hesitate to pick an insurance plan that covers psychotherapy.

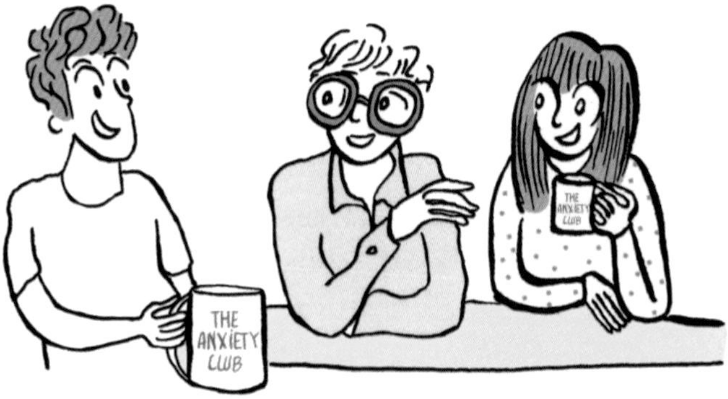
THE ANXIETY CLUB

A BRIEF
AND PRACTICAL
BIBLIOGRAPHY FOR ANXIETY

Here are a few useful books to guide you on your therapeutic journey.

BOOKS ON ANXIETY

→ David H. Barlow and Michelle G. Craske, *Mastery of Your Anxiety and Panic: Workbook*, fifth edition (New York: Oxford University Press, 2022)
→ David A. Clark and Aaron T. Beck, *The Anxiety and Worry Workbook: The Cognitive Behavioral Solution*, second edition (New York and London: Guilford Press, 2023)
→ Seth J. Gillihan, *Retrain Your Brain: Cognitive Behavioral Therapy in Seven Weeks: A Workbook for Managing Depression and Anxiety*, (London: Sheldon Press, 2020)

REFERENCE BOOKS

→ Aaron T. Beck, *Cognitive Therapy and the Emotional Disorders*, (New York: Meridian/Penguin, 1979)
→ Dennis Greenberger and Christine A. Padesky, Mind Over Mood: Change How You Feel by Changing the Way You Think, second edition (New York and London: Guilford Press, 2016)
→ Jeffrey E. Young and Janet S. Klosko, Reinventing Your Life: The Bestselling Breakthrough Programme to End Negative Behaviour and Feel Great (London: Scribe Publications, 2019)

USEFUL LINKS

UK:
→ www.nhs.uk/mental-health/feelings-symptoms-behaviours/feelings-and-symptoms/anxiety-fear-panic/
→ www.samaritans.org/branches/central-london/
→ www.mind.org.uk
→ www.anxietyuk.org.uk
→ www.mentalhealth.org.uk
→ www.youngminds.org.uk

US:
→ www.mhanational.org/conditions/anxiety
→ www.psychiatry.org/patients-families/anxiety-disorders/what-are-anxiety-disorders
→ www.adaa.org

Canada:
→ www.anxietycanada.com
→ www.canada.ca/en/health-canada/services/healthy-living/your-health/diseases/mental-health-anxiety-disorders.html
→ cmha.ca/brochure/anxiety-disorders/
→ www.camh.ca/en/health-info/mental-illness-and-addiction-index/anxiety-disorders

ABOUT THE AUTHOR

 As a qualified psychiatrist and psychotherapist, I have been practising Cognitive Behavioural Therapy (CBT) for the last thirty years. I trained at the University of Lyon 1 under Dr Jean Cottraux, a key figure in the promotion of CBT in France. During seminars in Europe, I have also had the privilege, throughout my career, to count as mentors the most eminent CBT specialists in the world: Aron Beck ("the father of cognitive therapy", Philadelphia); David Barlow (a pioneer of Anxiety Disorders, New York), Cory Newman; Christine Padesky (Cognitive Therapy, Los Angeles); Jeffrey Young (Schema Therapy, New York); Lucien Auger (Rational-Emotive Therapy, Quebec); Andrew Christensen (Integrative Behavioural Couples Therapy, Los Angeles); Frédéric Langlois (Laval University, Quebec); Roz Shafran (Oxford and UCL, London) for "perfectionism"; the late David Servan-Schreiber (EMDR, Pittsburgh and Lyon 1); and Jurgen Margraf (Ruhr-Universität Bochum).

The range and quality of my training and experience have allowed me to share and popularize my specialist expertise in CBT beyond the walls of the academy, and I am grateful to be appreciated for my teaching skills, which have allowed me to transmit scientific psychology to the general public in a simple, direct, and effective way.

Other books by Dr. Frédéric Fanget: *Oser: Thérapie de la confiance en soi* [*Dare: Therapy for Self-Esteem*] (Odile Jacob, 2003); *Je me libère* [*Free Yourself*] (Odile Jacob, 2013).